CROSS UPON CROSS

By the same author:

PERSONALITY AND READING

KING-DOCTOR OF ULITHI

WHAT'S YOUR CATHOLIC I.Q.?

CATHOLIC SHRINES IN THE UNITED STATES AND CANADA

Poetry:

ON WINGS OF SONG

BITTER WINE

Anthology:

RETURN TO TRADITION (A Directive Anthology)

Biography:

ALEXANDER POPE: CATHOLIC POET

THE BURNING FLAME (Life of Pius X)

SEA OF GLORY (A Story Of The Four Chaplains)

Cross upon Cross

THE LIFE of POPE PIUS IX

By

FRANCIS BEAUCHESNE THORNTON

BENZIGER BROTHERS, Inc.

NEW YORK

BOSTON   CINCINNATI   CHICAGO   SAN FRANCISCO

Nihil Obstat:

William Busch,

Censor Deputatus

Imprimatur:

✠ John Gregory Murray,

Archbishop of St. Paul

Paulopoli, die 15 Aprilis, 1955

Conforming to the decree of Urban VIII, the author protests that all that touches on the supernatural in this book
is to be accepted as resting on human faith alone.

TO MY FRIEND

MONSIGNOR PATRICK J. RYAN

Major General and Chief of Army Chaplains
On the 180th Anniversary of the Chaplain's Corps.

ACKNOWLEDGMENTS

THIS book took shape after months of research in Rome and on the Continent. Slowly the full magnificence of Pius IX was revealed to me: The depth of his holiness, the width of his charity, the heroic weave of his life, the towering height of his virtue.

Many kindly people helped me in assembling over a thousand pages of notes from which my book was written. I am particularly grateful to the following: Monsignor Tickle, Monsignor Charles Duchemin, Monsignor Peter Whittey, Monsignor Hugh O'Flaherty, Monsignor William A. Hemmick, Monsignor Umberto Dionisio, Monsignor Andrew P. Landi, Monsignor Morin, Monsignor Clapperton, Monsignor Macario Tinti, V.G. of Senigallia, Father Alan Clark, Father Rope, Father Leonardo Pavone, Don Segundo Pierpaoli, Sister Saint Joseph, Mr. Arthur Phelps, Timothy Murphy Rowe, Contessa Emma Augusti Orsilli, Mrs. Arthur Utz, Mrs. John P. Wilde, Mrs. Richard Cotier, Miss Janet "Toppy" Wilde, Miss Patricia Rossworn. The Librarians and Staff of the Vatican Library, the English College, Collegio Beda, the Scots College.

Above all I am grateful to Monsignor Vittorio Bartoccetti for his active interest and intelligent criticism during the whole course of the work.

CONTENTS

Chapter I

CHILDHOOD AND YOUTH

JOHN MARY walked slowly into the big square house. He could hear the rattle of pans in the kitchen on the first floor. His nose told him that old Marta was preparing a delicious supper. Sometimes he wished she would keep her hand out of the big-mouthed rosemary jar that stood on the kitchen mantlepiece. But his father liked the taste and because Count Mastai-Ferretti was complete master in his house no one complained. Sometimes John Mary expected his mother to speak out. After all she had been born Catherine Solazzi and was noble in her own right. A slight wrinkling of her nose was the only sign of distaste she gave. Then the placid square face returned to its half-smiling, almost German tranquillity.

Already at seven the boy knew what it meant to be a count of Mastai-Ferretti. Senigallia looked up to its first family, and even the Archbishop della Genga showed deference in the presence of John Mary's serious and stiff-backed father, Count Jerome. There was a blank haughtiness in the long face and uncompromising moustaches, that sat well in the village councils where as Mayor he presided, and at the annual games in the plaza below the castle of the Riarios.

The town folk of Senigallia thought it was a great thing to be a Count like John Mary Mastai. John Mary knew from the inside how difficult this was. It meant a day that started early.

1

His mother would help him to wash and dress. She spent a long time brushing his fine brown hair, but he didn't mind that because she was beautiful to look at, and she had so many funny comments to make even when she scolded him. She was particularly insistent that he should know his prayers. The *Pater* and *Ave,* acts of faith, hope, and charity—and the Creed. That was the hardest to learn. "You are like our silly parrot," his mother would tell him when he stumbled on the hard words. "All she can say is 'Poor Pol, Poor Pol.' " Then his mother would give him a hug and a kiss, and they would start all over again.

With the little boy clutching her hand she would go to the family chapel for the morning Mass. The hand of his mother was warm and friendly on the trip through the cold hall. At the chapel door they would stop. His mother made a loud "shushing" sound, widening her large, dark eyes in warning each time before they went in. Sitting on the rush bottomed chair John Mary could look up at the red plush priedieu where his father's uncompromising back and his mother's solid form dominated the little room and half blocked out the tiny altar with its engaging picture of the Virgin and Child. The candles were lighted and then the bell tinkled. Sometimes the priest was young, and the small tonsured spot in his thick hair looked incongruous; at other times it was one of the old Canons from the cathedral leaning heavily on the altar and seeming to mutter swiftly rather than saying the Latin words. One of his older brothers usually served, and John Mary would soon be expected to do so and take his turn with the others. Mass was always a pleasure to John Mary. It was quiet in the little room, and the Madonna looked as friendly and amiable as his own mother.

He remembered well how his mother had taken him to the cathedral last year. It had been cold then, and the bare reaches of the building had seemed like a great icy vault of the dead. They had knelt at the altar of Our Lady of Good Hope. The wonder-working portrait glittered with diamonds and rubies, and the crowns of the Mother and Child looked heavy above their painted heads. The face of the Mother had a secret sadness in it accentuated by her half-bent head. The Child in her arms, however, was almost laughing. His crown sat askew on his little head and one lock of hair had escaped from its gold band. Then his mother had said to John Mary in a solemn voice: "I give you to the Madonna. She will keep you. All your brothers have chosen the world, but I give you to the heavenly Mother." John Mary had never known his mother to be so solemn. "Love her, John Mary, and she will love you."

"I do, mamma; I will," the boy promised. His mother bent and kissed him. It was after that day that his mother had given him the little cross of lemonwood, bordered with an inlay of mother-of-pearl and studded with squares and diamonds of the same material. "It will help you to remember the promise to Our Lady," she said. "It's not a sad cross but the cross of triumph," she explained. "Now the sorrow of death is gone and Christ is risen."

John Mary had treasured the cross. Sometimes when he woke in the night and the darkness seemed filled with frightening things he felt for the hard outline of the cross on the night table. His precious cross of hope! The smooth feeling of the mother-of-pearl under his fingers made him think of the early morning sky. Suddenly the smile of the Infant in the arms of Our Lady seemed shining on him out of the darkness. Then before he knew it the morning light was in his eyes.

Lessons took up most of the morning. In spring and in early summer he didn't mind too much. Later there would be hours of delight wandering along the seashore. Sky and sea would be trying to outdo each other in shimmering blue, and there were a thousand things to discover on the beach under the amiable but watchful eyes of Guido, the strong young servant assigned to him for a playmate and guardian.

But in winter, sitting in the dark old winter parlor barely warmed with its braziers, John Mary's fingers seemed too stiff to accustom themselves to the copperplate writing he must learn; too numb to lift the picture book for the slow lesson in reading. From time to time John Mary's mother looked up from her embroidery to encourage him. "Remember you are young Count Mastai," she would say half satirically. "You must try to be smart. A count without learning is a no-account." John Mary didn't always follow her words but he liked the trill of her laugh and the warm feeling of her arms as she caught him up and praised him when the morning was over and it was time for dinner.

He would stand in a warm corner while the table was being laid. The old winter parlor with its long black settles against the walls seemed pleasant for the moment. The faint gold scrolls and swirling patterns on the seats seemed to fly up toward the four big pictures that covered most of the space on the wide walls. They had been painted by a local painter, John Anastasius, at the close of the seventeenth century, and his mother loved to tell John Mary stories about the painter and the paintings. "The Triumph of Constantine" was on the west wall, "Esther and Mardochai" faced in from the north. The east wall was covered with "The Vision of Ezechiel," and the south with "The Rape of the Sabines." The gigantic figures, the armor, silks, and flashing expanse of bare arms seemed to set all the walls in motion. The rich colors gave an autumnal note to the big room and somewhat relieved its coldness and lack of windows. It was the chief gathering place of the family in the winter months, and dinner was always a cheerful event that started with a rich soup, very hot, and a clatter of voices as John Mary's sisters and mother all seemed to be chattering at the same time.

Then, after the cheese, it would be time for a nap and more studies with a young, and somewhat stiff, professor from the cathedral, who came to teach John Mary Latin and his first sums in arithmetic.

With the advent of spring, and it always seemed to come with Easter, the entire house was opened to the sun. The rose-and-gold salons to the east and north were cleaned within an inch of their lives. Crystal and gilding caught the light. The prisms on the chandeliers tinkled. It seemed good once again to hear the musical chime of the ormolu clock. The hours, even those devoted to study, seemed to hurry by on swifter feet. There would be company from Rome. Uncle Paul, Canon of Saint Peter's, would spend hours with his brother, Count Jerome. Often, too, Uncle Andrew, Bishop of Pesaro, would come down to Senigallia for a few days in his heavy carriage. His visits were always a delight to the entire household.

Always the Bishop questioned John Mary. His ruddy face was serious but the boy noted a twinkle in the intelligent brown eyes. The black silk coat with its lace ruffles at the throat, and the matching black knee breeches spoke less of the bishop than the nobleman. But the sparkling ring on his expressive hand and the twinkle of the pectoral cross on his ruffles marked him for a prince of the church.

There would be the usual long inquiry about John Mary's facility in his prayers and the Catechism. Usually Uncle Andrew ended his queries with a great laugh that seemed to rumble up out of his capacious stomach. "After all, boy, I feel responsible for you. It was I who baptized you. I remember well how you squalled. You seemed quite reluctant to quit the devil. Your father is bent on making you a general at least, but your mother and I will fool him yet. What would you like to be?"

"A priest, Uncle Andrew."

"Ha, I knew it, and you will be too. Good boy!" He tweaked John Mary's thin cheek. "Then we'll have to put some fat on your bones."

Conversation among the three brothers was mostly about the Pope, Pius VI. He had been taken captive by the French republicans in 1798. The Papal States were dominated by the French armies after the looting of the great art treasures of Italy. Two hundred million lire had already been extracted from the impoverished nation, in addition to the art treasures.

John Mary gathered from the conversation of his father and uncles that the Pope was ill. "He will die in exile," his Uncle Paul had said.

"It looks hopeless," his father observed.

Bishop Andrew's face grew more red than ever. "Not at all! Not at all! The Church is old, she can wait. Napoleon and the French won't last forever. There's a new spirit in Italy. You'll see!"

"But how can a new Pope be elected if His Holiness dies in captivity?"

"You'll soon find out. The Sacred College has a plan and we'll have a new Pope shortly after Pius VI is dead."

"But Rome is in French hands."

"Not for long, I think, and the Sacred College is already gathering in Venice."

John Mary was upset by the conversation of his father and uncles. As usual he took his worries to his mother. "The French must be very bad people to do these evil things to the Pope." His mother smoothed out the wrinkle in his forehead with one hand and put the other on his shoulder.

"It's hard to judge people, John Mary. Only God can do that. Certainly it would be wrong of us to think that all the French are bad. We know that couldn't be true just as we know all the people in our town couldn't possibly be evil. Even of those we call bad it's hard to say what God may think of them."

"I see what you mean, mamma. But what if there shouldn't be another Pope? What would become of the Church?"

His mother laughed. "Don't you know, my darling, that

Christ promised Saint Peter that the Church would last forever and the gates of hell would not prevail against her? Remember! I explained that to you before in the Catechism. You may be sure that God will settle all these things in due time. If the Pope dies, the Cardinals will elect a new Holy Father. Now, you are not to worry any more. Come, say a prayer with me for all the enemies of the Pope. His Holiness prays for his enemies as Our Lord did. We must do the same."

Before his mother's reassurance about the Pope could come true John Mary was to undergo an unpleasant and frightening experience. It had been the custom in the summer that the Mastai family would leave the heat of Senigallia for a small villa in the hills above the town. It was a simple quadrangle of brick with a plain tile roof and a well in the courtyard. Such a villa permitted aristocrats to play at being peasants, somewhat in the fashion of Marie Antoinette at Versailles. Meals were served out of doors under an arbor, and the tension of being the Counts Mastai could relax a bit. Most of John Mary's brothers would be at home. His mother was perpetually occupied with guests, and John Mary and Guido were free to explore the pine woods and hills to their hearts' content.

One day in July, John Mary and Guido had gone further afield than usual. They had discovered a deep pond fed by a mountain brook. The strong Guido was gathering small branches to build a fire before they ate their lunch which John's mother had given them that very morning with the caution, "Remember, don't stay out in the noon sun, and you are to be home before mid-afternoon."

John Mary lay on his stomach on a ledge of rocks watching a school of silver fish flashing in and out of the shadows cast on the water by the thin pines above. The air was fragrant from the sun-warmed branches. One fish seemed to lag behind the others John noted. Wouldn't it be fun to catch it. He could just see Guido's surprised look. John Mary hunched up on his knees and bent over the water. His hand was poised to snatch the silver shape lolling there in the darkling water. His hand lunged down. He felt himself losing his balance. Then he plunged in. His mouth, opened to shout to Guido, was full of water and he seemed to be going down interminably. He rose to the surface, flailing his arms wildly and shouting in a faint voice. He had begged Guido to teach him to swim—but always the boy had put him off. Now John Mary would pay for that refusal with his life.

He struggled fearfully. Bits of prayers flashed into his mind. Suddenly he felt Guido's arms about him and the next thing he knew he lay on the rocks while Guido worked over him with a face pale with fright. John Mary vomited and vomited. "That's good," Guido told him.

Finally Guido propped him up against a large rock. He tenderly wiped the boy's face with a red-fringed napkin from the small wicker hamper and forced John Mary to swallow a few sips of wine, most of which came up. "What will your father say?" Guido lamented. "I'll be punished. I know I will."

"Don't worry," John said in a weak voice. "Father won't be home until tonight. I'll tell mother about it, and I'll ask her to say nothing to him. After all it was my fault. If anyone is to be punished it must be I."

By the time the two boys reached home John Mary's teeth were chattering. His mother was too alarmed to scold him. She gathered him up in her arms, stripped off his clothes, and covered him with blankets. Soon the cook came in with a glass of bitter herb tea. "Drink it all, you bad boy," his mother commanded. John Mary did as he was told. He felt himself drifting off into an uneasy sleep.

The experience left its mark on him. He was nervous and pale. Now night after night he dreamed of drowning, yet he half resented the way his mother continually fussed over him. Worst of all, Guido was exiled for the summer.

"You are to blame," John Mary's father said with a stern face. "You must be more careful. And since you are to blame and are fond of Guido, you will have to stay near the house the rest of the summer and not have the pleasure of his company. I'll find other work for Guido."

John Mary felt an impulse of bravery. "But you won't punish Guido, father. Will you?"

John could see that his father resented that question. After a long pause his father replied. "No I won't punish him. It's you that must be punished."

John Mary's time of punishment came to an end with the exciting news of the Pope's death at Valence in August, 1799. There were all sorts of alarming rumors that shifted family attention from John Mary to more important affairs.

The Cardinals, as Uncle Andrew had said, slowly gathered at Venice for the election of a new Pope. But it was not until the 16th of March, 1800, that Barnabas Chiaramonti of Imola was elected. The new Pope chose the name of Pius VII.

Uncle Andrew was jubilant. John Mary heard him exulting to his father. "Didn't I tell you it would come out all right. And you'll see the French won't be long in Rome. The new Holy Father is a fine man, a saint I think. Everyone is fond of him— so wise and mild he is."

The following year fairly throbbed with compounded excitements. John Mary could see that his father was forever busy with secret preparations of some kind. Gabriel, John's eldest brother, though he was only nineteen at the time, went on messages throughout the countryside. Finally the men in the family disappeared. John could see how worried his mother was. Her serenity was no more in evidence. She spent much of her time in the churches now, lighting candles and praying. Then in July the men came home bronzed and triumphant. A smell of baking and cooking pervaded the whole house; the rose-and-gold drawing rooms were gay with summer flowers.

John gathered that the troops of Naples and Austria had defeated the French. The Papal States were free again, and the Pope was back in Rome.

John Mary pursued his studies with uninterrupted regularity. All his lessons now centered about the Catechism, in preparation for his first Communion. His new and charming Aunt Victoria had come to live with the family. She had a sense of fun that captivated John Mary. They were often together, and Aunt Victoria took over most of the tasks connected with his education.

"You mustn't learn your Catechism like a parrot," she advised John Mary. "You ought to learn it so you can understand something about Our Lord and God. We have too many noble Catholics that know less than a hitching post. But even learning is not enough, John; you must pray. And if you forget your morning and night prayers then you might as well throw your Catechism out of the window."

Finally the day dawned. It was the Feast of the Purification, 1803. John Mary's mother and Aunt Victoria dressed him in the beautiful white silk suit with the high neckcloth and collar. When at last he stood ready for the carriage that would take them to the cathedral Aunt Victoria caught him up in her arms. "He looks like a little Pope," she said to John's mother, "a little saint."

The morning was like a dream to John Mary. He knew in his heart how great a day it was. He and Christ were to be one this morning. Like the first dawn ever to come upon the world there was a special beauty and importance in the day that would linger forever in his soul. Father wanted him to be a soldier, but he only longed to serve Christ in His army that came to heal and not destroy.

The altar of Our Lady of Hope was snowed with flowers. The perfume of stocks and carnations came to the boy kneeling on the white priedieu. The countenance of the Madonna promised him only the sorrow of knowledge, but the face of her Son held the bright smile that had always been a comfort to the boy since his early childhood. The flower-wreathed candle in his hand trembled until the moment of Communion. Then he felt himself in a great white silence with God.

Developing maturity brought an increase of responsibility. Already in the excitement of his first Communion morning his mother had told him he must go away to school. "Saint Michael's school at Volterra," she informed him. "The Scolopii Fathers are in charge. They will teach you all the new wonders of science and literature. I know you already love poetry, but you must learn the poetry of the new things that in these days are shaking the world."

"I promise to do my best, mamma."

"I'd rather you went to school in Rome, but your father wants you to be with the boys of your own class. Most of your schoolmates will be the sons of noble families. And you must remember you are Count Mastai and hold up your head among them."

John Mary found this last information odd. He loved his three brothers because they were all so kind to him. They had a special affection for this little brother almost ten years younger than themselves. But in goodness they were no better than Guido. Being a count meant being disciplined and kindly. Judged by these standards Guido excelled them all.

Going away to school was a sorrow. It meant being banished from the light of his mother's face, the company of the family, and Aunt Victoria. The Fathers were kind but strict. Sleeping in a dormitory brought a new kind of collected loneliness that led to pranks and nightly scuffles and eventual punishment.

La palla, a form of football, was a release and John Mary played it with a complete abandon and ferocity. He found his noble schoolmates quite as elemental as himself. The rough kindness of the playing field was in joyful contrast to the long hours spent in study. There was a heavy emphasis on science. John Mary found the study of physics especially delightful. It helped him to understand all the new inventions that were beginning to cause such a stir in the world.

The classics had always fascinated John Mary. Greek and Latin looked back into beauty. Science looked to the future. It seemed to John Mary that religion and poetry were the bridge between the two worlds. One gave it stability and order, the other expressiveness. Dante had combined both in his great *Comedy*. He had not hesitated to rebuke evil in high places, because he saw in the end it is holiness that walks the highest roads and sees the farthest even in the practical business of living.

Filing into the school chapel with his fellow students early each morning John Mary never ceased to be impressed with the well-balanced front of the little church. The simple columns were lovely in the pure light. The masked arches of black and white marble lent a note of gaiety to the bare piazza.

During the Mass John felt the complete wonder of the mystery of God made Man. It was simple like bread and wine. The ancient prayers called to his heart. Like Saint Michael himself, there above the altar, he was determined to serve in God's army. But how could he when his father was equally determined to make him serve in the worldly and destructive armies of princes?

On his first summer vacation John Mary could see that his father was pleased with him. "I have had a fine report on you, John Mary, from the French inspector of your school. He singled you out especially among all the students, but I'm not going to turn your head with all the good things he said. The Fathers are more than satisfied with you too, and you look strong and well."

"We play a lot of *palla,* father."

"Good, it's a sound preparation for the rough ways of armies. You must learn to ride well also, and if time permits this summer I'll teach you myself."

John Mary could see his mother knitting her brows at these words. She had been wonderfully pleased when he had told her of his ambition to be a priest. Perhaps then she would fight out the ultimate battle with his father that would give her son the freedom of action he wanted.

The five years at Saint Michael's school were filled with minor triumphs of study. Small occasions stood out. John could remember well the flurry of excitement when Queen Eloise of Etruria came on a visit to the school. He had been elected by his fellows to preside at the academy held in her honor in the study hall. He remembered with some pardonable pride the poem he had read; the white hand flashing with rings ruffling his hair as the queen expressed her thanks to him for the delightful entertainment.

Many difficult but repaying hours were spent in learning to play the violoncello. Its tone, deeply sonorous and so like a human voice, was a pleasure to direct and master. The boy had a feeling for beauty, and he showed it in the swift progress he made in music.

Yet, in spite of such small triumphs and the ease with which his studies progressed, there was growing in John Mary a feeling of tension. The struggle for his future between his father and mother was a part of it. Somehow it gave him the same sense of terror he had felt that day when he had almost drowned. Now that old dream revived again and made his nights hideous. Yet, with the coming of spring in the year 1808, he felt first a strange depression and then a sense of exaltation. The two moods were like a pulse in his nerves that moved him without his own volition.

One morning in the study hall a giddiness seized him. It came in ever stronger waves. He stood up at the side of his desk, gave a half inarticulate cry and suddenly fell into a fiery blackness.

When he awoke John Mary felt strangely calm and quiet. He was in the small infirmary and the Father Superior, the school doctor, and the brother infirmarian were grouped about his bed.

"What happened to me?" John Mary asked.

There was a pause while the three pairs of eyes seemed to be consulting each other. Finally Father Superior Inghirami spoke. His voice was kind and soothing. "You have been studying too hard, John Mary. You must rest now. When you are a little better Brother John will accompany you home in the stagecoach. Since you have excelled all the boys in your class I'm going to permit you to finish the year without examination. I shall write Count Jerome at once. Brother John will sit by you now. Anything you want, just ask him to get it."

John Mary stretched back on his pillows after they had gone. The homely face of Brother John was consoling. Strange. John felt so light and well. It seemed silly to be lying there with the spring sun bright against the half drawn blinds.

"Couldn't I get up, Brother?"

"Wait a little! You must rest. Father Superior said you must, and you know what a tartar he is when you don't obey him."

"Did I faint, Brother?"

"Yes, I suppose so. I didn't see you until they brought you in here looking like a wrung out sheet. If you'll just relax I'll fix you a nice glass of orange water. And who knows, you might be well enough tomorrow to play a hard game of *palla,* and you may not go home at all. Father Superior is a good astronomer, but no prophet. He's been wrong before." Brother John laughed at his own wit and John Mary joined him.

But he went home. He couldn't understand what it was all about and this frightened him immeasurably. His mother had cried bitterly though she tried to control herself, and his father looked at him with the strangest look that seemed made up half of pity, half of loathing.

Several doctors came to the house, one a famous specialist from Rome. They all left bottles of drops and pills and asked John Mary endless questions. It was the mystery of the thing that worried the boy. Propped up on a couch in the first drawing room he turned over in his mind what it could possibly be. His heart? Or lungs? Once he asked Aunt Victoria outright. "What's wrong with me, Aunt Vickie?" But she only shook her head. Her eyes were full of tears.

Long hours with his school books and the two small devotional volumes his mother had given John Mary soon became irksome. He begged his mother to let him sit up and walk around. She gave a reluctant consent and John Mary felt better once more. He took his drops and pills with better grace. Color came back to his cheeks. By the time the family was in residence at the summer villa the boy appeared to be well again. His father seemed particularly pleased by the improvement.

It was through a visit of Uncle Paul's that John Mary learned what was wrong with him. His uncle had come for a week. He and Count Jerome spent the evenings discussing the explosive political situation. The name of Napoleon Bonaparte was constantly in their talk. One evening when John was in bed and thought to be asleep, for the hour was very late, he heard his uncle and his father come into the little paved court below his bedroom window. From the scraping of chairs and the clink of glasses the boy knew they were having a glass of wine before turning in for the night. John Mary was relaxing into sleep when suddenly he heard his name mentioned. Instantly he was alert. In one movement he was out of bed listening at the window.

"He's been fairly well since he came home," his father said.

"Will he be able to finish his last year at Volterra?"

"Yes, I think so, if he doesn't get much worse. The fathers

are willing to take the chance because the boy is brilliant: he has a genius for mathematics and science. All the students are fond of him."

"Let's hope and pray for the best, Jerome."

"Yes, I try to. It's a great disappointment to me. He has a beautiful presence. It's plain he would have a fine career in the Noble Guard. But epilepsy! Who would want an epileptic officer?"

"But the doctor I talked to in Rome said it might possibly not be epilepsy but something that looks like it. Something that John Mary might grow out of."

"What's the difference, he has fits, and epilepsy or something like it—in the end the effect is the same. Poor boy, I pity him."

John Mary felt the tears jetting from his eyes. So that was it. He was an epileptic. The boy turned and took his lemonwood cross from the table. Holding it to his breast he knelt at the window and looked up at the stars. "Say it isn't true, God," he begged. "Say it isn't true." He leaned his chin on the sill and breathed in the scent of the pines. The wonder of the night seemed smudged. The faint sickle of the moon was like a sword in the sky.

The last year at Volterra had passed without too much embarrassment. John Mary maintained his first place in his class. But he was inexpressively sad that he was not permitted to indulge in sports. Even his walks were taken alone with Brother John. Most of his meals were eaten on the infirmary table. Under this regime his first two seizures of the year gave no cause for public comment but the third, near the end of the year, was public. Even more difficult to bear than the physical indignity were the frightened faces of his schoolmates who came to visit him afterwards. They brought him fruit and sweets; they pretended he was merely ill, but their eyes betrayed them.

In the long, lonely hours John Mary's cello proved to be a good friend. When heavy discouragement threatened he would play for hours the joyous music of Mozart. It cheered his heart and brought an occasional admiring student to the door of the infirmary where the sight of the slim figure in the fawn-colored suit with high neckcloth and Byronic collar was like a charming painted scene caught in a bar of sunlight.

With apathetic eyes John Mary saw the year coming to a close. His only hope seemed to lie in heaven. The boy spent hours on his knees in the chapel. He begged his father's permission to receive the tonsure. Perhaps it was his father's disgust with him that brought a speedy answer granting John the gift he had long desired. On the evening when Bishop Incontri came to the infirmary to cut the locks from the boy's thick hair John Mary saw both hope and happiness in the kindly smile of the venerable Bishop. At least, in spite of his illness, John Mary had taken the first step in the service of the Lord, and he would carry his cross with the help of his Master.

Uncle Paul gave John Mary great encouragement when he came down for his usual summer visit. "You are quite the young cleric," he said with an encouraging smile. "Now that God seems to be on the side of your mother and has permitted you to be tonsured I'll take you to Rome. You can live with me while you begin your philosophy."

"Thank you, Uncle Paul. You mean I'll live right in the Quirinal Palace with you?"

"Yes. Of course. My rooms are large and pleasant. And the Quirinal is the healthiest spot in Rome. If there's any sun in the city you will find it there, and the air is very sweet. You'll be practically one of the Pope's family. All the Cardinals that have remained in Rome will be as familiar to you as your own uncles."

"Aren't all the Cardinals in Rome, Uncle Paul?"

"No. Not now. You see, when that odious General Miollis

reoccupied Rome last February he still wasn't satisfied. In April he added further outrage by invading the Quirinal itself and occupied the Secretariat of State. As a result, many Cardinals have left Rome in order to be ready for anything that may happen. The Holy Father is certainly hampered and spied upon, but he is like a rock in his dignity and fearlessness. I tell you, John Mary, you'll love the man. He's a saint if I ever saw one."

"I know I'll love him, Uncle Paul. It will be wonderful to see him every day, and also fine to wear the cassock."

"Oh no, John Mary! You can't do that! General Miollis has forbidden students to wear priestly dress. I'll have your mother order you some dark clothes, and that's all you'll need." He laughed. "Of course I forgot your determination to study hard."

"I have that, Uncle Paul. That is, if I don't get sick."

"Well, if you do, there are splendid doctors available. But they don't know everything. Your seizures may be a passing thing that will soon clear up."

"That is what I ask the Virgin every night and morning. You pray for me too, I'm sure. Don't you, Uncle Paul?"

Uncle Paul was touched by the tears in his nephew's eyes. "Yes, yes, I do, John Mary. Indeed I do. And we must hope together."

John Mary was in love with his new life. The Quirinal with its vast series of quadrangles sprawling over the hill was a pleasant and happy place even under the French occupation. The tremendous outer courtyard with its fine belfry and sweet-toned bells was doubly lovely with the fresco of the Virgin set against a vivid blue background which faced toward the inner court. From the main gate that opened on the piazza, centered in the delicate obelisk with its gigantic horsemen, it was only a short walk to the opulent staircase of marble that led to the first floor and through a series of dazzling apartments to the simple quarters of the Pope.

Uncle Paul was known to everyone, and it seemed to John

Mary that his uncle had considerable influence. In addition to his canonry at St. Peter's he was sub-secretary of the *Memorialium*. He appeared to be on terms of familiarity with the whole Roman court.

The stately, ordered life, in spite of the French spying and interference, pleased John Mary. Through his uncle's influence he enrolled in the Roman College in October and started work on his course in philosophy. The reasons of the faith as advanced in St. Thomas and his compeers fascinated John Mary. Faith he knew was a gift of God, but it was pleasant to see that faith was reasonable, and it had its order and illumination that gave it subtle attraction for the mind.

At seventeen the young man attracted the attention of everyone. Tall and straight with a fine head and wavy brown hair, his narrow head had a note of command in it, amply enhanced by his intelligent eyes and mobile lips. His hands were particularly expressive.

Lectures began early. Serving Uncle Paul's Mass started the day in quiet. They both made their thanksgiving in the little chapel. His uncle, John Mary knew, was praying hard for the strength and health he needed: his own health was better, his seizures less frequent.

Then in May, 1809, Napoleon's decree from Schönbrunn Palace annexing the Papal States to the French Empire electrified the Papal Court. The Pope was quick to retaliate in his Bull, *Quum Memoranda*. In plain, and even scathing, language he excommunicated Napoleon without mentioning his name. The Bull was posted secretly by night on the doors of the great Roman basilicas, though the French had tried to prevent this.

Napoleon was furious at the action of Pius VII. He sent to Marshal Murat, who had taken over the kingship of Naples, an order to arrest the Pope at once. General Radet carried out the odious command. His soldiers forced the gates of the Quirinal. The Swiss Guards were disarmed and imprisoned.

Radet himself haughtily strode into the Pope's private apartments. The fragile white form rose from behind the massive desk and confronted the infuriated general.

"How dare you come here and use force on me and my household?"

"I am carrying out the Emperor's precise command. You must give up all claim to the Papal States or suffer imprisonment and go into exile."

The eyes of the Pope flashed. "I am prepared to do both," he said firmly. "God is with me." He touched his breast on which, in a beautiful silver locket, was the Blessed Sacrament.

General Radet, thinking the Pope referred to himself snorted, "Then you and your God must both be forced to do the Emperor's will."

"That is not so easy, General. The Papal States are not mine. They are the patrimony of the Holy See. I cannot give you what is not mine. Not for you, or his majesty, or anyone else."

General Radet took the Pope under a heavy guard, first to Genoa and then to France.

These events disturbed John Mary and his uncle. In the following October they were put out of Uncle Paul's rooms by rude soldiers who made obscene jokes as they went about their tasks of locking and sealing the rooms of the great palace. John Mary and his uncle took the stagecoach across the peninsula to Senigallia. After gathering funds and clothes they went in the Mastai carriage up the coast to Pesaro.

They found Uncle Andrew in a fine fury. He welcomed them into his palace with outcries of sympathy and outrage and kissed them both on the cheek in familiar and affectionate greeting.

"An outrage! An outrage!" He kept shouting. "Our poor Holy Father! Our poor saint! And that upstart Napoleon. Why he hasn't even the lineage of the Counts Mastai! I shall speak out, never fear!" John Mary and Uncle Paul had a difficult time in calming him.

Bishop Andrew was as good as his word. On Sunday morning at the Solemn Mass he rose from his throne and ascended the pulpit. The church was stony silent as he started to denounce the French, then a buzz of excitement went round. When the Bishop had finished the people applauded and many in the congregation shouted "Bravo!"

Uncle Andrew's electrifying sermons lasted only a few weeks. One evening while the three men were at supper in the Bishop's dining room they heard a tramp of feet on the stairs. The door of the dining room was thrown open by a frightened maid. Before she could say anything a French captain appeared in the doorway accompanied by two soldiers.

"Bishop, you are under arrest!" Uncle Andrew was led away from the table at once. He protested this new invasion of the Church in unmeasured terms. By the time John Mary and Uncle Paul had returned to Senigallia a secret message came to them that Uncle Andrew was in prison in the fortress at Mantua.

These continued alarms and excursions had an adverse effect on John Mary. He felt himself slipping once again into moods of alternating depression and exaltation. Then his old enemy had him by the throat, and he writhed on the ground.

"I will not give up, Uncle Paul. I must not." His uncle was almost in tears as he tried to comfort his nephew. "No, John Mary, you must not give up. Pray as hard as ever you can. I'll help you with your studies for a time, and when I leave I'll make arrangements for one of the priests here to take my place."

It was a terrible time for John Mary. His life of prayer and study was all directed toward the priesthood. But how could he be a priest if his illness persisted? Perhaps his father was right after all. Maybe God wanted him to lead an active life

and not one of study and thought. But Our Lord had condemned those men who put their hands to the handle of the
plow and looked back. He didn't want to be one of those people.

As if to test his resolve, Napoleon ordered Italian conscription in preparation for the invasion of Russia. John Mary received a summons to be examined for the Noble Guard. "Try
it," his father urged. "After all, your studies are practically at
a standstill. The outdoor life might be good for you."

"Very well, father, I'll do what you say."

The examining doctor at Ancona soon put an end to his
father's hope.

"Perhaps you're a lucky man, Count Mastai," he said, when
John Mary had answered his swift probing questions. "You
certainly won't have to take part in this stupid war. I could not
possibly certify you to become an officer of any kind. You are
totally unfitted for the soldier's life, as long as these attacks
persist. But there seems some chance you will outgrow your disease. Above all you are not to worry about things. Study. Be
quiet. And time will tell."

Such comfort as these words promised John Mary warmed
in his heart. At least God had indicated that he was not to be
a soldier in this war.

Napoleon's Russian excursion ended in his downfall. He had
boasted to Prince Eugene at the time of the Pope's Bull of
excommunication. "Does that old man think that his words will
cause the muskets to fall from the hands of my soldiers?"

Now on the plains of Poland the muskets dropped from the
frozen hands of defeated men. Napoleon's abdication was only
a matter of months.

The captive Pope started from Fontainebleau on the slow
journey back to his own country. Advance word came to Senigallia that Pius VII would pause briefly in the city en route to
Rome.

Count Jerome, as Mayor, swiftly planned a reception. Tapestries and decorations went up in the square and on the town hall with its stern old medieval clock tower.

People came in from the whole province clad in holiday costume. Singers and musicians greeted the Pope with an unrehearsed roar as his traveling carriage entered the piazza. The Pope gave his blessing to the people. His fine face was pale but joyful. Then Count Jerome, resplendent in his bright chain and sash of office, presented his family and notables to the Pope. John Mary kissed the shining ring and heard the Pope say: "Now you can return to our household with your Uncle Paul."

It seemed like a command, and John Mary was only too eager to obey it. He and Uncle Paul followed the Pope's carriage to Rome. The Eternal City, which had shrunk during the Pope's absence, was filling up again, and John Mary, after a short stay in the crowded Quirinal, went to live with the Devoti family who were friends of his uncle and related by blood to Bishop Devoti of Anagni, Secretary of Briefs to Princes under Pius VII.

Now under Father Conti's tutorship the young man made swift progress in his philosophical studies. With special permission of Pius VII, John Mary was then allowed to begin the study of theology with his friend, the Abbé Graziosi.

John Mary was overjoyed. These studies of God's ways with men were like a new world of light and resurrection.

Then he knew a further joy in finding an outlet for his energies at the hospice of Tata Giovanni. It had been founded during the reign of Pius VI, by John Borgi, a pious but practical workman, somewhat after the model of the French orphanages established by Saint Vincent de Paul.

Borgi noted the presence of large numbers of war orphans who came up to Rome in order to beg and make a living. They slept in odd places, in caves and the ruins. In rags and filth they haunted the city in search of a few pennies to buy food. Borgi gathered a small band of boys about him in an old house in the

Via Giulia. The boys called their protector Tata Giovanni (Father John) and his little establishment soon took the same name and caused something of a sensation.

The boys were neatly clothed and sometimes well-fed. Their quarters were clean as a pin. Borgi started the work of helping them to learn simple trades that would enable them to earn a living when they left his care. Borgi died in 1815, but his hospice endured and prospered. The establishment was moved to larger quarters in an old Visitation convent next to the Church of Saint Anne of the Carpenters.

John Mary was induced by Canon Storace, a close friend of his uncles, to help with the good work of Tata Giovanni. Now, between the hours of John Mary's own studies he returned to the hospice every afternoon and evening and gathered the boys about him at a long table. He questioned them about their prayers and gave them lessons in the Catechism. These tasks were followed by simple arithmetic, reading and writing. The boys loved this new teacher who had come to live and work among them. He was not merely pleasant to look at, but it was an unusual pleasure to be in his company. He told them such interesting stories, and if he made corrections they were always put in a witty form that made fun of the mistake but not the boy. Many of their teachers in the hospice had a large pinch of heaviness or ill humor. John Mary was never out of humor. His urbanity, politeness, and the joyful manner in which he organized games or debates among them had an air of spontaneity that never lost its charm for children. He often told them anecdotes about the great French Bishop, Saint Francis de Sales, and urged them to follow this saint because of his sweetness and perpetual amiability. The boys said among themselves: "Young Count Mastai is much the same himself. Nothing puts him out of countenance or makes him angry."

Yet had they known the way of the cross John Mary traveled they would have marveled the more at his unchanging humor.

They couldn't know how carefully he watched himself for the first signs of an imminent attack. Then he would excuse himself to Abbé Graziosi and seclude himself in his rooms with a servant. After being torn and ravaged John Mary spent hours reading the Passion of Christ. He was fascinated with that scene in the Garden of Olives. Christ too had groaned. "If this chalice may not pass!" Then the young man said the other words that rang like a bugle over the whole world, "Not My will but Thine be done."

Most of all, John Mary fought the discouragement that hung over him like a black cloud—never quite absent from the horizon of his mind. What if this was his lot to the end of his days? What if he never recovered? "Thy will! Thy will!"

Then he returned to God's Mother. "Let me serve your Son," he pleaded, "let me serve Him. It is so difficult this way. So hard to do the things I must do."

Coming to and from his tasks and studies John Mary stopped at every shrine of Our Lady that happened to be on his route. "Heal me for His work, Mother! Let me serve Him." Favorite among his shrines was the chapel of Our Lady in the great basilica of Saint Mary Major. In its wealth of marbles and exquisite fittings it was like a superb poem to the Virgin. Above the exquisite altar the old black portrait of Mary, said to have been painted by Saint Luke, looked down on his sorrow with comprehensive understanding. Coming out from the grilled entrance John Mary went down the steps to the confessional where the pieces of the Christ Child's crib were shrined in a splendid crystal reliquary. "I too am your child, Blessed Mother. Remember me! Help me!"

So the slow days went by. John Mary had been extraordinarily happy to wear the cassock but this privilege had been taken from him by an unexpected attack.

All day he had felt rather better than usual. Then, as he came into the piazza near Tata Giovanni, John Mary felt the onset of that terrible compulsion. He almost ran along the cobblestones, praying as he went. His agonizing eyes looked toward the entrance of his refuge. He must get there. He knew he must!

At this moment he fell to the street and writhed in the filth of the gutter. The coachman of Cardinal Fontana, driving his master along the street, suddenly pulled up his horses. "Eminence, there seems to be a young student dying in the street." The carriage came to a full stop and the Cardinal jumped out and bent over the writhing form. "Good God!" he said. "It's young Count Mastai!" Everyone knew him. The Cardinal supported the boy against his knee. "Run to the porter of Tata Giovanni. We must get this young man to bed at once."

This unfortunate episode caused much talk: so much in fact that John Mary was asked not to wear the cassock any more in public. It was a terrible blow. He might console himself by remembering that Christ had fallen in the filth of Jerusalem on his way to Calvary. He too had been a public spectacle, but there was a revolting character in John Mary's illness that caused comment and a kind of pity with a note of distaste in it wherever he went in public. "Thy will be done! Thy will be done!" the boy repeated with iron courage.

Yet, strangely enough, his public humiliation brought him some relief. Word of his seizure went to Senigallia and his father was quick to tell him: "I had hoped you would have a fine career in the army. This terrible disease has proved that I was wrong. You are free to do what you want with your life." Time and time again John Mary's father had urged him to apply for an army post. First it had been the forces of the Grand Duke of Tuscany, then Napoleon's army, later he had suggested the Noble Guard of the Pope. Now all that was over. John went into the church of the Bona Mors in the Via Giulia. Before Mary's altar he knelt down. "I am free to serve Your Son. I vow myself forever to you and Him."

John Mary made plans to go home until the talk of his sei-zure died down, but before he could carry out his intention he was summoned to an audience with Pius VII. The talk of Rome had reached the Pope's ears, and he who had known intimately so many sorrows was as always, quick to respond to the sorrows of others.

Uncle Paul took John Mary to the door of the Pope's study. Then with a pat on the back he turned away and left his nephew to himself. John Mary made the three genuflections then kissed the reliquary cross on the Pope's slipper. When he raised his head his eyes met the deep-set eyes of the Pope fixed on him with a look of fatherly pity. Tears misted John Mary's eyes, and he forgot all his polite defenses. His words poured out in a torrent.

"Holy Father, for my vocation to the priesthood everything seems to be finished. Every avenue, every hope I had seems to be destroyed."

The delicate hand of the Pope with its gleaming ring of the fisherman rested on John Mary's head. A deep voice rang in his ears.

"Rest easy, my son. We have been neighbors in fact when I was in Imola, and neighbors in sorrow. In this last condition I found it helpful to resign myself to the will of God."

"I have, Holy Father. Oh, I have."

"Continue then, my son. Confide in God's goodness. And confide in the heart of that beloved Mother whose name you bear. Recommend yourself to her powerful help. I feel sure this cross will pass from you. Take courage, then."

The Pope's assurance made John Mary joyful all the way home to Senigallia. From the windows of the stagecoach the very hills seemed rayed with light. He told his mother about the Pope's reassurance over and over again. "I feel I must still pray more strongly to Our Lady."

"Why not take a carriage and go to the Holy House at

Loreto? I'm sure the monks will be glad to receive you. There is ample time for you to make a retreat and a novena at the same time."

"It's a wonderful idea, mother. When may I start? Let me go today!"

"Very well then, I'll arrange everything with your father. Guido can pack your things and go along with you and do the driving."

John Mary was silent most of the way to Loreto. Guido respected his silence. John Mary had always loved this countryside with its alternating fields of wheat and squares trellised with vine lattices. Groups of lopped pines bordered the fields and the Adriatic showed gray-blue through the humped-up sand dunes that bordered the left side of the road. Stopping overnight at Ancona John Mary felt something particularly attractive in the plane-bordered squares of the town and its great mole challenging the sea.

Sometime near noon the next day John Mary's eyes caught the sight of the towering dome on the hill and the clustering buildings round it.

"There it is, Guido. Our Lady's house set inside a great church."

Guido's eyes sparkled. "I had never hoped to see it. It makes me happy to think that I shall see Our Lady's house today. I'm really excited, John Mary. What it must be like I can't even guess. They say angels carried the house here from Dalmatia."

"It may well be, Guido. It's certain that Our Lady has granted many favors to her children in this spot. Help me to pray, Guido, during these days while I am telling God's Mother my troubles."

"I will, John Mary. Believe me, I will. I always think of that day you almost drowned in the little lake, and I wonder if that shock might have caused your illness."

"I don't think so, Guido. It doesn't seem likely at all."

"Just the same it does bother me, and I blame myself for not watching you more carefully. For this reason I'm going to join your retreat. I'll beg Our Lady to cure you this time for sure."

John Mary was used to being alone, though he loved people. His illness had drawn him aside from the world because he was unwilling to cause embarrassment to his friends or the public. If he went out to lunch or dinner he always feared to upset his hosts. Yet, in the eight days at Loreto he experienced a loneliness he had never known before. It seemed to the young man that he had entered a great plain enveloped in a mist of impenetrable silence. There was a dryness in him that stood between his heart and his lips. The wonderful marble screen about the Holy House, with its delicate carvings telling stories of Our Lady's life, moved him to the same admiration he had known from his childhood, when he had first visited this place. The little dark house of sun-dried brick inside the gorgeous shell had the old subtle atmosphere of mystery. Here Mary had cared for Joseph and her Son. Here she had measured out her life in labor: in cooking meals on the tiny hearth, in washing the worn clothes and mending them, in sweeping and dusting— all those simple tasks that make up the daily poem of motherhood.

The treasures heaped upon Our Lady by grateful princes and clients had been looted by the French. But the black, rather wooden face, said to have been carved by Saint Luke long ago, perhaps in this very house, had a mysterious sweetness far beyond the power of any treasure to enhance it. John Mary's heart was dry, yet like the saints he forced himself to pray. His two books of devotion given him by his mother provided fuel for his lips, though they failed to move his heart.

"Cause of Our Joy, Spiritual Vessel . . . Tower of Ivory . . ." he said them over and over. And the burning words of Saint Bernard, "Remember, O most gracious Virgin Mary . . ."

For seven days the dryness persisted. The Virgin seemed deaf to his pleading. Then on the morning of the eighth day, after Mass and Communion, John Mary's heart awoke. The monks had been singing the Office and suddenly the *Salve Regina* echoed in the high dome and spoke to him like a celestial voice. "Hail, Holy Queen, Mother Of Mercy . . . O clement, O loving, O sweet Virgin Mary!"

It seemed to John Mary that he was being shaken by a great warm wind. Hardly knowing what he did, he rose from his kneeling chair at the edge of the choir and went through the door of the marble screen into the dark house of Nazareth. He felt the sharp edge of the altar step under his knees and looked up through the ruby radiance of the lamps to the face of the statue.

"Our Holy Father has told me to trust in you, dear Mother. I have fulfilled his command. Heal me, make me well enough to do the work of your Son. Then let me carry my crosses with a calm heart so long as I am your servant and His. Make me well, Mother! Make me well! I will glorify your name all the days of my life!"

The noise of his own heart was the only sound he heard in answer. Though the Virgin answered nothing John Mary felt as if a gentle hand had touched him with healing. He got up from his knees and almost ran to find Guido outside on the sun-bathed steps. "I feel I am cured, Guido. I know I am." Suddenly the gates of relief opened and tears poured down his cheeks.

His cure was indeed an accomplished fact. The attacks did not cease at once in a completely miraculous fashion, but they lessened in force, and the intervals between them grew greater and greater.

The return to Senigallia was joyous. John Mary and Guido sang much of the way. The Mastai household heard the good news with demonstrative pleasure. Senigallia was in the midst of a fiery mission preached by three famous priests, Monsignor Strambi, Monsignor Firrao, and the still better known Odescalchi who later became a Cardinal and joined the Jesuits, after their revival under Pius VII.

Young Count Mastai was drawn to this brilliant and ardent spirit. So strong was the effect of Odescalchi's fiery sermons on the love of God that John Mary took a mission cross on his shoulders and went along the curving Corso of Senigallia, an ever-growing crowd following at his heels. Having reached the main bridge that spans the river Misa, John Mary set up his cross and preached to the throng. His words were swift and telling. His white hands flashed in dramatic gestures. The people stood in silence under the spell of the warm magic of his voice.

"He is the best of the lot," one woman said. "And so beautiful and graceful. Our young Count Mastai will be a great bishop some day. I feel sure of it."

Chapter II

PRIESTHOOD

B ACK in Rome John Mary fell on his studies with a kind of holy fury. Abbé Graziosi and Uncle Paul were quick to help him. By autumn he was ready for minor orders which he received from Archbishop Peter Caprano in his private chapel in the Doria Palace. The Church is ever cautious in dealing with illness in her prospective priests. The private conferring of orders on John Mary was a sign of the care she took in guarding against a public scandal should John Mary be seized with a fit during the ceremonies.

The subdiaconate and diaconate followed swiftly on December 18, 1818, and March 6, 1819.

The Pope had received John Mary on March 28, 1819, the eve of Palm Sunday.

"I hear you are cured, my son."

"Yes, Holiness, Our Lady has granted my prayer at last." John Mary poured out the whole story. After thanking the Holy Father for the dispensations that had cleared his path to the priesthood he asked the further favor of being allowed to celebrate Mass without the presence of another priest at the altar. This was the normal condition attached to the ordination of those who had suffered as John Mary had. Pius VII lost no time in consideration.

"Dear son, I freely grant you permission to celebrate the

holy Mass alone, because I am sure that you will never again be attacked by your malady."

On April 3, the formal document of permission had arrived. Then on Palm Sunday, 1819, John Mary began his final retreat in preparation for the priesthood.

He was in a ferment of joy and exultation. The words telling the Passion of Our Lord rang in his heart with a particular meaning. The cross was at the heart of the great revelation Christ had made. Through the cross and suffering came the morning of resurrection.

In the Holy Saturday liturgy blended of light and shadow that suited well with the thoughts of his heart, John Mary was made a priest, April 10, 1819. Once again the ceremony was in the private chapel of Archbishop Caprano.

John Mary's mother watched the anointing with tears in her eyes. John Mary knew, in the midst of his joy, how thoroughly his mother felt the nature of the triumph. It was the heavenly answer to her nights of prayer when the drama she witnessed this morning seemed so impossible of attainment.

Breakfast under the delicately painted ceiling of the great hall was a gala affair. It surprised John Mary that his father appeared to enjoy the occasion equally with his mother. For once Count Jerome came out of himself. Smiles flashed from under the cloud of his heavy moustache, and he made pale jokes with Uncle Paul about John Mary's future.

For the new priest only one place could possibly be selected for the offering of his first Mass, the Church of the Carpenters next door to the hospice of Tata Giovanni, where he had so often heard Mass surrounded by his orphans.

Wasn't it strange, John thought. Easter and summer had always been linked in his mind. At home the old winter parlor would be forsaken while the family enjoyed the color and beauty of the rose-and-gold drawing rooms. Now on this Easter morning he himself was like one risen from the dead into a new life infinitely more beautiful than the bright drawing rooms he had loved as a child.

The Mass was sung by the boys of the hospice of Tata Giovanni. They filled the arches of the little church with robust sound until it seemed ready to explode.

When John Mary came to the reading of the Easter sequence he stopped for a few moments overcome by emotion. The question asked of Mary Magdalen seemed addressed directly to himself.

"What did you see on the way, Mary?"

"I saw the grave, the sheet, and winding cloths and the witness angels. I saw the risen glory of Christ, our hope, Who has gone before us into Galilee."

The *alleluia* at the end of the last verse was a cry of triumph in the young priest's heart. Its sweetness was so powerful that it could almost be tasted with the tongue.

Uncle Paul stood at John Mary's side in the cope of the archpriest. How long he had been at John Mary's side, encouraging him and helping him with good advice and consolation!

At home in Senigallia the first Masses of young Count Mastai were attended by all the notables of the city and the poor who had loved the young man for years because of his unobtrusive and constant charity. With the permission of Cardinal della Genga, John Mary gave a mission to which the whole city responded. Some idea of its success may be summed up in the remark of a sailor who attended and was said to be a friend of the Mastai family. "In Senigallia there is a Mastaia who preaches like the very devil." It was the description of himself that Father Mastai was to remember for many years with laughter.

Soon after this, while he was still at home, John Mary was appointed by the Holy Father as assistant to the director of Tata Giovanni. It was wonderful to throw himself into the work without being overshadowed by fear of a sudden seizure among his pupils. Now he was among them on the same old plane of comradely companionship, but the cassock and bands he wore had real meaning. In the morning he could offer Mass in the midst of his children, and in a more positive sense could lead them directly to Christ in new and thrilling ways.

There are two ways of attacking a new job. One is to accept without question the pattern already laid down and make it work as well as possible. The second is to take the pattern, enlarge and amplify it, or even change it radically in order that it may work more efficiently.

In his capacity as assistant director of Tata Giovanni, John Mary chose the second or creative way. Simple trades had been taught the students, such as carpentry and mechanics. John Mary introduced the study of surveying and all the new avenues to scientific progress. He also brought in experts to teach drawing, painting, sculpture, and pottery making. If a mathematics teacher could not be had, the young priest taught the subject himself. He also expended his own private income on the clothes and food of the orphans. To them it seemed that their friend was always with them at work or play. During free time his door was open, and many a boy was privately tutored or helped with his problems by the young, ardent priest. "Don't say I helped you. Just pretend you learned it yourself."

John Mary had an intimate fashion of giving religious instruction. His wit, invention of stories to illustrate his point and the warmth of his voice helped the boys to see how important religion was as a key to daily living. When he spoke of God's Mother his words really caught fire. He led his orphans to see her simply in every enchanting aspect of her life and theirs. Not as a heavenly Mother far away, but one who walked among them tender-hearted, loving and affectionate as the mothers they had never known.

There were other ways in which John Mary used his talent for direction. Waste and duplications of all kinds were eliminated, and the money given to run the establishment was stretched to its farthest. Every year an exhibition of the best works of the students was held, and Rome was astonished to see how much was being done at Tata Giovanni.

Much of the time John was in complete charge of the place, and his name was often mentioned at the Papal Court as one of the coming young men.

In 1823, Joseph Ignatius Cienfuegos, Canon of the Cathedral of Santiago, in Chile, came to Rome on an important mission. He had been sent, the Canon informed Pius VII, to ask that an Apostolic Delegate be appointed to straighten out ecclesiastical affairs in Chile, Peru, Mexico, and Colombia. The Spanish colonies had but recently secured their independence from Spain. In the rough outbursts of revolutionary fury and coarse liberalism the Church had suffered severely. Many, even of the largest cities, were without bishops, and the life of the Church was almost at a standstill.

Pius VII was filled with anxiety for his children in the Americas and he was only too happy to comply with Canon Cienfuegos' request for a settlement.

The Pope chose the commission with care. Monsignor Giovanni Muzi, secretary to the Nuncio of Vienna, was consecrated Archbishop and made Vicar Apostolic of Chile, Peru, Mexico, and Colombia. He was given the widest possible faculties to be used in reconciling the churches with Rome.

Muzi chose as his assistants, Count John Mary Mastai and Don Giuseppe Sallusti. John Mary was to be auditor, Sallusti the archivist. Archbishop Muzi had been one of John Mary's collaborators at Tata Giovanni, and it was the most natural thing in the world that he should have selected his old friend, long admired for his brilliant talent and delightful manners.

To John Mary the news of his appointment was something of a shock. For four years he had been happy with his orphans, and only now was his management of Tata Giovanni coming into its fullest flower of usefulness.

John Mary took his doubts to God in the church next door. Kneeling before the altar he suddenly remembered his promise to the Virgin at Loreto. "Only remove this cross from me to work for your Son. I am ready to carry any cross after that." Now he was allowing himself to fear the cross sent him by his beloved Father, Pius VII. He felt ashamed of himself. Suddenly he realized the splendid mission opportunity given him in his assignment to South America. His old missionary zeal awoke, and he accepted the position with cordial gratitude to God.

One thing he was sure of. His mother was getting old. She would hate the separation beyond measure. During all the years of his trial she had prayed for him with the constancy of Monica. This parting would be a bitter blow.

Parting from his orphans would also be a trying affair. He loved them, and they loved him and depended on his continued presence and advice.

In the evening when John Mary came into the dining hall all the boys could see at once that something was weighing on his mind. His usually smiling face was grave and he seemed to be preoccupied. He said grace in a low tone and then sat at the head of the table merely picking at his food. When the dinner was over he tinkled the little handbell. In the ensuing silence John Mary made his stunning announcement:

"The Holy Father has named me auditor on a commission to South America. I must leave almost at once." A great groan came up from every voice in the dining room. Then, forgetting all rules of decorum, teachers and orphans rushed to the top table and gathered around John Mary. They were crying and begging him not to go. Such was their importunity that they followed the young priest down the hall and invaded his rooms, still protesting, still crying out against his departure. It was a shattering experience to the tender heart of the priest.

His final interview with Pius VII had also touched John Mary. The Pope had received him with a special warmth. After a long discussion of the mission the Pope finally said. "Your mother, the Countess, has written asking that we should not send you to South America. She fears the danger for you. But we have written her a letter reassuring her that you are sure to return safe and sound."

John Mary had already written his mother telling her of his mission. It had rather surprised him to have no reply from her. He smiled to think how shrewd his mother was. She wasted no time in writing to the Pope himself. She knew John Mary's respect for that authority. Would she accept the Holy Father's reassurance? Perhaps John Mary could make her see it was prophetic like the Pope's first promise of his cure. The South American journey would be a hazardous trip, ships being what they were. After all, Chile was halfway across the world.

Archbishop Muzi and his two assistants met at Genoa on July 3, 1823. The bark *Eloisa,* bound for Chile, waited in the wide serenity of the harbor. They were all busied with the heavy task of stowing away their numerous trunks and hand luggage. In John Mary's eyes the ship looked pitifully frail and not the kind of conveyance fit to face the immensity of ocean before them. But they were venturing out on the water at the express command of the Holy Father. They would normally expect the favor of heaven and blessing on their voyage. Genoa was full of memories of Columbus. He had not feared the fury of the seas. Even with the added handicap of a rebellious crew, the great navigator had reached America.

Canon Cienfuegos was full of consolations on the subject of the trip. "We may have some rough weather at first, but, after all, we are sailing south and can expect a quiet voyage once we get below the Canaries. Our crew of thirty-two men are all expert sailors."

The captain of the *Eloisa* waited from day to day for a favorable wind. One morning a small boat came out to the ship. One of the men in the boat handed up a document to the captain. "It's for Your Lordship," the captain said to Archbishop Muzi.

The Archbishop broke the heavy seal. His face grew pale as he read the message. "Our beloved Holy Father is dead!" Muzi announced to his companions. They knelt together on the deck and prayed for the repose of the Pope's soul. While John Mary's lips prayed, his mind went back through his memories of Pius VII. How many favors he owed this Pope, who was perhaps the architect of his cure; certainly the architect of his priesthood and the great model of his life!

Until a new Pope could be elected the mission would have to wait. Perhaps the new Pope might cancel the mission altogether. Archbishop Muzi, after some discussion with his assistants, made a quick decision. "We must move our things ashore and throw ourselves on the hospitality of Cardinal Lambruschini."

The distinguished Prince of the Church received them cordially. John Mary was charmed with the Cardinal's courtly manners. "Of course!" he assured them. "My palace is your home until new orders arrive. I am going to Rome at once for the conclave, but I feel sure whoever is elected Pope will be favorable to your mission. Rest here, then. I'll give orders to my steward. If you have any messages to send I'll be glad to carry them to Rome."

News of the new Pope's election came before the Cardinal's return to Genoa. John Mary was elated that Cardinal della Genga had been elected. Cardinal della Genga near Senigallia was an old friend of the Mastai household. John Mary had known him well for years. He was pleased that the new Pope had chosen the name of Leo XII. John Mary would have preferred the name of Pius, but if the new Holy Father formed himself in the great Leonine tradition his reign promised well for the Church.

Cardinal Lambruschini arrived with fresh authority for their mission. They were all anxious to be off. The wind and tide seemed favorable for their plan. On the 5th of October, under full sail, they slid out of the harbor of Genoa into a freshening sea.

Wind and waves were against them from the first. After nine days of adverse winds they were driven into the port of Palma, on the island of Majorca. Here new trials awaited them. The Chief Magistrate came on board. He was furious to find that the Pope was sending a mission to the rebellious colonies. Quickly he placed the ship under quarantine for twenty days. Its distinguished passengers were rowed ashore and locked up in the military hospital.

Archbishop Muzi was a patient man, but after a week of constant interrogation he got indignant. "I appeal my cause to the Archbishop of Palma," he said wrathfully. "Believe me, Your Honor, if you dare impede my appeal you will not long be the Chief Magistrate of this place. How dare you delay an embassy of the Holy Father?"

The protest achieved the desired results. The ship was freed from quarantine and allowed to sail almost at once.

Storms and near shipwreck made the following days hideous. In the small, dark and evil-smelling cabin the important passengers could do little more than clutch their rosaries and pray for better weather. The most frightful storms of all met them off the coast of South America in the early part of December.

Then, suddenly, on Christmas Eve, the sea calmed and the weather grew moderate. An awning was set up on the main deck. Under it John Mary and Father Sallusti erected the portable altar they had brought. All these stormy days they had been without the consolation of the Mass, but now God was sending them the best Christmas gift of all.

At midnight, Archbishop Muzi offered the first Mass of Christmas. The candles guttered in the slight breeze. The immensity of the sea was all about them, a waste of dark water. But the sky above the stars was like music. The Southern Cross seemed to be a gigantic chandelier of rejoicing.

John Mary and Father Sallusti offered the Christmas Masses in their turn the next morning. John Mary recalled how often he had prayed at the gorgeous manger-shrine in Santa Maria Maggiore. Now the only splendor he could offer to God was the manger of his heart. He prayed not only for his mother and the family but for all those, like Pius VII, who had assisted him toward his unfailing good health and the chance to serve God.

On New Year's day the *Eliosa* anchored in Montevideo's harbor for repairs. The ship was in Buenos Aires on the fifth of January. Many distinguished citizens came to the dock to receive the Pope's legate, but in a few days the mission was to feel the full hatred of the civil authorities. Archbishop Muzi wished to confer the sacrament of confirmation, but he was curtly and rudely told it could not be done.

John Mary refused to be moved by the hatred of the republicans. He spent every free moment hearing confessions and teaching Catechism to the children. His old missionary zeal had found an outlet. He would cheerfully have taken the mission cross on his back and spoken in the public square, but he could plainly see that would be more resented than anything. It had amused him to see that some deference was paid to his title, even by the most hot-headed liberals. What a stupid world was coming into being where men respected a title more than the priesthood!

Archbishop Muzi soon decided to go overland to Santiago rather than face the voyage around Cape Horn. They were weary of the capriciousness of the sea and it was thought a land voyage would do them all good.

It was a decision the Archbishop later regretted. With a long train of pack mules the courageous priests set off across the pampas. Some nights they slept in rude and dirty inns along the road; at other times they put up a large tent and found what comfort they could in makeshift beds. The heat and insects made the days and nights horrible.

Strangely enough, John Mary was exhilarated by the voyage. Christ had not promised his priests lives of ease, but only the cross and martyrdom. But martyrdom and the cross were useless unless they were gladly received. It was for these reasons that John Mary looked for and found amusing slants in every aspect of the day. And when he couldn't find them he discovered other reassurances as they jogged along on their mules.

"Come, Don Sallusti, I will hold a contest with you. What do you remember of your classics and Dante? Better still we'll choose sides. You and I will be on one, Canon Cienfuegos and our good Dominican, Friar Raimond D'Arce, will be on the other. Archbishop Muzi will be the judge among us, and keep us in order."

Over the insufferable miles it was amazing to see how many quotations they could fish out of the pond of memory. Tags of verse from Virgil, Tasso, and Metastasio, long passages from Dante. Often they read their Office in common or recited the rosary. When most disheartened they sang all the old hymns to the Virgin. To these religious distractions Don Mastai added jokes and riddles. With their minds occupied, the day was somehow bearable.

One night when the tent had been put up on the wide prairie and the candles in their tin screens had been lit, Don Mastai was reading his breviary on a makeshift cot under the shelter of his mosquito net. He was so absorbed in his prayers that he failed to notice a huge toad that had crawled up and nestled on the pillow behind the top of his head.

"Look!" Don Sallusti said to his companions. "Look! Count Mastai has a living *zucchetto*. It is easy to see what that promises. He will be a bishop at least."

There was a general laugh while Don Mastai drove the animal out of the tent. Returning to the safety of his frail screen the young man observed: "For me it's only a warty omen. The new Holy Father knows me too well for that. He will choose men of might for his bishops."

Another incident from the passage of the pampas deserves mention. At one of the rude taverns where the party stopped they were informed that an Englishman had stopped in the place and was lying there ill of a fever. John Mary went in immediately to see the man and found him in a terrible state of mind and body. By dint of using both his French and Spanish, Father Mastai established communication between them. Eventually, he discovered that the stranger was named Miller, whose chief worry was the fear of dying in this forsaken place. "We have quinine with us and I'll get a supply of it for you," Don Mastai promised. "And you must not drink any more water here. You must try to eat a little."

The man demurred. "I can't eat."

"Yes you can! Try it even if it's only a bite at a time. You'll live to laugh at this episode yet. I feel sure of that."

The next morning Miller was better. John Mary sent his own party on ahead. "I'll keep one of the guides with me and catch up with you before nightfall. I want to get this man started back toward Buenos Aires before I leave."

The journey through the Andes was both terrifying and thrilling to John Mary. Day after day they went through the deep mountain passes, fording rivers, crossing the narrow-slatted bridges that swung to and fro and looked too frail to support the weight of even one man. Above them were the towering peaks, austere with snow; below them were the endless canyons through which a froth of river boiled.

Coming down from the heights they saw Santiago afar off. They were worn with travel and fatigue. The towers and domes on the skyline were like welcoming hands beckoning them to rest. On the feast of St. Patrick they entered the city. Archbishop Muzi and his little band went to the cathedral and intoned the *Te Deum* in thanksgiving.

What followed their arrival was more or less an anticlimax. Except for the priests, nuns, and religious people of the district, the Pope's envoys were studiously ignored. Months were wasted. After many weeks of waiting, cramped quarters were assigned the Pope's embassy in one of the public buildings. So small was the space given them that Father Sallusti had to set up his office in a draughty corridor. Canon Cienfuegos' description of conditions had proved to be almost entirely wrong. In Chile, Peru and Mexico, the liberal authorities wanted nothing to do with a Church they considered outmoded and totally out of joint with the new age of unfettered freedom.

John Mary was too busy to be discouraged. Religion was at a low ebb in Chile. Yet many people were hungry for the word of God, and they longed to see the Church free again to administer the sacraments. Frequent preaching and the work of the confessional took up much of the young priest's time. The poverty of the people appalled him. He longed to remain among them, helping them with the things they needed both for their bodies and souls.

On one occasion John Mary was sent to observe the conditions in Peru. With a kind of intrepid joy he set sail in a small fishing boat. The weather promised well upon leaving Santiago. It was exhilarating to run before the wind while all about them light worked its magic on the tumbling water.

Off the coast of Peru they struck a sudden squall. Light was drained from the sky and low-flying wind clouds beat the waves to a gigantic froth. The Spanish members of the crew seemed petrified. The boat was in danger of turning over with every slap of the waves. The sails rattled and slammed like cannon shot. John Mary was drenched to the skin. The rosary in his hand was slippery with water. Then a gigantic black crewman, named Bako, suddenly took command of the boat. He seemed to be everywhere, taking down the sails, giving orders, speeding the small crew to action. Had it not been for him the ship would have gone down. As it was, the battered craft limped painfully into Arica, the great silver port.

John Mary felt that he owed his life to Bako and he was quick to reward him with a handsome present of four hundred piastres. Later, when he became Pope, John Mary sent double the sum he had first given Bako. The Pope was delighted with the reply, not written by Bako, but some hired letter-writer, which told the Pope that Bako had made himself rich through John Mary's first gift and would apply the second sum in building a chapel in honor of his patron.

Peru, John Mary discovered at first hand, wanted nothing to do with the Holy Father's Vicar Apostolic. On his return to Chile, John Mary's report to Archbishop Muzi was gloomy indeed. It bore out every other indication that it was a waste of time for the three priests to remain longer in South America. In one last effort Muzi made a series of sharp protests to the authorities, threatening them with possible censure and interdict. This bold attitude achieved absolutely nothing.

Muzi announced his conclusions to his confreres. The Canon's rosy view of the possibilities was obviously mistaken. "Our mission here is a failure. Our ship has come around the Horn and there's nothing to do but return to Italy. At least we will be able to give His Holiness a full and accurate report on conditions here, and an analysis of liberal intransigeance."

Not one of the priests wanted to face the prospect of the long journey overland. "Far better to trust the inconstant sea," John

Mary said. "And I know from experience just how terrible a prospect that is."

Once again their trunks and boxes were loaded on the *Eloisa*. The government gave no sign; the people themselves seemed largely unconcerned at their departure on October 9, 1824.

From the deck of the little craft they watched the mountains pale into the burning sky. The hills of Genoa did not come into sight before June 5, 1825. It had seemed an endless voyage. But this time the sea had been kind to them.

Chapter III

BISHOP AND CARDINAL

JOHN MARY was at home in Senigallia when a new assignment came from Leo XII. He had been appointed coadjutor to the pastor of Saint Mary's in the Via Lata and director of the Hospital of Saint Michael, a vast institution on the Ripa Grande.

John Mary's mother was disappointed at what she considered a poor reward for the exhausting services of her son.

"I'm surprised at della Genga," she said. "When he was Cardinal here in Senigallia we were kind to him. I don't think this appointment is worthy of your rank, John Mary."

Her son smiled at her. "My rank, dear mother? I'm a priest and only the favor of Our Lady has achieved that. The hospital of Saint Michael calls to my heart. After all, it is something to be a man."

John Mary had been anything but idle when he returned to Senigallia. In a series of brilliant lectures recounting the perils of the South American voyage he had charmed crowds in the cathedral. His missionary ardor was like a summons to his people to do everything they could for the missions.

Taking over his new assignment in Rome was an interesting experience to the young priest. The job was anything but small, and it demanded the utmost of his talent for administration. Saint Michael's had been founded by Innocent XI. Four later

47

Popes had endowed it. Its revenues brought in an annual income of fifty thousand dollars. John Mary's charge consisted of an orphanage for boys, and one for girls, with large schoolrooms for study, and shops for learning trades. It also housed a home for the aged, a reformatory for wayward girls and boys, and a prison for political offenders.

Father Mastai's long experience at Tata Giovanni proved to be of tremendous importance. His government of Saint Michael's was inspired by love and an intelligent grasp of human psychology.

Young Mastai did not sit in his office to wait for intelligence of progress. He was everywhere from morning till night, inquiring, encouraging, giving words of advice and praise. Though he had always loved the young, he was deeply moved by the loneliness of the aged. Happiness seemed to have passed them by; their days had little of the affection that makes life bearable. Father Mastai poured out his heart on them. Every evening he visited with them, making them laugh with unexpected jokes about their lives and most intimate hopes.

There was no ceremony about him. To the aged he seemed a kindly son, to the wayward an inspiration, to the young a brother and companion. Some idea of his improvement of Saint Michael's comes to us when we recall the trades begun there under his devotion: engraving, woodcarving, lithography; handweaving of silk, woolen and cotton fabrics; cabinet and pottery making, in addition to the simpler trades like carpentry and mechanics. In two years Father Mastai wrought a revolution of order that was to affect the lives of thousands.

Leo XII watched the transformation of Saint Michael's with extreme interest. Obviously here was an intelligent administrator of the highest order. He seemed to live up to every word of the praise his teacher and advisor Graziosi had expressed to Leo: "He is a young man of penetrating knowledge and unsullied virtue. In him beats the heart of a Pope."

Pope Leo XII had ample need of such a man. The French Revolution had inspired a fiery republican movement in Italy. "We have been too long under foreign domination," the revolutionaries said. "The time is ripe for Italy to be great and unified." Austrians and French were both despised and resented. "Italy for the Italians!" was the secret slogan. So deeply had the movement affected young and old that it swept into the Papal States and led to small incidents of rebellion even there. The diocese of Spoleto was particularly infected with the spirit of rebellion and when its archbishop died, Leo XII astonished no one in naming John Mary Mastai to the trying post.

The bishop-elect again endured the emotional regret of his children in Saint Michael's and he was secretly appalled at the task before him in rebellious Spoleto. But the Holy Father had chosen him to reform the city and he must obey, and carry his heavier cross as he had promised Our Lady.

His open-handed charity at Saint Michael's had mortgaged his income, and it was necessary for him to borrow a large sum from a Roman banker. His brother Gabriel stood security for the debt in order that John might be able to finance the expense of his new dignity.

John Mary Mastai was consecrated bishop by Cardinal Castiglioni on June 3, 1827. This much loved and saintly prelate was to ascend the papal throne two years later as Pius VIII, and it is a strong reflection of John Mary's importance that the noted Cardinal was chosen for the consecration. It seemed strange to John Mary that his mother and father should be kissing his ring now and calling him Lordship. He much preferred the old, unceremonious ways of the past.

Spoleto at once appealed to him. Perched on a spur of Monteluco and famed as a fortress all through the Middle Ages, the old town looked down on the lower hills rich with marble quarries and mines. The cathedral, begun in 617, had a noble dignity that Bernini respected when he planned its restoration in 1640. The frescoes of Pinturicchio and Fillippo Lippi gave it warmth and color worthy of the seat of an archbishop.

John Mary loved the beauty of his See, but his first interest was in the social condition of the town. The coal miners and stoneworkers were underpaid, but even more than that were underprized as if they had been beasts of burden.

Archbishop Mastai didn't announce any program but started out to see things for himself. Coal miners and pastors were suddenly astonished to see a gracious form in their midst. Before they had time to recover from their surprise John Mary was asking a thousand intelligent questions. He examined parish books minutely and his reproofs for waste, for negligence of any kind were made with a smiling urbanity that attracted rather than commanded obedience.

He was at once governor and bishop, and he did not forget his dual role for a minute. How did his people live? The bishop went into their homes and found out at first hand from those most concerned. He revived the sodalities and a new form of the old guilds. By his example he taught peasants, nobles and the emerging middle class to work in harmony together. They all noticed how he stood with his head cocked slightly to one side while he spoke or listened. His comments were always creative and the doors of his palace were never closed to men with a grievance or an idea. Those men who felt themselves burning with new projects found their bishop had a wide sympathy with them.

"Italy would be better off by herself," he stated. "She does not need foreigners to tell her how to act. We can solve our problems if they will let us alone. Italy once led the world in invention and art. She can do it again and become a great nation."

Spoleto had been disturbed by warring factions and these suddenly found their differences blunted and reasoned away like the petty quarrels of children. The city had needed a father and a director and in her new archbishop she found both.

The source of his power and influence was obvious to all. They could see him day after day kneeling in his church with the humility of a peasant. When he spoke of Christ or His Mother his words went beyond the instruction of the mind into the realm of the heart.

There are many stories told of John Mary's humor and republican simplicity. One day in spring, coming through the steep and miry upgrade of the Pass of Spoleto, the bishop's coach was having difficulty in getting up the hill. The peasant coachman reasoned with the mules and when that achieved very little result he turned to Bishop Mastai.

"Your Lordship, these are stubborn animals and lazy to boot. They are not doing their best. Give me permission to curse the lazy beasts."

A chuckle escaped the bishop. "Well now, Giuseppe, I realize I am Bishop of Spoleto. I know well the faculties the Holy Father has granted me. But cursing mules is not one of them, so of course I can't give you that permission." He opened the door of the coach. "Give them a flick of the whip, and I'll put my shoulder to the wheel." The coach with difficulty went forward up the steep hill. At the very top the bishop got into the carriage dusting his hands. "Remember, Giuseppe," he said as he settled back on the cushions, "that there are limits to a bishop's power but not to his strength."

Bishop Mastai was sad to receive the news of the death of Leo XII, in February, 1829. He preached a great panegyric on the Pope's virtues at a requiem Mass in Spoleto's cathedral. He spoke of the Pope, in glowing human terms, as his old friend and advisor. His audience could see no distant figurehead in the portrait Bishop Mastai painted. This was the picture of a man who in strength and holiness had lived up to his high title.

John Mary was not surprised to receive the news that his old friend Cardinal Castiglioni had been elected Pope and had chosen the title Pius VIII. Before the new Pope could formulate a policy he died suddenly on November 30, 1830. Cardinal Cappellari was elected Pope and chose the title of Gregory XVI.

Bishop Mastai was so busy with affairs in and around Spoleto that he had little time for speculation of any of these great or sudden changes.

The year 1831 brought him trials that were to test to the full his high qualities as administrator and priest. He had completely pacified Spoleto and brought tranquillity to its squares, streets and the surrounding countryside.

The unexpected revolution of 1831 was an attempt to drive the Austrians out of the north of Italy. The surprise of the attack seemed to promise well, but when Austria had thrown in the weight of her well-trained troops and generals the rebels were slowly driven south and were at the very gates of Spoleto. The city seemed on the point of being plunged into a war that threatened to outrival her bloody struggles during the Middle Ages. Bishop Mastai saw his whole program going down before the storm. He was advised to withdraw from the city until tempers died down and order was established. The Pope had sent him here to heal not to add fuel to the fire, and if his absence from the city would lead to a happy result then he must not let his pride stand in the way.

As a result, he left Spoleto in the night and went south to Leonessa. He arrived there on Palm Sunday and participated in the mystical re-creation of Christ's triumph and the beginning of His Passion. Two days of meditation were enough to show John Mary that the advice given him was bad. He should be in the midst of the struggle, and if that meant his death then it would mean following the good tradition of his crucified Master.

On Tuesday of Holy Week John Mary rode back into Spoleto. He found there both panic and confusion. The four thousand rebels below the town were on the verge of attacking the ancient city. The Austrian general pursuing the rebels was threatening reprisals if the gates should be opened to the new insurgents.

With a flag of truce John Mary went to the rebel camp and spoke to the men and their leaders. He was able to convince them that they had committed a great crime against the authority of the Pope, and that further struggle was hopeless. It would bring reprisals against themselves and their families and lay waste their homes and farms. If they would disband in peace and lay down their arms the bishop would guarantee them a safe conduct home for Easter. As a proof of his disinterest he had brought a gift of twenty thousand francs to distribute among them.

The last statement brought forth a general cheer. After some further discussion the rebels agreed to the bishop's terms. Muskets, pistols and knives were stacked in great piles. Pickets were withdrawn and the men melted into the surrounding countryside. Everyone seemed happy except the Austrian general.

"I will report Your Lordship to Rome and to Vienna," he announced to John Mary.

"That is your privilege, General."

"I shall use it. Had it not been for you I would have captured these rebels and punished them. After all, you must remember that I am here at the request of Cardinal Lambruschini."

"Yes, I know that. But your master in Vienna is a master of wars. Mine is a master of peace and suffering. I could not have done less than I did."

Easter came. All Spoleto rejoiced. The hill town was hung with lights and tapestries in memory of the peace that came in with the risen Lord. That feast, so memorable to John Mary, had taken on fresh meaning this year. His voice when he spoke in the cathedral seemed warm with the promise of a world grown young again.

One trying problem remained. Among the leaders of the rebellion was Prince Louis Napoleon, son of the former King of Holland. The Austrians had set a price on his head and they tried to catch him at all hazards.

Shortly after the day of the truce Prince Louis Napoleon appeared in the bishop's palace with his mother, Queen Hortense, and asked John Mary for refuge. Bishop Mastai listened carefully to the young prince's long story. "Your Highness, I can't agree with either your prudence or your sentiments, but you are a son in trouble. I offer you the refuge of my palace for the present and a safe conduct through the Papal States to freedom." To this assurance John Mary added a sum of money that he could not afford to spare from his mortgaged finances.

Later in the year, on a cold, rainy day, an Austrian detective asked an audience with Bishop Mastai. He was admitted to the bishop's study where John Mary sat before a blazing fire, going over the disordered accounts of his diocese.

"Sit down," the bishop said, indicating a chair near the hearth. The detective sat down, reached into his pocket for a paper, and handed it to John Mary. Noting his air of smug solemnity the bishop fixed the man with a penetrating glance.

"This is an important document I take it."

"Most important, Your Lordship. In that paper are the names of the ring-leaders of the conspiracy. Many of them, most in fact, are subjects of Your Lordship. With this evidence you can have them brought to Rome and tried for treason against the Pope-King."

A look of horror fixed itself on the handsome face of the bishop. When he spoke at last his voice trembled with emotion.

"My poor man, and you are poor, for you know nothing of either your profession or mine. Don't you know that a bishop is a shepherd? Have you never heard that when the wolf comes to grab the sheep the shepherd must prevent it?"

With a quick flick of the hand the paper was in the roaring

fire. It fairly exploded in the blaze and its ashes were drawn up the chimney.

The detective's face was working with rage. "This will be reported to the Cardinal Secretary of State." The bishop said no word of reply or farewell. He sat and stared into the fire with a sad look on his face.

The rescue of Louis Napoleon and the destruction of the master list of rebels soon brought a letter summoning John Mary to Rome. He went with a clear conscience, but in some fear of the vigorous reproof he knew was in store for him.

After making himself at home in the rooms always kept ready for him by the Cavaliere Filippani and his family, Bishop Mastai went up to the Quirinal. He was kept waiting in the Pope's antechamber much longer than usual while secretaries and messengers hurried in and out with that air of mystery which usually means important affairs.

John Mary expected a strong rebuke from the Pope. The tirade that broke over his head before he had raised it from kissing the Pope's slipper fairly withered him. He had to kneel there while the lava of words poured over him. He was allowed no word of defense and was dismissed curtly from the Pope's presence.

To the gentle heart of the young bishop the blow was a massive one. He returned to the Filippani house; his pallor frightened his hosts. They put him to bed at once and sent for a doctor who diagnosed a fever.

To John Mary it seemed that he had been beaten with clubs. Numb in mind and body he lay there tossing about, going over the Pope's words, trying to accuse himself. Yet in spite of any reason he could dredge up John Mary could not see where he had been wrong.

During the days when John Mary was recovering, a Noble Guard came to his bedside with a message. "His Holiness is sorry to hear you are ill. When you are well the Holy Father wishes to see you. He sends his blessing." The last part of the Pope's message did more for John Mary than his medicine.

On the day of his second audience Gregory XVI refused to let John Mary kiss his slipper. He rose from his chair and embraced the bishop. "Now! Now!" he said consolingly. "Don't be alarmed, my son, but why did you do these things?"

"Holy Father, the reason is simple. I did it because I was a pastor and must protect my sheep at all costs. That is my only defense."

Gregory, who had been a devoted monk, looked at John Mary with tears in his eyes. "You were right! You were right!" he said at last. "I would have done the same in your place."

The year 1832 brought John Mary further trials. A terrible series of earthquakes shook the province of Umbria. So frightful was the disturbance that people fled from the cities and their homes. They camped in the fields and hedges, terrified and desolate. John Mary went everywhere among them. He collected money and food for distribution and opened wide his depleted purse to those who had lost everything. Physicians and nurses came at his invitation to begin the work of rescue. The bishop had no time to think of himself: he was too busy consoling and encouraging his people, too occupied with his prayers among the little groups camped in misery at every crossroad.

Gregory XVI was impressed with the young bishop's resourcefulness. Word was brought from Rome to John Mary promoting him to the See of Imola. His enemies and those who hated the character of his good works said the appointment was a demotion because Bishop Mastai had fled from Spoleto in the first days of the rebellion of 1831. The bishop's partizans also pretended to consider it a demotion. They could not bear the thought of losing this friend and father. Several committees went up to Rome. They begged the Pope to keep John Mary in Spoleto. The appointment to Imola they maintained was quite unworthy of the great qualities that had been shown by Bishop Mastai.

The truth is that the Bishop of Imola was usually honored with the rank of Cardinal. The promotion of John Mary to Imola was a promise of that honor, but it was also a test. Imola was at the time even more disaffected than Spoleto had been when John Mary had gone there. It was torn apart by revolutionary intrigue. The social problems requiring solutions were many and grave.

In appointing a liberal archbishop to Imola the Pope depended on John Mary to duplicate his triumphs in Spoleto. Many things were on his side: religious fervor, an imperial kindliness and an imaginative approach to current problems. Best of all, John Mary was from the neighboring town of Senigallia. In giving the Imolans a bishop who was a neighbor, the Pope was promising them one who could sympathize with their own ideas and way of life.

John Mary saw very clearly what the assignment would entail. Endless labor, endless vigil, endless persuasion of dissidents. He loved Spoleto and its people. He had lived in the midst of their joys and sorrows, and he hated to leave the gracious old town. It would be like transplanting his heart.

It was a further trial that he would be going into a veritable wasp's nest of intrigue. He knew it well, that town of Imola, the narrow little streets, the evil-smelling old houses packed with people, the furtive, closed-in squares. Alone in his chapel John Mary reproached himself. Christ had lived and walked in the midst of a leprous civilization. Yet, He had brought joy and peace wherever He went.

Now John Mary longed to be gone; to throw himself into the work of moving the mountains of ignorance and hatred in his new charge. Whether the Imolans received him well or ill, it really didn't matter. His heart would be sad enough with the farewells in Spoleto, and Christ's work was a tonic that could take him out of himself.

One day in February Bishop Mastai sat in his carriage turning over the plans he had made on his brief visit to the family in Senigallia. His mother had particularly encouraged John Mary. "The Pope has selected you. In Imola they are devoted to God's Mother, and you bear her name. What more could you ask?" In the wide plain before John Mary's carriage the tiled roofs of Imola were pinkish red with the morning sun shining through the February mist. "Look, Your Lordship," the coachman cried. John Mary followed the line of the pointing whip. He saw a huge crowd of Imolans. They were like one solid block of black on the bridge spanning the river; they spilled out over its banks and back along the road as far as his eyes could reach.

The horses were urged forward, and the crowd soon came in sight. John Mary observed that everyone was in holiday dress; they were shouting and waving flags and winter flowers. Groups of strong young men with wreaths of flowers round their necks ran out and unhitched the horses. Twining ropes through the front of the carriage, they drew it through the shouting crowds to the cathedral square. There, under an arcade, the mayor and the city council waited.

John Mary was deeply touched. Never before had he met such a spontaneous outpouring of cordial welcome. There was verve and force in these people, and the Lord would show him how to harness both in His service. "Give me a loving heart," the bishop prayed in the midst of the music and tumult.

In his first days John Mary made a quick estimate of the things to be accomplished. The people were poor, he could see that, and they badly needed instruction. Imola was a populous market town. It had provided a refuge for all the strays and orphans of war. Its morals were appallingly loose. Well, he knew the answer to those things. Like John Borgi he gathered the orphan boys around him and started the work of reform and teaching they so badly needed. Every penny he could scrape up from his family and friends went into charity. He was content to see his home bare because he spent most of his hours in the schools he established, much in the pattern he had directed at Saint Michael's. His orphanages and schools soon proved to be growing concerns, along with the protectory for girls who had taken to the streets in the rebellion against moral life and family authority.

Above all, the Bishop of Imola tried to make his people see that the restoration of their spiritual life was the key to all their problems. He had a compelling magnetism about him that was of great importance in private interviews and in the pulpit. Looking into the bishop's sparkling eyes, and hearing the warm measure of his sentences you felt how beautiful the world could be when it was informed with spirit and prayer. Christ was in their midst, and John Mary showed them His face and the beauty of life and healing that came from the merest touch of His garments.

The sodalities took on new members and new power. Under their colored banners they helped to make processions and feasts a telling witness for Christ again.

The week before Lent was carnival time. At this season the people were accustomed to fling off all restraint. The narrow streets and squares were filled with shouting people in fantastic costumes. They all drank wine to excess, and old quarrels were warmed by drink to fever pitch. Brawling and the easier forms of vice were commonplace.

John Mary did not at first rail against his people's intemperateness and folly. He attacked the problem in another way by starting Forty Hours Devotion on the last three days before Lent. "It will be a test of your devotion to Our Lord," he told the sodalities. "Christ approves of simple pleasure and laughter. His religion is one of joy, but He hates excess of all kinds."

Many, both young and old, responded to the bishop's appeal. He watched them kneeling there before the monstrance hour after hour while the noises of the carnival eddied about the silent cathedral. Many of the night watches were kept by the bishop himself. The few who came into the cathedral during those hours noted the graceful figure kneeling motionless on the red prie-dieu. On his face was a look so benign, so utterly lost in the beauty of contemplation that he seemed oblivious of everything but God.

One night as John Mary knelt there alone, he suddenly became conscious that a quarrel was in progress on the very steps of the cathedral. He heard a chorus of horrid shouts and imprecations, a shriek, and then cries of distress. John Mary rushed to the dimly lit porch in time to see the last of the scuffle. A young man lay on the floor moaning. Several of the men standing over him had knives in their hands. There was blood everywhere.

The bishop faced them with a look of horror. "How dare you profane the house of God with bloodshed and crime? It is a wonder He does not strike you dead this minute."

Through their fog of alcohol the bishop's words came like a flash of lightning. In a moment the men were running away and the bishop was left alone with the dying man.

John Mary snatched up the holy oils, heard the man's last confession, and then anointed him. Before he could say the last prayer the man was dead.

This terrible experience gave the bishop fuel for the denunciation of all the excesses and hates that had disfigured the season. Once the full story of the bishop's bravery was known, the people of Imola were so in admiration of John Mary's courage that they readily listened to his advice for keeping the carnival days in a more seemly fashion.

John Mary's greatest sorrow of the year was the death of his father on December 1, 1833. Count Jerome had been a man of stern justice, but his enlightened ideas had earned him the respect and admiration of everyone in Senigallia. He had lived up to the brightest ideals of the minor nobility. Watching his coffin being lowered into the family vault in the Church of the Magdalen, John Mary sorrowed more for his mother than for any member of the family. They had known a kindly father, but his mother remembered him in the bright colors of romantic love and courtesy that had never faded through the long years of their married life.

All John Mary's love and tenderness would have to magnify itself in order to lighten her sorrow and fill the vacant places in her last years. He could thank God he was in Imola. The distance from Senigallia was not great, and he could see his mother often.

The resolve was difficult to fulfill because of the bishop's many burdens and reforms. The establishment of a seminary had been one of John Mary's first concerns. Before his time the young men studying for the priesthood in Imola had lived with private families or their own people. This circumstance led to many abuses. Often a newly ordained priest was found to have little or no formal training in the spiritual life beyond his own somewhat desultory gleaning from spiritual books.

Now that was changed and John Mary himself watched the students' progress with a fatherly eye. He often dropped in and delighted the students by taking over a class, joining them in their meals, and exercises of piety. He gave them an open invitation to his house at any time, and asked them to sit in on the discussions of the Scriptural Academy that met each Sunday in his palace.

John Mary seemed more like an elder brother than an archbishop. No formality of approach, no stiffness of manner inhibited any of his actions. His own joyous optimism was the source of the tremendous influence he had on both clerics and people. They had never known anyone like him in their lives before, and his manly frankness and tranquil exterior gave them an insight into a greatness not based on worldly ideas.

At the time of the yearly retreat John Mary followed every exercise like the humblest of his priests. But he shone among them by the depth of his concentration and the ardor of his devotion. He knew how to deliver a reproof with courteous indirectness, but those of his priests who had found him wrong in any of his quick decisions were amazed to hear him admit his mistakes with equal quickness. To them he seemed a kind of Saint Peter in the disguise of a prince.

Gregory XVI knew John Mary's worth by the state of Imola itself. The once divided town had become a model of order. John Mary had rather cut the ground from under the feet of the liberal and revolutionary group by wishing the Austrians out of Italy. Italian affairs he could discuss with fire and good sense. John Mary read all the new authors like Gioberti: their good points, and bad, he could enumerate with critical directness. His friendship with the noted liberal, Count Pasolini, brought him in touch with the most enlightened group in his diocese. This group of people were amazed to find how their apostolic bishop shone out in their company and made them seem a bit dated or harebrained in the uninformed way in which they reasoned about coming things.

The whole diocese fairly turned itself inside out with joy with John Mary's nomination to the Cardinalate, December 23, 1839. John Mary received the news with a sad heart summed up in his iron saying, "The office of Cardinal will aquire scant glory from my nomination."

It was not until a year later that John Mary actually received the honor, on December 14, 1840. On the following day he took possession of his titular church, Saints Peter and Marcellinus, near the basilica of Saint John Lateran.

John Mary's mother was enormously pleased with the honor. "It is too bad your dear father didn't live to see this day. He always wanted you to be a general. I'm sure he would have been satisfied that Christ and Mary knew what was best for you."

"To be a Prince of the Church is nothing," her son replied, "unless there is a pure soul and a worthy heart beneath the purple. Pray that God will strengthen me, mother."

Three years later, in January 1842, John Mary looked down on his mother's dead face in the coffin. She was like the great mothers extolled in the Scriptures, strong in love and virtue. She had vowed him to the heavenly Mother, and now she would pray for him and keep him worthy of his calling. But there was a piercing sorrow in her departure. She had been first to show joy and interest in all his concerns and plans. He would miss the mirror of her eyes in which he always saw reflected the true image of himself. Life would never again have the same fullness.

Three years remained for his work in Imola, and they were years of tremendous burdens and continued activity. His appointment to various Roman Congregations drew him frequently to the Holy City. It was clear that Cardinal Lambruschini, Secretary of State, didn't care much for the "liberal Cardinal" but he had to admit that John Mary was a man of ideas, well loved by his people. Seldom had a Cardinal worn the purple with greater beauty of form and manner. He seemed a natural prince among the many who held that title, but lacked the innate majesty that went with it.

For his part, John Mary's sense of humor saved him from any sense of hurt at Lambruschini's coldness. In his own eyes he was an amusing nothing that God had seen fit to use. No one laughed harder than himself to hear the opinion of his family expressed by the Cardinal Secretary, "Even the cats in the Mastai household are liberals."

Chapter IV

ELECTION AND CORONATION

CARDINAL MASTAI received the news of the death of Gregory XVI shortly after June 1, 1846. At once he prepared to go to Rome for the conclave. Baladelli, his valet, said to him in the midst of packing: "Your Eminence, there's only one thing I fear about this journey. I'm afraid you won't be returning to Imola." The Cardinal's eyebrows went up in a quizzical manner. "I am going to Rome to help elect a Pope, Baladelli. I hardly expect God to work a great miracle. The Sacred College can boast many distinguished prelates who are worthy of the papacy. For them God does not need to work a miracle."

John Mary saw only too well the terrible responsibility that lay upon the shoulders of himself and his brother Cardinals. Gregory XVI had been a man of deep spirituality. He had kept his eyes squarely focused on the spiritual concerns of the Church. Any comprehension of the popular movements of the day was quite beyond him. The rising tide of Italian nationalism seemed to him simple rebellion. All forms of liberalism were suspect in his eyes, and the era of modern invention and progress appeared an abomination to him. On seeing a working model of a railway engine in Rome, the Pope had exclaimed, "What a diabolical machine!" This statement fairly well represents his general outlook on the world.

While other kingdoms were modernizing themselves and

their machinery of government, Gregory had refused to consider political reforms of any kind. A considerable number of his subjects were in papal prisons because of their political opinions. Backed by the strong arm of Austria, the Pope's Secretary of State, Lambruschini, had held with astute realism the line laid down in the Congress of Vienna. Yet it must be confessed that the Papal States were the most backward in the kingdom of Europe. Lack of railroads and good postroads made trade and travel difficult. Repression had cost far more than modernization. The papal treasury was heavily in debt to the Rothschilds.

John Mary realized that something creative had to be done. To live was to grow along with the good things of the times. So often he and Count Pasolini had been over this ground: discussing, arguing, planning what should be done. The States of the Church cried aloud for a Pope who would be liberal enough to try his hand at utilizing the new movements in the service of the papacy and the service of God. The old static and repressive ideas had proved themselves impossible.

As John Mary jolted over the bad roads to Rome in the lumbering coach painted with his coat-of-arms, he stopped to chat with his friends along the way in the little towns and villages. They were all concerned, like himself, with the seriousness of the conclave. In true Italian fashion they made jocose remarks about Cardinal Mastai's surety of election and the Cardinal made equally funny retorts about the rewards they could expect after his accession. There is every indication that John Mary never considered himself a papal possibility. He was happy among his own people. The heavy tasks God had thrust upon him in Imola demanded the full exercise of his talents. His responsibility to Christ for the good he accomplished or the evil he did had long been in his mind since his mother had first taught him a prayer that he said every day of his life:

"Humbly prostrate at thy sacred feet, O most holy Virgin,

we confess our sins, so many, so grave! By them we have earned the wrath of the Divine Justice. Because of this we are filled with sorrow and repentance, and beat our breasts. Because of this we have recourse to thee, refuge of sinners.

"Ah, Mother, full of kindness, do not refuse us thy help in obtaining pardon from our merciful Lord.

"Pardon us, O Lord for our great sins. Pardon the sins of all weak Christians. Grant us pardon by the merits of Thy Precious Blood and through the merits of Thy Holy Mother. Grant us pardon through the merits of Saint Joseph, her chaste spouse, Thy father protector and our help in the agony of death! Grant us pardon through the merits of all the saints of heaven!

"Peace, Lord! Peace, Virgin most merciful! Peace between us and God! Peace between all Christians! Amen!"

Rank and station meant nothing, that was obvious. They were merely an indication of the weightier cross God and His Mother had asked John Mary to carry, the weightier responsibility he would have to answer for.

At Fossombrone a white dove flew down and rested on the top of John Mary's coach. This portent evoked a fresh volley of quips from his coachman and the members of his suite, and caused much talk at all the places where they stopped.

John Mary had hardly time to greet Cavaliere Filippani and Victoria his wife before he was caught up in the meetings and ceremonies attending the burial of the Pope and the interim government of the Church.

The College of Cardinals was fairly small at the time. John Mary, because of his long residence in Rome, the eminence of his family in the Papal States, and his socialized and liberal outlook was well known among the members of the Sacred College. Most of the Cardinals were older than John Mary. They had known him as a young priest and a good bishop. Now he was standing among them with a repose and princely bearing that fairly put them all in the shade. His analyses of the political situation were brilliant: they showed that he had given world affairs and papal policy deep thought and had some interesting solutions to advance.

Sunday, the 14th of June, was the day set for the opening of the conclave. The skies were flawless blue, the sun blazed in the warm air.

After his Mass was over and the Cardinal was having breakfast with his hosts and their six-year-old daughter Julia, the house was suddenly inundated with visitors: Cardinals, important heads of Congregations, members of the nobility and the priesthood. Among them was Father Ventura, the most celebrated preacher of the day. They all came to pay their respects to the Cardinal of Imola.

The card of Monsignor Pecci (later Leo XIII) was brought in to John Mary on the heavy silver tray.

"Tell the Monsignor to come in," John Mary informed the butler. "I shall be happy indeed to meet the distinguished young prelate."

The morning passed in excited discussion of the dangerous state of the public mind: wildly disturbed in the legations or provinces, restless and excited in Rome itself, which was heavily guarded with Papal troops.

In the late afternoon John Mary stood in the courtyard of the Filippani house in the Piazza dei Ara Coeli. He was bidding his old friends a brief goodbye. "I don't think we'll be long at this election," he told the Cavaliere. "The political situation is too explosive."

Donna Victoria, holding her daughter Julia by the hand, broke in on their political interests. "It is always such a pleasure to have you in our house, Your Eminence. Whatever you do, be sure you don't change the color of your *zucchetto*."

John Mary broke into a full-throated laugh. "Oh, Donna Victoria, you needn't worry about that. There isn't the remotest danger."

John Mary stepped from his coach in the great courtyard of
the Quirinal. His eyes saluted the fresco of Mary on the tower.
The Cardinal's grave face was warmed with a smile at the
thought of her long kindness to him. Carriages of prelates constantly rumbled in through the gate discharging Cardinals and
their attendants. The great staircase was agitated with a veritable river of purple.

The great hall had been prepared for the conclave. All
around the edge of its vast expanse had been erected the tiny
cells which were to be the living quarters of the Cardinals until
a new Pope had been elected. The cells were about eight feet
square, of heavy purple serge. Each cell was furnished with
austere simplicity. This provision followed the rules laid down
by Gregory X in the General Council of Lyons. It was hoped
by this somewhat Spartan arrangement to impel the Cardinals
not to linger over the choice of a Pope.

Somehow John Mary was suddenly reminded of his old
cubicle in the dormitory at Volterra. He thought of his days of
pain there when everything had looked so hopeless. Now God
had made his path clear, and he was to have the privilege of
electing a Pope. The straitened quarters would be like camp-
ing out. Heaven knew he was used to that from his childhood.
The South American voyage, too, had prepared him well for
such an austere interlude.

He walked down the narrow aisle between the purple cells,
greeting his friends among the Cardinals and then went through
the tremendous door to the Pauline chapel, with its neat thrones
arranged in order for the actual conclave. Kneeling before the
altar John Mary dropped his head into his hands. His prayer
began in direct fashion. "Inspire me, Lord, to do the right thing.
Show me Thy will. . . ."

Late in the evening the heralds went through the halls ex-
cluding all externs from the conclave. There was a ringing of
bells from the tower, last hurried goodbyes, a scurrying of feet.

Then the Cardinal-Dean turned the inside lock, and the Prince Marshal the one on the outside. A sudden silence fell on them all. They were alone with their thoughts and the Holy Spirit.

Until a Pope had been elected they would all be under the most careful surveillance to see that there was no communication with the world outside waiting with burning curiosity to hail the election of a new Pope. Latecomers among the Cardinals would be admitted under minute scrutiny and cause a brief flurry of excitement.

There would always be a murmur of amused laughter at the hour when the Cardinals' meals arrived in the outer courtyard. John Mary himself could laugh at the prospect of the baked chickens that would ride in his coach these days through Rome and would appear on one of the dumb waiters under the violet veil Donna Victoria had embroidered with his coat-of-arms.

The committee of prelates appointed would look under the dishes, and they wouldn't hesitate to examine the insides of the fowls or fish, so rigid were the rules of secrecy.

The officials of the conclave were quickly chosen by ballot. John Mary was pleased to be teller of the votes. It would be his duty to announce to the waiting Cardinals the mounting totals in favor of the candidates. In his own mind John Mary favored Cardinal Gizzi, who in recent years had spoken out strongly in favor of liberal policies. The people of Rome were sure Gizzi would be elected, and they went about the city whispering their surety until they considered it an accomplished fact. The conservative Cardinals were opposed to Gizzi. They favored a continuation of severity, and could be expected to stand solidly behind Lambruschini.

At the end of the morning vote John Mary's forecast of the election was almost completely nullified, with the addition of a staggering surprise. Lambruschini had fifteen votes, Gizzi two, and John Mary thirteen. He found it impossible to believe his voice, but he repressed his rising excitement with the thought that the early votes were ballots of orientation and meant very little.

Cardinal Mastai's confidence was shaken by the evening vote called the *accessus*. In this vote the Cardinals in those days were not allowed to vote for their candidate of the morning. Yet in this balloting John Mary read off his name seventeen times. His closest competitor, Lambruschini, had thirteen votes.

The morning scrutiny of the 16th of June, bore out the conclusion of the night before. John Mary received twenty-seven votes, Lambruschini thirteen. John Mary couldn't doubt the eventual conclusion now. He had asked Christ for health to carry any cross. The shadow of the heaviest cross in Christendom loomed before him.

The late night vote confirmed his fears. Thirty-four votes were required to provide the two-thirds majority required. On the twenty-eighth reading of his name John Mary turned white, his voice shook and faltered. "I beg you, Cardinal-Dean, allow me to retire from my task of reader."

The Cardinal-Dean shook his head. "To retire would invalidate this election which is the work of the Holy Ghost. Let His Eminence of Imola sit down for a moment and compose himself. Then we will proceed."

John Mary dropped his shaking hands into his lap. The demand had come. What kind of a son was he to deny his Lord?

His hands showed no tremor and his voice was clear while he read off the remaining votes. He had been given thirty-six, two more votes than the thirty-four required.

John Mary prostrated himself before the papal altar. When he arose he appeared to be strengthened with new vigor. To the question of the Cardinal-Dean asking his acceptance of the will of the Sacred College, John Mary's words seemed to be the words of the submission he had just made to Christ. "Behold Thy unworthy servant, O Lord. Thy will be done! I accept the result of the election."

After the clothing of the new Pope in the white cassock and the formal homage of the Cardinals, John Mary announced his name. It could be none other than Pius because of his profound love of Pius VII. The hour was too late for the announcement of the election to the people. Except for a few stubborn watchers, the crowd had retired for the night, and it was thought best to keep the news secret until the next day.

The new Pope went into his cell and prayed longer than usual. Then, asking for pen and paper he wrote a letter to his brothers in Senigallia:

> Rome, 16 *June, quarter of an hour before midnight.*
> Dear Brothers: The blessed God, who humbles and exalts, has been pleased to raise me from insignificance to the most sublime dignity on earth. May His most holy will be ever done. I am fully conscious of the immense weight of my charge, and I also feel my utter incapacity for it and the nothingness of my talents in the face of it. Ask everyone to pray for me, and do you also pray. The conclave lasted forty-eight hours. If the city of Senigallia should wish to make any public demonstration on the occasion, I beg you to take measures—indeed it is my command—that the whole sum set aside should be applied to purposes that may be judged useful to the city by the chief magistrate and the council. As to yourselves, dear brothers, I embrace you with all my heart, in Jesus Christ. Instead of exulting, pity your brother, who gives you his apostolic blessing.

When he had signed the letter, the new Pope committed his soul to God, got into his narrow bed and slept like a child.

The morning of June 17th was ushered in with a salute of guns from the Castle of Sant' Angelo. Hearing it the people of Rome knew that a Pope had been elected. From every section and street of the old city they came rushing and panting up the steep hill to the Quirinal. The big square was soon a solid mass of humanity. Some climbed to the pedestal of the slender Egyptian obelisk; bolder spirits perched on the backs of the gigantic marble horses ornamenting the fountain in the square. All eyes were fixed on the large balcony from which the announcement would be made. They were all sure it would be Cardinal Gizzi and his name went buzzing among them in whispered sentences.

At last there was a movement in the walled-up window at the rear of the balcony. Slowly the masons took out the stones, one by one, until the space was completely free. The papal cross came to the front of the balcony, the purples of the Cardinals made it blossom. Then the Cardinal-Dean gave the traditional announcement in Latin.

"Romans, I announce to you a great joy. We have a new Pope, the Most Eminent and Most Reverend Giovanni Maria Mastai-Ferretti, Bishop of Imola, who has assumed the name of Pius IX." Before he retired the Cardinal-Dean threw a paper to the people containing, in Italian, a translation of the Latin.

An imperial figure clad in the papal robes came to the front of the balcony. He seemed young and fair. His hair was thick and dark. It wasn't Gizzi after all, but another Cardinal, vigorous and somehow hopeful. The people all fell on their knees. A singing voice of great beauty was giving the papal benediction, then the new Pope opened his arms wide in a dramatic gesture as if to embrace them all.

On the morning of his coronation, June 21, 1842, Pius IX rose with the dawn. It was the feast of Saint Aloysius, the patron saint of purity. Meditation for John Mary was not a duty, it was the very breath of his spiritual life. In the presence of God he would somehow find the vigor to carry him through this morning of splendor to the mountainous tasks before him in the papacy. God had appointed him to this eminence of responsibility, and perhaps if John Mary listened closely enough to the voice of God he would not make too many mistakes. The successor of Peter would always need the gift of tears.

The young Pope's heart was quiet as they robed him in the full pontificals of his power. He seemed to be still in contemplation as he was borne across the city from the sun-washed slopes of the Quirinal to the palace of the Vatican across the Tiber. Sky and trees and water saluted him with summer serenity. They were like a thousand voices calling to him out of his childhood, telling him how little he was, how frail and defectible. The houses along the way were not decorated in his honor, but to pay tribute to the Vicar of Christ.

The rondure of Saint Peter's dome was an outline of perfection in the morning sky. The great square before the church was thronged with people who had come out to see the untarnished splendor that attended the coronation of the last Pope-King.

Formed in the great hall of the Vatican palace, the coronation procession descended the grand staircase and emerged into the piazza. A vast silence seized the great crowd. The courts of Spain, Austria, and England knew something of pomp, but their knowledge of ordered pageantry was cast into the shade by the oldest kingdom in Christendom with its living memories of Rome and Byzantium.

Pages, procurators, choristers, consistorial advocates, auditors of the Rota advanced in waves of color. Then came the papal cross borne by the Apostolic Subdeacon. The image of the Crucified was turned in the direction of the Pope, a living reminder of his fate.

A flash of gold and crystal in the sunlight—that was the seven gilt chandeliers borne by red-robed acolytes. Penitentiaries, commanders of the Holy Ghost, archbishops and bishops, mitred abbots in their turn, prepared the eyes of the spectators for the splendor of the College of Cardinals, the cloth-of-silver of their capes held by chaplains.

After them came the chiefs of the civil government. The senators were like sheaves of fire in their robes of gold; the governor of the Eternal City seemed a pillar of snow in his ermine cloak. The Prince Assistant to the throne brought back a note of severity with his black silk dress of ceremony foaming with exquisite lace at wrist and collar.

Swords, maces, the shining tabards of the heralds, the halberds of the Swiss Guards held high and glinting in the sunlight, were like the final chords of a prelude that led to the climax of the procession—the hieratic figure of the Pope borne aloft on the chair of state. Here the red of the mantles of the chairbearers seemed refracted in every shade of rose and crimson worn by the surrounding dignitaries bearing the staves of the heavy gold canopy and the great feathered fans that seemed old as Egypt, magnificent as Persia.

From the shoulders of the Pope a jeweled cope rippled in folds about his shining cassock. A precious stole caught the light and refracted glints of color on the serenely smiling face. The noble head was crowned with a gold mitre, the right hand was raised in continual blessing.

The crowd flew into a frenzy of demonstration. "Long live the the Pope-King! Long live Pius IX! *Viva il Papa! Viva il Papa!*" Back and forth across the square swept the storm of sound.

Behind the Pope's chair the procession still came forward: the high officers of the Pope's army in blazing court dress, the official members of the Pope's household in their full livery of office, staffs, and shining chains. The generals of the religious orders closed the procession that seemed like a river of color and fire under the dazzling sun.

A temporary throne had been erected in the porch near the Porta Pia—the door that is only opened every Holy Year. The procession halted, and Pius IX descended from the *sedia*. He seated himself on the throne for the homage of the Cardinal Archpriest of Saint Peter's, the Canons, and officials of the great fabric. They all kissed the Pope's slipper. Then the Pope was carried once more through the great central door of the most splendid church in Christendom. A salute of silver trumpets rang through the reaches of the vast temple and was lost in the far shadows of the dome.

At the chapel of the Blessed Sacrament Pius left his chair of state. Bareheaded, and with affecting humility he lost himself in prayer. Let no one deceive himself. Here was the Master of the World, and the servant must kneel before Him. That act of homage, which looks into the heart of life, prepared the Pope for the triple ceremony of the quickly burning tow held high on the silver stick with the warning, "Holy Father, so passes the world and its glories!"

Through the noble church the Pope was carried in state to his great throne, and the Master of Ceremonies assigned the ranked dignitaries to their proper places. It seemed that all the glories of the world were gathered in this hierarchy about the golden chair. The chandeliers of lights were placed on the altar. They cast a soft glow on the massive silver-gilt cross, the candlesticks, and twisted bronze pillars of the tremendous baldachin.

With mystic pomp the Pope was vested for the Mass of coronation. It was like a dream of beauty. Gold, silver, jewels, all the arts and artifices of mankind had been sacked for this moment. It was no vulgar display, but more nearly like a page torn from the Apocalypse to signalize the glory of Christ's descent upon the altar and the luminous splendor refracted from Him upon His Vicar.

After the *Gloria* was finished, the first Cardinal-Deacon, with the red rod of office, accompanied by two officers of the Rota and the consistorial advocates arranged themselves in two files. Across the apse they went and descended into the Confession above the tombs of Saint Peter and Saint Paul. From the vault of the chapel, like a voice from the past was heard three times the cry, *"Exaudi, Christe!"* Three times the choir answered with a ringing burst of melody, *"Domino nostro Pio Nono, a Deo decreto summo Pontifici et Papae, Vita!*

Then began the litanies of the coronation calling the holiest names of history to strengthen Christ's Vicar and to witness the continuity of Christ in the world.

At length the Sacrifice was accomplished: the incense still rose in clouds through the shafts of sunlight, the music took on a new note of aspiring splendor—the moment for coronation had arrived. The Pope was bowed before the altar making his thanksgiving. Once more he got into the chair of state. The Cardinal-Dean of Saint Peter's knelt before Pius and presented him with a gold and white purse filled with antique gold coins as an offering from Saint Peter's Chapter. The procession then re-formed, and following the papal cross went back through the nave of the church. The Pope once more stopped at the Sacrament Chapel, bent his knees in adoration, and was carried to the large balcony of the loggia overlooking the square before Saint Peter's.

The roofs of the galleries and colonnades were packed with noble visitors from all the nations of the earth: kings, princes, the famous and the wealthy. The blaze of jewels and silks seemed to go in waves to the far reaches of the piazza, where it was once more caught up in a riot of flags, tapestries, lights and flowers that framed the balconies and windows of the surrounding houses. Circled with this glory was the swaying, dark mass of the watching crowd.

A rush of song from the papal choir began the magnificent melody of the coronation hymn, *Corona super caput ejus.* The Cardinal-Dean then recited the *Pater* and the choir responded. The Cardinal-Dean approached and repeated the usual Latin oration. At its close the second Cardinal-Deacon removed the mitre from the Pope's head.

The first Cardinal-Deacon, to whom the right of crowning belongs, lifted the superb triple tiara, given to Pius VII by

Napoleon. With a graceful, sweeping gesture the deacon placed the crown on the Pope's head with these words: "Receive the triple crown, and remember that thou art the father of princes, and the guide of kings upon the earth, the Vicar of Our Savior Jesus Christ, to Whom be honor and glory forever. Amen."

The *sedia* continued its progress toward the people. Two bishops knelt down, one holding the book of the Evangelists, the other a lighted taper, while the Pope said the following prayer: "May the Holy Apostles Peter and Paul, in whose authority we place our confidence, intercede for us with Our Lord.

"May the prayers and merits of the Blessed Mary, ever Virgin, of Blessed Michael the Archangel, of blessed John the Baptist, and the Holy Apostles Peter and Paul, and all the saints, and God Almighty have pity upon thee, and Jesus Christ conduct thee to life eternal.

"Thus be it—indulgence, absolution, and remission for all thy sins, a time of true and abundant repentance, a heart always penitent, and the correction of thy life, the grace and consolation of the Holy Spirit, and the perseverance in good works accorded to thee by the almighty and merciful Lord. Amen."

After this prayer, which the Pope pronounced with great emotion, Pius IX, standing up in the *sedia,* lifted his eyes to heaven. He opened his arms, as though he were about to clasp all mankind in one paternal embrace; then, after making the sign of the Redemption with his hand in the air three times, he three times repeated, *"Benedictio Dei Omnipotentis, Patris et Filii et Spiritus Sancti, descendat super vos et maneat semper."* The whole multitude responded with a shouted *Amen* that was counterpointed with a deafening chorus of bells from Saint Peter's, and the roaring of cannon from the Castle of Sant' Angelo.

Before the Pope quitted the loggia, he gave the last blessing. The whole procession once more got under way, while the people rushed into the avenues of the porticos in order to receive the Latin and Greek formulas of the plenary indulgence just given to all who had fulfilled the required conditions.

The Cardinals returned to the church and divested themselves of their copes, which they replaced by the large red mantles of their rank. They followed the *sedia* of Pius IX to the robing hall of the Vatican. There the Pope put on his ordinary costume. After this, the Cardinal-Dean complimented him in the name of the Sacred College, expressing the wishes of all for his happiness, prosperity, and a long reign. Pius IX in an affectionate reply thanked the Cardinals and asked them to pray for him. Then, proceeded by the pontifical cross, the Pope left his palace of the Vatican and was carried through the shouting crowds back to the sun-haloed hill of the Quirinal.

Chapter V

THE POPE BEGINS HIS REIGN

PIUS IX spent the first ten days of his reign surveying the needs of his spiritual and temporal kingdoms. Heads of both realms were summoned for consultation. The Pope had a thousand questions to ask about procedures, administration, funds, and spiritual outlooks. He asked his questions rapidly and then courteously gave full rein to the answers. His head was cocked to one side, his fine eyes filled with intelligent and con-centrated interest, while the pen in his beautiful fingers flew over the paper. The Pope made extensive notes on things to be done—tentative measures that might or might not be successful.

The Pope also chose his advisors with care. The names of his ministers came as something of a surprise to all those who feared that a "liberal" Pope would sweep out the old wisdoms with a careless hand. Cardinal Gizzi was appointed Secretary of State, but the Pope's council was headed by Cardinals Macchi and Lambruschini, and by Mattei, who had been Secretary of State under Pius VII. The most intimate members of the Pope's household were drawn from the ranks of prelates noted for their wisdom and charity.

Among the new appointments was a canonry at Saint Peter's. A long list of titled candidates was presented for the Pope's choice. He scanned it swiftly and then looked up at his advisors with a grave glance, with just the faintest twinkle of merriment in it. The Pope drew his pen through the names to show that he had cancelled them. Then poising the instrument, he observed in that melodious voice that never lost its charm: "One name is missing on the list, the Abbé Ponzileoni. He is neither count, marquis nor Roman prince. But he is a learned priest, zealous and charitable. The Abbé has consecrated his life to good works, and he will be of good service to us. He is the person I have chosen for the vacant canonry. Men of his stamp are dear to us. We should and will recompense them."

It was the same appreciation of talent and holiness that caused Pius IX to make Abbé Graziosi a Canon of Saint John Lateran and his confessor. Guido, too, had to be remembered, and Bako his savior far off in South America. Baladelli, his faithful valet from Imola, was settled in Rome with his wife and children.

John Mary received his own family with unaltered affection, but his brothers and relations knew him well enough to expect nothing but a cordial welcome and good advice. The advancement of his family was allowed no place during the Pope's long reign or in his many gifts.

The Pope's first interview with Countess Victoria Mastai was both charming and humorous.

John Mary could see that Donna Victoria was deeply impressed with his new honor. She bent to kiss his ring and then rose and said nothing. The Pope's eyes were dancing but his face was grave. "I hope you remember to say your night and morning prayers, Donna Victoria."

A look of perplexity and near panic passed across his aunt's face. "Remember," the Pope said, "you told me if I didn't say my prayers I might as well throw my Catechism out of the window." The Pope was laughing. He rose from his chair and kissed his aunt on both cheeks. What a joy she had been to him!

Officers, friends and relations were all surprised to see the humble atmosphere in which the Pope chose to live. His bedroom was furnished with simplicity. The iron bed was un-adorned. A prie-adieu completed the furniture, with the little lemonwood cross his mother had given him hung above it. There was not a single strip of carpet on the tiled floor. His study contained a great desk, adorned with a crucifix, a massive chair behind the desk and several small occasional gilt chairs for guests. There was a tiny strip of carpet under the desk alone.

Pius was quick to declare his policy to the first inquiring visitors. "My people may expect justice and mercy from me, for my only guide is this book." The Pope placed his hand on the New Testament.

Between talks on policy, reform, and the engrossing tasks that fell with increasing heaviness upon the new Pope, he some-how found time to visit the entire Quirinal. He inquired into all the departments of the huge building. Among them was the papal stable. The unaccompanied Pope was amazed at the huge number of beautiful horses standing in the well-kept stalls.

"How many have you?" he asked the Farrier Major.

"Sixty, Your Holiness."

There was a look of horror on the Holy Father's face. "Sixty horses," he cried. "We need horses for the honest work of Christ's Vicar. But sixty! You must sell half of them immedi-ately."

This was only the beginning of reform. The huge staff of gardeners was cut, the queues of guards, and the superabundant lackeys with their powdered hair and bulging silk-clad calves.

The Pope seemed to be all over the place—curtailing, arrang-ing, giving precise directions. His complete lack of ceremony filled the papal household with amazement. His speech was direct and kindly, but it had an elusive magnetism that gave force to his slightest word.

On one occasion the Pope, in his study, was discussing for-eign affairs with Cardinal Gizzi. The Holy Father felt thirsty and asked his secretary for a glass of lemonade. Two silver-gilt trays arrived almost at once. They were fairly loaded with varied drinks, little sandwiches, and cakes.

"What's all this?" the Pope inquired. "Didn't I ask for a glass of lemonade?"

"Yes, Your Holiness, but it is the custom always to offer the Pope something that might give him a choice or tempt his appetite."

"It's a bad custom then. Get me a glass, some water, a lemon and sugar."

The request was fulfilled with speed. The Pope thanked the servant, himself squeezed the lemon, poured in the water, sweetened the drink and tasted it. "That's good," he told the servant. "And in future when I ask for something please forget all the old customs and bring only what I request. Meanwhile, take this food and all these drinks out into the square and give them to the poor."

On another occasion, the Pope was quick to remark to his chef, after a dinner of many courses, "The Pope is not Lucullus. His diet should be that of a simple priest. No more is necessary." In explaining his wishes about food to his chief steward the Pope observed with wit: "It wasn't my stomach that was crowned Pope."

Those nearest to the Pope could understand his economies, for they all began with himself. They came into being not from some Utopian theory but from the spiritual bases of his existence. His long meditation, the Mass he offered and the Mass of thanksgiving he heard after it, were the beginning of a day broken by short prayers and, whenever possible, two or three hours of meditation before the Blessed Sacrament. One of his suite who thought the length of time excessive questioned the Pope about it. Pius looked at his interrogator with a piercing glance that was almost a rebuke. "The poor Pope has the greatest need of all to spend a little time with Our Lord. I have so many things to tell Him. So much light, so much counsel, so many graces to beg of Him."

The Pope's wisdom garnered in the personal visits with his Lord ran quickly into word and act among his close associates. The moment the Angelus bell rang Pius stopped all work and rose with his suite, took off his *zucchetto,* and began the ancient prayer. At its conclusion the Pope recited the *De profundis* for all the faithful departed of the world.

Next to his own responsibilities the Pope thought first of his priests. He planned a central Roman seminary to care for the needs of students from every section of Italy. They were to have the advantage of brilliant professors and every resource of spiritual direction.

A further reform was added in legislation that made it obligatory for priests, students, and prelates to wear the cassock. In former reigns there had been a careless disregard for clerical dress. Some great prelates had far more resembled princes than clerics, and the Pope's sweeping reform in dress put a stop to these abuses.

Yet it is not to be presumed that Pius IX was trying to raise barriers of formality between priests and people. The Popes preceding him had kept themselves at a distance from their subjects. Pius wanted nothing of this, and his own actions soon showed the simplicity, friendliness and humanity he expected his priests to show at all times.

On the second of July, 1846, the Pope walked out of a side entrance of the Quirinal. He wore the dress of an abbot and was accompanied by two monsignori in simple black. Pius loved to walk and he moved briskly along the street toward the Convent dell'Umiltà, where the feast of the Visitation was being celebrated. It wasn't long before some of the people recognized the young Pope. They knelt for his blessing and then followed after him toward his destination.

By the time Mass was over a tremendous crowd had gathered outside the convent. When the Pope emerged the people cheered him again and again. Some peasants, in naive fashion, gave fulsome expression to their admiration for his youth and handsome bearing. "What a lovely Pope!" "How handsome he is!" "What beautiful manners!" The Pope, undisturbed by the din, gave his blessing, received petitions, and with the aid of his two companions distributed medals and alms. The police tried to break up the demonstration but the Pope rebuked them. "Let the people come to me! Don't keep them away! A father can't be too near his children!" This statement evoked a wilder volley of cheers that followed the Pope all the way back to the Quirinal.

This casual appearance which shocked the more conservative members of the Pope's household was the first of many. John Mary wanted to see everything in Rome for himself. He actively loved his people as he had done in Imola and Spoleto. His social work in the hospices had taught him the value of getting his information personally. Night schools, prisons, hospitals— the Pope visited them all. He would appear suddenly, unaccompanied, or with one or two priests. A black cape covered his white cassock, a broad clerical hat shaded his serene face.

At one school the principal did not immediately recognize her distinguished visitor. "Why should you observe the classes?" she said. "I'm sure the Pope would not approve of this disturbance." The Pope threw back his cape and revealed his white cassock. "The Pope thinks you're wrong. But don't be disturbed. I just want to see how the good work goes forward." The Pope went into the classrooms and spoke to the children. He questioned them about their work and studies and gave medals and prizes to those who answered well.

In prisons and hospitals he visited the sickest patients, encouraged them and, if necessary, heard their confessions and anointed them in their last agony. Always he inquired about the administration and endowments. Nor did he hesitate to suggest, on the spot, improvements he thought necessary.

Often enough on such errands of inquiry the Pope was asked for special favors. On one occasion a small boy approached the tall figure. The child was crying. The Pope, who had always loved children, stooped down and put one arm around the boy. The tears fell less fast. "Why are you crying, my son?"

"I'm crying, my father," answered the lad, thinking the Pope was a simple priest, "because I have no father."

"Come now, don't cry, my son. I will be your father." The Pope made the proper inquiries and discovered that the child was an orphan. He placed him in a school and provided funds for his education and care.

Of the hundreds of stories of the Pope's friendly benevolence that circulated in Rome, one has a charm above all others.

The Pope, without state, was driving through the street in a simple black carriage. He observed a crowd gathered about the figure of a man lying on the cobblestones. No one seemed to be helping the man. With a quick command the Pope halted the carriage, got out and approached the scene. A stocky, dark-haired man lay stretched on the blazing stones. "Who is it?" the Pope asked.

"It's a filthy Jew," one of the bystanders said, spitting as he spoke.

All the indignation of his heart was in the Pope's stern answer. "It's a man!"

With the aid of his coachman and some of the shamed bystanders the Pope carried the man to his carriage and put him under the care of his own physician.

The sequel to the story is an astonishing one, for the Jew grew to love the Pope and became a Christian. In baptism he chose the name of Pio Manuele.

One day, years later, when the Pope was driving out on one

of his private visits to his people, the horses bolted and ran away. The Pope was in some danger as the carriage careened over the rough street. Suddenly a bystander leaped from the footpath. He caught the bridle of one of the horses and with some effort and damage to himself brought the team to a halt. The man was bleeding badly and some bystanders helped him to a nearby fountain where he could wash his wounded wrists and feet. The Pope went over to help. To his amazement he discovered the Jew he had rescued long ago. "Why, it's my good Pio Manuele," the Pope cried embracing his benefactor. "Come, my son, once again I'll take you to my own doctor."

The Pope had, as a matter of fact, gone out of his way to help all the Jews. He had ordered the gates of the ancient ghetto to be left open day and night. Pius enlarged the civil and political privileges of this much-abused segment of his people. But he did far more than that.

Shortly after his coronation a group of distinguished Jews was received in audience. Opening a soft linen cloth they unveiled a superb chalice. It had been preserved in the ghetto for two hundred years and was a triumph of the goldsmith's art. The Pope turned the beautiful vessel about slowly, admiring every part of it. He stroked the delicate relief work with his fingers.

"It is kind of you, my sons," he said at last. "I accept your magnificent gift with pleasure. Thank you for it. I realize fully," the Pope continued, "that the piece is far beyond price, but what would you say is its value?"

The chief of the delegation thought for a moment. "It weighs five hundred Roman crowns, Your Holiness."

The Pope reached for a slip of paper, wrote on it, and gave it to the leader. "Please accept this small sum for the poor of the ghetto."

Written on the paper were the words: "Good for one thousand crowns, Pius IX."

The Pope's imperial benevolence and ready friendliness were balanced with an impartial justice that reveals the virile core of his manhood.

Looking out from his window one day the Pope saw a long queue of people waiting for their passports before the Secretariat of State. Over an hour later he saw the same crowd of people still waiting.

He at once sent a messenger to inquire into the reason for the delay. The Pope's messenger was told that the officer in charge was out to lunch. Upon the official's return the Pope summoned him to an interview.

"You have kept these simple people waiting for hours. It's a shame and a disgrace."

"But I was having my lunch."

The Pope snorted. "They were being robbed of time while you lunched. I order you to reimburse them by distributing 50 pauls among them."

"But I haven't got that much money, Holy Father."

The Pope reached into a drawer of the desk and counted out the required sum. "Here it is, then. Take it to these people. I'll order that amount to be struck from your wages."

The officer obeyed the Pope's command. "It was the most expensive lunch I've ever had," he complained to his friends.

In a gesture of paternal kindness on the opening of his reign the Pope had set aside a sum of money to be used as a dowry for young women too poor to get married. The sums were to be assigned by lot to one girl from each of the parishes in Rome. In one parish the pastor was displeased with the first name he drew from the bowl. He discarded the slip of paper and drew out the name of another young lady to whom he gave the dowry.

The father of the first girl complained personally to the Pope. The man had protested the injustice done his daughter, but the pastor had refused to receive him. Pius listened to the story.

His face was grim. "Stay here in the anteroom, my good friend. You will not be one too many for the conversation we are about to have with this good pastor."

The Pope sent a carriage to summon the pastor at once. When he arrived, somewhat overcome with fear, the Pope had the girl's father ushered in. Then the Pope addressed the priest.

"Do you recognize this man?"

"Yes, Holiness, he is one of my parishioners."

"Why did you refuse to receive him when he went to complain of your injustice?"

"I was not free, Your Holiness, I had a penitent to reconcile with God."

"You should have first reconciled yourself with God, my father, by making amends to this man. Why did you refuse to give his daughter the amount that her good fortune assigned her?" The priest said nothing.

"So you don't answer. Then you acknowledge your misconduct?"

"Yes, Holy Father."

"Very well. This is your punishment. First, you will beg this man's pardon. Then you will give to his daughter the sum assigned to her by lot. And out of your salary you will pay the second girl the sum of money you so graciously chose to give her."

In estimating the effect of the first year of the new Pope's pontificate historians are accustomed to make the Pope's popularity depend on his granting of an amnesty in July, one month after his election. The truth is that Pius IX was a new kind of Pope. The center of his life was religious and mystical. In the best tradition of western mysticism, as Bergson has pointed out, personal graces and enlightenment flow out into social channels. Pius loved God and His Mother with a tremendous personal love. Because he loved them so ardently he loved mankind on which they had poured out their love. The Pope's political action in declaring an amnesty cannot be understood unless we first understand the Pope's piety, personal benevolence, and love of justice.

Because he wanted to be the father of his people and must forgive them seventy times seven as commanded by the Scriptures, the Pope felt that he must do something for the political offenders of the last reign. When he first brought forward the idea to his Council a great many of the Cardinals were in violent and vigorous opposition. In order to appreciate their point of view it is necessary to understand something about Italian patriotism of the time.

Italy had long been divided into warring groups and kingdoms. Like the Poland of our day and the Israel of the Old Testament, she had been trampled by the greedy armies of the great powers. Under the astute leadership of Charles Albert of Piedmont, ably seconded by his minister Cavour, and Mazzini, the leader of the revolutionary party, new slogans came into being. "Italy must be unified. Foreigners must be driven out. Austria and France must be pushed back to their own borders." This rising tide of nationalism pleased every class. The poor saw in it a hope for a better future. The rich and the princes who loved to play at being republicans in cheap inns thought of the consolidation of their influence under a king who would control the entire peninsula.

Pius IX sympathized with a great many of the republican ideas. Anyone with half a brain could see that Italy should be allowed to manage her own destiny. But Pius remembered with equal force the words of his beloved model Pius VII to General Radet: "I cannot give away the patrimony of Peter. It is not mine to give!" The Pope was later to propose an astonishing solution, but in the first days of his reign he was pained to discover how many men had been imprisoned for having revolutionary ideas, many of which he himself sympathized with.

Some fifteen hundred were actually in prison. About the same number had been banished from the Papal States.

The young Pope's reading of men corresponded with his experience in Spoleto and Imola. If you treated a man like a beloved son he frequently became one. Now, as the universal father of the faithful, Pius IX was determined to usher in a period of forgiveness and liberality.

Even more than the members of his Council, the Austrian and French ambassadors reacted violently to the Pope's plan for an amnesty. Both countries were intent on keeping their influence in the peninsula. They were equally intent on hanging on to the Italian land they already occupied.

In particular, the Austrian ambassador, Count von Lutzow, pointed out to the Pope the danger of an amnesty. By it he would release a horde of the most noted malcontents in the kingdom. They could be expected to reward his generosity with a resumption of the plotting and intrigue that had brought about the revolution of 1831. The Pope smiled at the warning.

Austria was obviously more determined to serve her own purposes than she was in thinking of Italian justice or human justice. But as Pope he had a responsibility for both. Forgiveness had always been the cornerstone of his policy. Was it not also the cornerstone of God's providence and Christ's life?

In the final vote on the amnesty in the Pope's Council, a leather pouch was passed along the table. Into it the Cardinals dropped either a white or black ball: white if they favored the project, black if they were against it. When the pouch came back to the head of the table where the Pope sat, he could see at once that the black balls far outnumbered the white. They were all watching him for an expression of displeasure. The serenity on his face showed not the slightest alteration. He rose from his chair, took off his white zucchetto and covered the top of the pouch. "Now they are all white. The amnesty is carried."

The amnesty was posted on churches and public buildings, July 17, 1846. Briefly it embodied the following points:

1. All political offenders still in prison were to be granted full remission of their sentences if they would give their written word of honor to be good citizens.
2. All exiles from the Papal States were to be readmitted on the same condition.
3. Those excluded from holding municipal office and those under police surveillance were absolved of all further suspicion.
4. All criminal proceedings for political crimes were to stop, unless the accused themselves chose to clear their names in court.
5. The amnesty did not apply to those very few ecclesiastics, military officers, and employees of the government who had been condemned for actual crimes, had fled the Papal States, or were under trial for serious political crimes.
6. The amnesty did not apply to offenses committed against the common law by those men also under judgment for political crimes.

In a matter of hours the amnesty had been read by every grown person in Rome. At once the people fell into a veritable delirium of joy. Men cried and embraced each other. Public buildings and monuments blazed with flares as the evening drew on. Groups of torchlight processions converged on the Quirinal hill. The piazza was one sea of light. Roar after roar echoed until the Pope appeared on the balcony. On three different occasions during the course of the evening the white-clad figure raised his hand in benediction and then waved in a friendly gesture toward his excited subjects.

From this time forward, every public appearance of the Pope led to the wildest excitement. On one occasion the young men of the city unhitched the Pope's horses, pelted him with flowers, and the Pope's carriage was forced under two triumphal arches, one telling his virtues; the other composed of great sheaves of carnations and roses.

The decent people of Rome loved the Pope for his holiness and kindness exemplified in a wealth of stories told and retold in every meeting place and *albergo*. It was this good enthusiasm that the well-organized republicans were to twist into an instrument for overthrowing the Papal government.

It was a fine thing that the Pope's subjects should appreciate his good deeds and show enthusiasm for his person. Such spontaneous demonstrations might well have channeled into the many reforms the Pope had already planned: the liberalizing of government, the building of roads and railroads, customs reforms, public service utilities, and the ultimate and peaceful unification of Italy.

But there were groups of disciplined men determined to defeat the Pope's designs. These men caught up the popular enthusiasm of the mob and used it to achieve their own ends. Little by little this well-organized group twisted the popular enthusiasm for the Pope into evil ends that still plague us and Italy in our own day.

Liberals and freethinkers were in central control of the so-called republican movement. In London, particularly, Mazzini and Garibaldi laid their secret plans that envisaged the downfall of the Papal government and the destruction of the Church.

The instrument of their power was the Society of the Carbonari. It met in secret, had its own passwords, and punished defection with death by assassination. Hovering over the scene in the background were the ambitions of Piedmont for a unified kingdom of Italy. King Charles Albert, and his minister Count Cavour waited like vultures to take advantage of each bloody struggle for power.

All these evils seemed far away in the first honeymoon year of the new Pope's reign. The newspapers of the world were filled with his praise. In Protestant England and America he was held up as an example of all those qualities that mark an enlightened ruler of his people.

The first year was not without severe challenges to the Pope's decisive manliness.

The first of these was a crop failure in the Papal States. The Pope's treasury was almost empty but he met the crisis by abolishing all duties on foreign grains and cereals. With the removal of this barrier necessary supplies fairly poured in. All threat of famine was averted.

Then, in December, 1846, a long series of torrential rains caused the Tiber to overflow its banks. The whole southern end of the ancient city was covered with water to a depth of six feet. The Pope collected money among every class of citizens. Princes and peasants responded with alacrity. Soup kitchens, clothing depots, and hospitals were hurriedly set up. The Holy Father directed the rescue in person. Everywhere he went his appearance led to demonstrations of popular affection.

The evil genius of the Pope's first years was a man by the name of Angelo Brunetti. Brunetti was born poor, but through his cunning and shrewd investments he became a wealthy man. Always he posed as the people's friend, an old trick sure to attract a numerous following. Brunetti gave good advice free; he loaned money without security, but at a good rate of interest. His greatest asset was a talent for fiery oratory in the best tradition of the rabble rouser, that could sway the crowds in any direction. It was this last quality that earned him the nickname of "Ciceruacchio." On the surface this has an echo of Cicero, but actually in Italian slang it means, "the man with the fat jowls." Brunetti had a short neck and figure that good living had done nothing to improve.

Ciceruacchio was an ardent follower of Mazzini. The little fat man saw in the Pope's popularity a chance to increase his own influence and bring about the chaos desired by Mazzini.

All through the first summer and fall of the Pope's reign Brunetti and his lieutenants watched every movement of His Holiness and organized tumultuous ovations to celebrate his public appearances. When he paid visits to state schools or colleges the mob was encouraged to make a wild public demonstration. When occasions were lacking Ciceruacchio created them. The people of Rome were kept in a continual state of excitement. The Pope departed for a short holiday at Lake Albano. Throngs of people, screaming their benedictions, impeded his carriage to the city walls. The same undignified outburst of popular acclaim accompanied the Pope's return. In the midst of all was Ciceruacchio like Bacchus in a tail coat. He was loudest in his fulsome flattery of Pius IX, and he was always sure to be at the center of the spotlight. Sometimes he leaped on the front of the Pope's carriage, encouraging the mob to a madder transport of joy.

The Pope and his advisors were quick to see where these demonstrations were leading. On October 8, the Pope begged his Roman subjects to stop or curtail these noisy celebrations which constantly took people away from their work. The Holy Father asked the people to use the money spent in honoring him in the service of the poor and forsaken.

On November 8, the Pope, accompanied by his whole court, took possession of the Lateran Basilica, the oldest church in Christendom. The following day the Pope's first encyclical letter was addressed to the Universal Church. It shows only too clearly how little the Pope had been fooled by the wild demonstrations in his honor.

Pius did not hesitate to state his policy: he intended to fight to protect every right of religion. As a successor of Saint Peter it was his duty to guard the patrimony of the saint and to preserve intact the rights and privileges handed into his charge. Next the Pope lanced out at the errors of the day, described in detail the terrible condition of society, "which ought to arouse all the bishops of the world to vigilance and zeal." He forcibly condemned the assault on the celibacy of the clergy and the bad influence of all false teachers.

The conclusion of the encyclical was directed to the rulers of nations. The Pope reminded them that their power came to them from God. It was not only their duty to direct civil affairs. Their most grave responsibility was to protect, encourage and foster religion.

The encyclical is interesting because it brushes away many misapprehensions concerning the policies of Pius IX. He realized that his chief task was the struggle against modern errors and the religious indifference of his own people and the world. The preservation of the purity of the priesthood was necessary for the santification of men. Without these safeguards modern reforms were the ornaments of a whited sepulcher filled with dead men's bones.

As if to emphasize his drift, the Pope, on the 20th of November, issued a plenary indulgence to all the faithful who would go to confession and Communion and pray for his intention. The churches were thronged, and the manipulators of revolution were quick to see that Pius had unmasked their faces with his encyclical, and had indicated the true remedy for the evils of the time. The plotters gnashed their teeth in secret.

The celebration of the Pope's name day on December 27, indicated the deep reverence the people had for their ruler. When on New Year's eve, with the cheers of the crowds eddying about his coach, Pius IX drove to the Gesù for the annual *Te Deum* of thanksgiving, he could look back on a year of glowing triumph. As he knelt in the vast church with its decorations and statues in upward motion like restless flames, the Pope realized only too well that the whole year had been a veritable Palm Sunday of acclaim. He was deeply learned in the wisdom of the cross and he knew like his Master that the dark shadows of Gethsemani yawned before him.

Chapter VI

REBELLION

THE year 1847 was a prelude to the year of revolution and fury that followed it. Early in January of 1847 the Pope issued a *motu proprio* which set up a committee of censorship for all newspapers and tracts coming into his dominions. Five responsible censors were appointed. The measure was a necessary one. The fires of irresponsible revolution had been fanned to a blaze from abroad. In handbills and careless journalism the Church had been exposed to a campaign of slander, vilification, and outright lies.

The censorship was furiously condemned by the revolutionary party and their allies among the fellow-traveling liberals who followed much the pattern of the "liberals" of our own day. Though the censorship was obviously the work of Pius IX, his enemies pretended it had been forced on him by a group of repressive and conservative Cardinals. The Pope was still popular with the great mass of people. Any denunciation of him at the time was sure to rebound on the heads of his enemies. The revolutionaries were content to wait until they had moulded the mob to their own likeness and iron purpose.

Later in January the Pope himself went to the church of Sant' Andrea della Valle. Father Ventura, the most influential preacher of the day, gave over his pulpit to the Holy Father, and Pius preached a strong sermon against blasphemy. It followed much the same trend of thought expressed in a later talk in which he said: "I know that there are some few in this city—the center of Catholicism—who profane the name of God by blasphemy. . . . I have no hope for such men. They cast against Heaven the stone which crushes them as it returns. To blaspheme the name of their common Father, who gives us life, and all the good we enjoy, is filling the measure of ingratitude brimful. Tell such of my people who offend by these outrages, that I beg they will no longer scandalize the Holy City."

The political problems of his own realm pressed on Pius from every side. His treasury was practically empty. Yet, the Irish famine brought out in Pius IX every resource of tenderness and active charity.

The Pope himself ordered a triduum of prayers at Sant' Andrea della Valle. The persuasive eloquence of Father Ventura moved vast audiences to contribute to the fund for the relief of Ireland. Pius himself gave the sum of three thousand francs; the contributions of princes and commoners followed his good example. The bishops of the world were further requested to hold a triduum in every diocese. They were also ordered to make a collection in behalf of the Irish people.

The terrible reports from Ireland wrung the Pope's heart. The people dying in the hedgerows, the mass emigration of thousands to the United States, Australia, and Canada—all these made him cry out in anguish and sent him to his knees in his chapel. If only his purse were as big as his heart.

The drama of the time was further heightened by the death of Daniel O'Connell in Genoa. The great Irish emancipator was enroute to see the Pope at the time of his sudden death. His body was sent back to his unhappy country, but his heart, according to O'Connell's direction, was placed in a silver casket and journeyed on to Rome, which had always been the center of the great man's affection.

The Pope ordered a solemn requiem in O'Connell's honor,

and with tears in his eyes spoke of the man with affection while he mourned Ireland's loss.

The high regard in which the Pope was held the world over moved the Sublime Porte to send an ambassador to the Holy See. The French did everything in their power to sabotage the project in Constantinople and to prevent the Pope from receiving the Sultan's envoy. France had long posed as the protector of Christian interests in Turkey. Actually she was merely intent on serving her own imperial interests and did little or nothing to settle the many vexing religious problems. In receiving a Turkish ambassador at his Court the Holy Father served notice that he was by-passing France to deal directly with Turkey in solving the questions that concerned the Church in the Holy Land and the Near East.

In spring the secret revolutionary party set going a rumor that soon had all of Rome disturbed and uneasy. The Pope, they said, was about to be imprisoned and deposed by the reactionary Cardinals, Grassellini, the governor of the city, the commander of the militia, and counsellors Freddi, Nardoni, and Minardi. The plot was supposed to be carried out on June 17, the anniversary of the Pope's election.

The mob was wildly excited at the news, and the whole city was disturbed by rioting bands. Father Ventura, on the night of February 11, was awakened by Ciceruacchio and some of his lieutenants. The noted preacher was informed that the people's party intended to murder five of the Pope's enemies the next day. In the early hours of the morning Ventura hastened to the Quirinal with the terrible message.

The Pope, awakened from sleep, went into immediate action. He sent messages to all the men concerned, begging them to leave the city at once. All complied with his request with the exception of Minardi, who lingered on in Rome for two days. Tracked down by secret operatives he would have been killed had it not been for the vigorous intervention of Father Ventura in calming the mob. Cardinal Lambruschini, the popular whipping boy of the revolutionaries, also thought it prudent to leave the Holy City.

Rumor and riot still disturbed the atmosphere. New concessions were demanded of the Pope every day. Most important of these was the establishment of a Civil Guard, recruited from the people. The Pope was in general favor of the measure. The Papal States were inadequately policed. Pius saw in the creation of a Civil Guard, trained and controlled by officers of his own choice, a safety valve for popular frenzy and an instrument that would enable his more prudent subjects to control the rising passions of the mob.

Cardinal Gizzi was against the measure. To him it promised nothing more than a preparation for utter chaos. In this the Cardinal proved to be right. He signed the proclamation creating the Guard and at once resigned as Cardinal Secretary.

The Pope chose Cardinal Ferretti, his own cousin, to replace Gizzi. Ferretti had been a vigorous but liberal upholder of the Pope's authority in disturbed Pesaro, where he was the Pope's Legate. Before that, in the rebellion of 1831, when revolutionists threatened to lay siege to Rieti, of which he was bishop, Ferretti rallied his people about him, mounted a horse and successfully led them against the rebels.

Ciceruacchio and his friends received the new Cardinal Secretary with a flamboyant reception upon his arrival in Rome. For the moment the Cardinal was elevated to a liberal status he had never desired nor approved.

The Cardinal's true sentiments were published in a circular letter the following day. In this letter Ferretti appealed to the prudence and moderation of the Roman people. He also pointed out a passage in the amnesty, in which the Pope declared his determination to follow a course of strict justice and to punish with severity all those who were enemies of law and order.

Cardinal Ferretti's strong hope of establishing order in Rome was soon nullified by events beyond his control. Austria invaded the rebellious city of Ferrara, the most northerly "legation" of the Papal States. From this town, for some time, revolutionary elements had plagued the Austrian government of Venezia.

The Austrian capture of Ferrara and the threat of further reprisals brought out again the mobs. The wildest excitement prevailed. The Civil Guard opened public recruiting offices in the city and went into intensive training for a move against Austria.

The Pope with admirable coolness drafted a protest to the Austrian Emperor. Such was its vigor that the Austrian Commander in Ferrara was confined to keeping order from the Citadel while the gates of the city remained open and free from interference.

The Pope added to his political stature by reviving the ancient Council of State that had been, before the French Revolution, responsible for the government of the Papal States. It was to be composed of a Cardinal President, also a prelate, and twenty-four councillors named by the provinces. These were to be selected by the Pope from lists presented to him by the provinces.

The functions of this body were to assist the Pope in the administration of the Papal States and to advise him in the drafting of laws, taxes, tariffs, and general reforms.

This measure was roundly applauded by all men of good will who had followed the Pope's cautious drafting of liberal policies for his people. The revolutionary party, however, scoffed at the measure. They said it was not democratic enough, in spite of the fact that the Pope went out of his way to choose from the lists presented him the men most acceptable to the various provinces.

The year closed on notes of tragedy and menace. In November, word came to Rome that civil war had broken out in Switzerland between the radical and Catholic Cantons. General Dufour, in a series of lightning-like movements, captured the seven Catholic Cantons and took Lucerne. The Catholic Cantons were forced into a unified government dominated by radicals. The civil war, like all struggles of its kind, was marked by brutality, cruelty, and sacrilege. Most noted of its effects was the expulsion of the Jesuits from Switzerland.

The revolutionary orators in Rome were quick to praise the radical Swiss. They gave voice to a demand for the expulsion or death of all Jesuits in the Papal States.

The Pope took note of these events and expressed his grief to the Cardinals in an allocution on the 17th of December,

"We were deeply grieved on learning, a few days ago, that some few individuals, devoid of sense and of a due appreciation for true manliness, had the presumption and bad taste to openly express in our city, the center and citadel of the Catholic religion, their delight at the sad civil war now raging in Switzerland. We deplore this war from the depths of our inmost soul, partly because of the shedding of brothers' blood, and because of the dreadful and protracted feelings of hatred it will engender; and again, on account of the injury already suffered by the Catholic Church, and the great injury to be inflicted on her in the future; finally, on account of the shocking sacrileges perpetrated in the heat of passion by the belligerents."

The mob took to the streets of Rome on the 20th of December. In the square before the Quirinal they screamed and shouted. The banners they carried summed up outrageous demands for further concessions.

The Pope, apparently unmoved by the popular fury, drove on New Year's eve to the Church of the Jesuits. His hand was raised in blessing on the crowd as he descended from his carriage. For the first time since his accession, the blessing of the Holy Father was answered with a hiss.

On New Year's day, Ciceruacchio presented to the Pope a list of new demands from the "Party of Unlimited Progress." Some of them were reasonable: the formation of an Italian confederacy, the complete emancipation of the Jews. Others were outrageous: the abolition of convents, the exclusion of all prelates from the ministry, the banishment of the Jesuits, the absolute pardon of twenty-four political agitators excluded from the amnesty.

January saw revolution in the Two Sicilies, Piedmont, and Tuscany. The demands of Ciceruacchio were a hint to the Pope of threatened revolution in the Eternal City.

The Swiss Guards of the Quirinal were alerted and reinforced. Ciceruacchio and his friends tried to force their way into the palace but were firmly turned away. Cardinal Ferretti was not intimidated by their boisterous mouthings. He received a delegation and denounced the rebels to their face. He told them they were a mob of unscrupulous scoundrels. To gratify their own passions they were willing to see the whole country desolate and in ruins.

Many feared the hour of revolution had struck. Senator Corsini begged the Holy Father to ride through the streets of the city. "For you, Holy Father, are the only one who can quiet the people."

The Pope, ever a man without fear, complied. All through the days of alarm he had gone his serene way; he slept soundly and his smile was as frequent as always. But he spent more time than usual in his chapel. At the Mass of thanksgiving, after his own, he seemed completely absorbed in the prayers of the two books of devotion his mother had given him in his illness long ago.

The Pope's appearance led to a frenzied reception from the people. They shouted his name in a delirium of joy and called down blessings upon him. In the Piazza del Popolo the crowd was so dense that the Pope's carriage had to stop. At this precise moment Ciceruacchio leaped on the boot of the carriage and flourished over the Pontiff's head a gigantic banner, *"Holy Father, Do Justice To Your Friends Who Stand By You!"*

By February 7th, the rioters brought about the fall of Cardinal Ferretti, now more scorned and hated than formerly he had been praised. Cardinal Bofondi, elevated to the sacred purple only a short time before, succeeded Ferretti as Cardinal Secretary on February 7, 1848. The Pope granted a further measure of indulgence to his subjects on the 12th day of the same month by nominating three noted laymen to be his chief ministers. They were Count John Pasolini, Counsellor Sturbinetti and Duke Gaetani.

A few days before their appointment the Pope clearly declared his policy to an excited crowd demonstrating in the piazza before the Quirinal. They were all clamoring for his blessing.

Finally after an hour of incessant shouting the French windows were thrown open, and the Pope came out on the balcony from which he had been proclaimed the day after his election. He stood there quietly, and it finally dawned on the crowd that the Pope had something to say to them. The noise grew less and less until a deep silence fell. Then they heard the powerful voice of the Pontiff speaking. He was appealing as a father and friend for peace, moderation, and unity.

He solemnly charged them to be on their guard against the lawless political demagogues who were leading them away from their duties and inspiring even good men to make demands which he could not grant and would not grant. Then lifting his arms in a wide prayerful gesture the Pope begged God to bless Italy and preserve its greatest good—divine faith.

The Pope had declared himself, but his words of warning did little to quiet the excitement of the mob. Ministry succeeded ministry and each proved as unsatisfactory to the revolutionary leaders as the former had been.

That Pius IX was sincere in his attempt to modernize his government appears in the granting of a constitution on March 15, 1848. Most important of its measures were the following:

"The Council of State is to be composed of a Cardinal-President, a prelate, vice-president, and twenty-four councillors, nominated by the Sovereign Pontiff, and selected by the people.

"The College of Cardinals shall continue to be the Pope's personal cabinet advisors.

"For the framing and enacting of laws two houses shall be established; the higher council called the Senate, and the lower the Chamber of Deputies or House of Representatives. Both Houses shall be convened and adjourned by the Pope. The session shall be public, and the proceedings printed and published. The members of the higher council shall be appointed for life; the deputies shall be elected by the people, every thirty thousand souls being entitled to one representative. All persons paying a yearly tax of twelve dollars or over, and having attained their twenty-fifth year, shall be entitled to vote. To be eligible for office any candidate must have reached his thirtieth year. The House of Representatives shall choose its own President.

"Church matters do not come within the province of either House, neither the diplomatic nor ecclesiatical questions of the Holy See. Both Houses may legislate on questions of finance and commerce, may levy taxes, imposing direct taxes for each year, and indirect taxes for several years. Only the House of Representatives has a right to demand the impeachment of any minister. The civil list of the Pope is established at $600,000. Justice must be untrammeled, personal liberty protected, a moderate taxation enforced upon all citizens.

"The Civil Guard shall be a State institution.

"Official censure in political matters shall cease; the Chuch shall continue to be above and independent of the civil power. The theatres shall be subject to government surveillance."

It was a liberal constitution for the times; it went as far as possible in giving privileges to the people without impinging on the dignity and power of the Pope-King.

Some time before this Pius had also suggested a plan for the unification of Italy. He proposed that each of the Italian duchies or kingdoms should send delegates to a central government under the nominal headship of the Pope. Every section would preserve its own autonomy, but in the affairs that concerned all Italy, the various states would act in concert. The Pope also proposed a customs union for the whole of Italy that would guarantee the free flow of goods between the separate kingdoms and would erect barriers for the protection of Italian industry.

It was the suggestion of a genuine statesman, far in advance of the time. Masaryk employed the same plan in the unification of Czechoslovakia. It worked with wonderful success until the dominating personality of Benes nullified the cultural autonomy Masaryk had guaranteed. The Pope's plan is also essentially the same as that advanced for a United States of Europe.

That it was not tried was owing to several reasons. The first of these was the attitude of Piedmont. Cavour and Charles Albert were convinced that the great majority of Italians wanted a strong and unified Italy. To the King and his astute advisor this meant but one thing—a democratic monarchy ruled by the King of Piedmont. They were willing to use the high-flown rhetoric of Garibaldi and the careful plotting of Mazzini in bringing about a state of chaos in Italy. Then when the time was ripe, Piedmont would step in to impose order and carry off the spoils.

The role played was an easy one because of the revolutionary ferment of the times and the Austrian occupation of Venezia. Where others merely talked, Piedmont showed its super-patriotism by plunging into war with Austria, an act which brought the great mass of Italian patriots to enroll under her banner.

Pius IX had been variously criticized for dabbling in politics.
The truth is that he could not help himself. His reign began at
a moment in history that demanded liberal concessions. The
Pope made them in good faith but those who demanded the
concessions were not in good faith. They understood only too
well that the Pope could grant nothing that would condition
the freedom of the papacy. He could not destroy what he had
been elected to guard. In forcing the papal government to go
beyond that point they prepared the way for the planned
destruction of both the temporal and spiritual power of the
Pope.

Had Pius IX been as wise as Solomon and as bold as Gregory
VII he could not have done more or less than he did. The times
were out of joint, and men refused to listen to either statesmanship or common sense.

On February 23, 1848, revolution began in France. Louis
Philippe was toppled from his throne and fled in the night to
England. In early March the revolutionary ferment was at work
in Austria. Metternich was rudely jolted from power. Everywhere liberalism and revolution seemed to be on the march.

In Rome, the chief hatred of the revolutionary party was
directed against the Jesuits. In pamphlets and broadsheets they
were attacked and vilified. All the ridiculous and stupid old
stories were trotted out which pictured the Society as an ag-
gregation of monsters. So successful was the campaign that on
the 28th of March the superintendent of the police informed
the Pope that he could no longer protect the Jesuits from the
mob. On the advice of the Pope, the Jesuits quietly closed their
houses. Some of the Fathers left the Papal States, others went
into hiding in Rome.

The passions of the Roman mobs were fanned to further
heat when Charles Albert of Piedmont, who called himself the
"Sword of Italy," crossed the river Ticino with his troops on
the 23rd of March, and invaded Venezia. The move evoked the

wildest enthusiasm in Rome. Led by several patriotic monks a gigantic crowd assembled in the Colosseum to listen to incendiary speeches. These led to a demand that the Pope should send immediate reinforcements to fight side by side with the forces of the "Sword of Italy."

To the harassed Pope it seemed a heaven-sent opportunity to get a crowd of malcontents out of the holy city. He allowed General Durando to depart for the provinces with twelve thousand troops, most of them newly recruited by the Civil Guard. The Pope expressly charged Durando to proceed to the borders of the Papal States, but no further. His job was to protect the Papal dominions from attack. He was expressly commanded not to attack the Austrian troops.

Once in the field, Durando, most likely carried away by Italian patriotism, began actual hostilities with Austria and joined the troops under the banners of Piedmont.

In an allocution to the Cardinals on the 23rd of April, 1848, the Pope expressed his displeasure and the horror he felt of this disobedient act of his general and his troops.

The Pope maintained that his office demanded paternal good will toward all rulers and their subjects. Under the compulsion of Italian patriotism the Pope had allowed the Civil Guard to proceed to the borders of the Papal States, but the troops had been forbidden to make war on Austria. They had disobeyed his orders. The Pope completely repudiated their action. He also exhorted the subjects of Italian princes to respect their rulers and their governments. Any other course, the Pope maintained, would create civil war and bring about the permanent disunity of Italy. Two days later the Pope added to the force of his allocution by threatening the disobedient with censure and excommunication.

There could be no doubt, now, exactly where the Pope stood. The leaders of the people, who up to this moment had pretended to picture the Pope as a revolutionary liberal, took off their masks and called the Holy Father the "enemy of his country" and the "friend of despots."

Behind the scenes the "People's Association," in cooperation with the disloyal Civil Guard, took over the government of the Holy City. By the end of June the Pope was practically a prisoner in Rome. Revolutionary leaders, working on the emotions of the Chamber and contrary to the will of the Holy Father, declared war on Austria.

Meanwhile, the war against Austria had proceeded with more than doubtful triumph. Charles Albert was at first successful, but his troops suffered a stunning defeat at Custozza on July 25. Previous to this, General Radetzky had taken Vicenza, Padua, and Treviso. The well-disciplined troops of Austria had administered a sound trouncing to the green papal troops of General Durando.

The news of these defeats did little or nothing to dampen the Italian ardor of the revolutionaries. Under the leadership of Mamiani the Chamber voted the conscription of twelve thousand men, the establishment of a foreign legion, and an assessment of four hundred thousand dollars on the citizens and clergy.

Pius IX abruptly rejected all these measures. Their rejection caused the fall of Mamiani.

Several succeeding ministries having proved abortive, the Pope took advantage of the reverses in the field to place in power a layman as his chief minister. The radicals had long declaimed against the domination of clerics. They made repeated demands that a layman be appointed to head the Pope's council. Now the Pope acceded to their demand with a vengeance in appointing one who was noted for his integrity and strength. The man was Count Pellegrino Rossi.

Rossi was an Italian. He had been a noted lawyer and for years had represented France at the papal Court. In his younger days Rossi had been something of a revolutionary. His Catholicism had been lukewarm, to say the least, but with maturity he had returned to the outward practise of his religion.

The Pope's command that Rossi organize a government must have come as a surprise to the talented Count. He hesitated for several days and then gave his consent out of sheer admiration for the kindly and harassed Pope.

Rossi grasped the reins of power with a firm hand. He chose as his assistants two Cardinals and four noted laymen. With lightning speed the departments of the civil government were reorganized and strengthened. The revolutionary party was informed abruptly that no further mob-intimidation of the Holy Father would be permitted. To this end irresponsible public assemblies were severely curtailed. The notorious ex-monk Gavazzi, who had openly preached rebellion against the Pope, was arrested and put in prison. Revolutionary journals were outlawed, the police and military forces were strengthened. For the first time in over a year the Holy City was quiet. Honest people could once more go about their business and could sleep quietly at night. The revolution seemed to have met its master.

Rossi next turned his attention to the Italian question. He revised the Pope's plan for an Italian confederacy under the honorary presidency of the Pope. Approaches were made to Naples, Florence and Turin in the hope of bringing the confederacy into reality. It was chiefly the ambition and envy of Piedmont that defeated the delicate negotiations.

The revolutionaries in Rome were cowed but not without resource. At a secret meeting they decided to assassinate Count Rossi on the 17th of November, 1848, the day appointed for the opening of the Chamber.

On the evening before that day, the active conspirators met in the Capranica theater. Three of their number, chosen by lot, were appointed to carry out the crime. A corpse was brought in from a neighboring hospital. They stood it in a corner and for several hours the three assassins, under the direction of a surgeon, practiced on it with their poniards until they had learned perfectly how to sever the jugular vein with a perfect, single stroke.

On the morning of the 17th, Rossi had several warnings of disaster. A woman came to his house with important disclosures. She was received by the minister in secret. What she told him was never revealed.

The Countess Rossi begged her husband to remain at home for the day, but Rossi made light of her fears and set out for an audience with the Pope at the Quirinal Palace. He found the Pope equally worried. "I have reliable information that an attempt will be made on your life today. It would be better if you stayed away from the Cancelleria."

The first minister calmed the Pope's apprehensions. "I have taken adequate measures to insure my safety," he assured the Holy Father. "These people are cowards: they will talk a lot and make threats, but when faced without fear they will slink away."

In this frame of mind Count Rossi got into his carriage and drove to the Cancelleria where the opening session of the Chamber was to be held.

The carriage drew up at the entrance to the beautiful old building. Rossi gave a quick glance over the small group at the entrance to the staircase that led to the second floor. They seemed to be the usual crowd of idle men who hung about at all public assemblies. Clutching his leather portfolio in his hand, Rossi boldly made his way through the crowd and put his foot on the first step of the grand staircase. At this moment he was suddenly jostled by men from every side. He saw a flash, and felt a sharp pain in his neck. "Oh my God," he half whispered. Blood poured from his mouth and throat. He fell on the second step and died.

The screams and shouts that attended the murder cloaked the escape of the assassin with well-simulated confusion.

The body of the minister, covered with blood, was taken into the rooms of Cardinal Gazzoli. A messenger hurried to the Pope with the dreadful news.

The Pope put his head in his hands and wept. When he had found his voice at last he said. "Count Rossi was a martyr and died a martyr's death. God will reward him. May his soul rest in peace." The Pope went at once to the chapel to pray for his friend. He sent a tender message of condolence to the Countess Rossi.

That night a ghoulish mob screaming and shouting with delight carried the dagger of the murderer in a torchlight procession through the city. Around the streets they went, past the house of the minister itself, where a weeping woman heard their screams of delighted triumph.

From the headquarters of the revolutionary party messengers rushed out to the inns and albergos where the Civil Guards were numerous. The plotters were well-heeled with money and well-versed in threats, both of which they used lavishly to overcome the last hesitancy of those responsible for public order.

The next day in the full glare of noon the revolutionaries, accompanied by the Civil Guard and a band, escorted Galletti, a follower of Mazzini, to the Quirinal. He had arrived in Rome the day before with the latest instructions from Mazzini.

Cardinal Soglia received the delegation in the name of the Pope, while the mob rioted outside in the square. Galletti demanded among other things: a declaration of war against Austria, the establishment of Italian nationality, the summoning of a popular assembly to frame a constitution, and a completely lay ministry of radicals who were to be in charge of public order and government.

The Pope sent a message to the delegation that he refused to receive those who had fraternized with the murderers of Count Rossi. However, he would consider their demands. Galletti was empowered to form a new cabinet.

Galletti went out on the balcony and shouted down to the sullen crowd the news of the Pope's concessions. Far from being pleased the mob set up a clamor for immediate action. To this the Pope replied that he was still King and would not give consent to any measure wrung from him by force.

This courageous stand completely infuriated the mob and its leaders. With hoarse roars they cried again and again, "Down with the Pope" and "Long live the republic." Spurred on by the revolutionaries, the mob rushed forward to storm the main gate of the Quirinal. Guns and revolvers were brought into play on the outer windows of the palace. A part of the chief gate itself was set on fire. Several of the Pope's household were struck by stray bullets. One of the Pope's secretaries, Monsignor Palma, was instantly killed by a rifle ball.

A cannon was brought up to blast the main gate. The situation was so filled with menace that the foreign ambassadors who were with the Pope, in the hope that their presence would strengthen his hand, advised the Holy Father to give in to the revolutionary demands. The Pope reluctantly followed the advice.

Galletti announced to the mob that the Pope accepted the ministerial list and permitted the Chamber to legislate on the other demands. With a loud shout of triumph the well-disciplined revolutionary crowd dispersed from the square. A sinister quiet fell like a velvet curtain.

The Pope called upon the foreign diplomatic corps to give witness to the fact that the concessions had been wrung from him by force. He could not and would not give in to such outrageous demands.

The Pope then returned to his chapel, where he had been

praying most of the day. Now he knew, as never before, how heavy was the cross of his Master. It had bowed Him down on the way to Calvary and in the end He had been fastened to it and held up for all the world to see. Christ's Vicar must follow the same way, but with the same serenity and courage. All those about the Holy Father were amazed at the Pope's tranquillity.

Chapter VII

THE FLIGHT TO GAETA

THE quiet about the Quirinal did not last for long. The new ministers disarmed the Swiss Guard, and put into their places disloyal forces of the Civil Guard. Detectives were set to watch the entrances of the Quirinal. They did not hesitate to invade the building and spy on the activities of the Holy Father himself.

It was rumored that the Pope was to be deposed on November 27th and imprisoned in the Lateran. This moved the diplomatic corps to advise the Holy Father to leave Rome at once, before he could fall into the hands of his enemies. Count Spaur of Bavaria and the Duc de Harcourt were especially vigorous in urging the Holy Father to hurry his departure, because they feared he would be assassinated.

Pius IX was unmoved by this advice. As he had all his life long, he waited for a sign from God that would indicate what he must do.

The sign came on the 21st of November. It was a letter from Monsignor Chatrousse, the Bishop of Valence in France. In the letter Bishop Chatrousse said he had a silver pyx that Pius VI had used for reservation of the Blessed Sacrament during his exile. The Bishop of Valence offered the pyx to Pius IX, the heir of the virtues and the cross carried by Pius VI.

The Pope saw in this letter the answers to his hours of prayer asking for light on the course he should pursue. It was as if he had been answered by the very voice of the Pope of his childhood.

Several places of refuge were open to the Pope. He considered them all and decided to go either to Spain or the island of Majorca. The Spanish gunboat which was supposed to be in waiting at Città Vecchia failed to arrive, and the Holy Father altered his plan. He proposed to escape to Naples. From that point he would proceed to Spain.

The day of his departure was set for November 24th. Only four men knew of the full plan: the Pope's old friend, Cavaliere Filippani; Count Spaur, the Bavarian ambassador; the Duc de Harcourt, the representative from France; and Cardinal Antonelli. This Cardinal, newly created, had stood by Pius IX in a memorable fashion all through the recent days of terror.

On the evening of the 24th the Duc de Harcourt came in full state to an audience with the Holy Father. Harcourt carried an important red leather dispatch box. His lackeys opened the door of his coach in the great courtyard. Harcourt strode past the watchful civil guards and detectives, and ascended the grand staircase. Attended by the chamberlains on duty he was ushered through the gorgeous anterooms to the cabinet of the Pope. The door closed, the lock was discreetly turned: so softly that only the faintest click was heard.

Inside the Pope's study the Holy Father, Count Gabriel Mastai, and the faithful Filippani awaited. Harcourt immediately went to the Pope's desk. He pulled out a French newspaper from the red leather dispatch box. Seating himself in the Pope's chair the duke began to read in a singsong voice. Any detective who might be listening at the door would think that the Holy Father was hearing some involved complaint.

Gabriel Mastai and Filippani accompanied the Holy Father to his bedroom. Spread out on the simple bed was the costume Filippani had assembled for the Pope's disguise. Black knee breeches and coat, black stockings and shoes, a long black cape, a great pair of tinted blue spectacles, a three-cornered hat. A false beard and moustache completed the disguise. "No," the Pope said, "I won't use those. They are ridiculous. Besides, if they came loose they would be sure to betray me."

The Pope took off his white soutane and robed himself in the black coat and suit. He was so calm and deliberate that Filippani, his nerves stretched to breaking point, exclaimed, "Hurry up, Holy Father, please hurry!" The Holy Father looked up at Filippani with a sad smile. "Ah Filippani, my hands are as heavy as my heart. For me this is a bitter chalice—a veritable Gethsemani."

"There is a difference, Holy Father. You won't find me a new Judas; of that you may be sure."

"I am sure, Filippani. Indeed I'm sure."

At last the Pope was dressed. His hair was heavily powdered and he put on the long cloak and the three-cornered hat. A little powder rose in the air above the flames of the candelabra on the dressing table. Putting on the blue spectacles, the Pope looked at himself in the dim mirror. He was surprised into a smile. "You have done beautifully, Filippani. I look just like a country doctor. Let us go, then."

Gabriel Mastai knelt for his brother's blessing and kissed the Pope on both cheeks. He said no word of farewell, but his eyes were filled with tears of sympathy. It would be Gabriel's part of the plot to sleep in the Pope's room that night and eat the meals sent up for His Holiness.

As Filippani and the Pope went across the study Harcourt stopped his reading in surprise. "I should never have known you, Holy Father," he whispered. "You've done well, Filippani. Very well indeed!"

Filippani, carrying a single lighted candle, preceded the Pope into the darkness of his chapel. The Pope unlocked the tabernacle, took out the silver pyx, knelt a few moments in silent adoration and then hung the pyx around his neck beneath the black ruffles of his shirt front.

Outside the chapel there was a secret passage in the darkness of one of the great audience rooms. It would enable the fugitives to get over to the servants' courtyard where Filippani's carriage awaited. Filippani tugged at the spring again and again. His hands shook with nervous tension. He was almost crying with vexation.

"I can't get it open, Holy Father, I simply can't."

"Perhaps we should return and give up the whole idea tonight," the Pope said.

"No! No! Holy Father!" Filippani cried passionately, "there is another door, not a secret one. I'm sure I can open that, even if it's locked. Meanwhile pray, Holy Father. Pray to Our Lord!"

At this point the single candle went out, as Filippani lifted it from the floor. They were in complete darkness except for the starlit sky refracted in the tall windows opening on to the courtyard.

"I'll go back for another candle," Filippani whispered.

"No, Filippani. It makes no difference. We'll go on."

Feeling their way cautiously the two men came to the small door. "It's locked," Filippani said, "I felt sure that it was, but the pins that hold it are well oiled. I can remove them and we can easily lift the door out and replace it again."

Filippani had already lifted one pin when the Holy Father clutched him by the arm. "Listen!"

The two men waited as if paralysed. Sure enough they both could hear it now—footsteps! Someone was coming. The two men drew back in the shadow of the room from which they had just emerged. The footsteps came nearer.

In the dim light they recognized the figure of a Civil Guard making his rounds. They hardly breathed until the footsteps died away in the marble distance.

Then Filippani removed the second pin. With the help of the Holy Father the door was pulled open. They lifted it out with great care, climbed through the opening and swiftly drew the door back into place.

In a few moments they were in the servants' quarters. Filippani was at home here. He went swiftly down the stairs to the small courtyard where his carriage stood ready. "We mustn't hurry too much," the Holy Father cautioned. "That would be sure to give us away."

There was in the heart of Pius IX a piercing pain at leaving this house so long associated with his life. Here he had begun his studies in philosophy under the kindly direction of Uncle Paul; here Pius VII had assured him he would be cured. Lovely days when the windows of the courtyards barred the reception rooms with long shafts of sun. Gracious occasions. Courtly people. Would he ever see them again?

The coachman opened the door of the light carriage, known as a *bastardo*. The Pope and Filippani settled back in the shadows. "Where to, Cavaliere?" The coachman shouted.

"Home, Tonio! Home!"

The carriage moved slowly across the courtyard. Several servants shouted, "Goodnight, Filippani. Goodnight!" At the gate, where the Civil Guards stood with their guns, Filippani leaned out of the window and waved. The flaring lights on the gate showed the face the Guards knew so well, and some other servant with him who appeared to be busily engaged in blowing his nose.

Once the carriage had got out of sight of the Quirinal it was turned about in the opposite direction. No orders were given. The coachman had been instructed well. He whipped up his horses and they raced through the night toward the Piazetta of Saints Peter and Marcellinus. Here the heavy traveling carriage of Count Spaur waited in the shadow. The Count had the door open. The black-clad figure in the long cape entered the coach. Filippani slammed the door. "Goodnight, Doctor!" he shouted. "Goodnight, cher ami!" No reply came. The coach of the Bavarian Minister rumbled through the shadowed streets.

"Follow them cautiously to Saint John's gate," Filippani ordered when he had climbed up beside his coachman. "I must know that they have got safely out of the city. I must know, or I won't sleep tonight."

Count Spaur pressed the Pope's hand with a firm grip of encouragement. They said nothing, but the Pope's lips moved in constant prayer.

Saint John's gate came in sight. The various delays that had attended the Pope's departure had taken them beyond the curfew hour. The gate was shut for the night. A guard of soldiers waited beside it. The carriage halted. Count Spaur had never been more haughty and imperious. "I'm on urgent business for my master, the King of Bavaria." He extended his passport. On it was written, "Minister of the King of Bavaria and his doctor." The Captain scanned the passport briefly.

"Very well, Excellency!" He gave a sigh. The heavy gates were unbarred and folded slowly back. The carriage with its six horses rumbled through the opening and went forward on the old Roman road under the cold stars of the November night.

The carriage swayed and jolted along the road. The noise made by the hooves of the horses was the only sound in the stillness, but Count Spaur continually looked back through the small slit of a window. Always he made the same comment. "Thank God, we are not being followed."

Both men knew the danger was far from over. In an hour or two they would be fairly safe; at least no one from Rome would easily overtake them. But suppose someone recognized the Holy Father. Suppose they should be detained until word came from the revolutionary committee in Rome. At each little village the horses were slowed down for safety's sake.

In Genzano the coach halted. Countess Spaur, her son Maxi-

milian, and a Jesuit priest, Don Sebastian Liebel, were waiting
there. Greetings were in whispers. The Countess was weeping.
She had all she could do to restrain herself from falling on her
knees before the Holy Father.

"I have Our Lord here with me," the Pope said reassuringly.
"Don't cry! Don't fear!"

Count Spaur hurriedly placed the new passengers in the
coach. "It will be too crowded with five, so I'll go up on the box
with the coachman. My greatcoat will protect me against the
cold and I can keep my eye on the road behind us better up
there."

In a moment the coach was in full motion. Outside the village the Count had the coachman whip up the horses. The wild
ride through the night continued. The coach lights had been lit
and the little inside lamp. It cast a dim glow on the strained
faces of the passengers. The Pope, who had been saying his
rosary, took off his blue glasses and with Father Liebel began
the recitation of the Office of the day. The moving Latin phrases
of the Psalms were like a river of consolation. David too had
fled from his capital, but he had returned in the end to reign in
triumph.

By the time the carriage reached Galloro the horses were
lathered with foam. The moon was up and they stopped in the
shadow of the church. The Pope, Count Spaur, and Father
Liebel walked up and down to exercise their cramped muscles,
while the coachman wiped down the smoking horses.

Countess Spaur and Maximilian watched the three men from
the safety of the carriage. The Countess shuddered with alarm
when a group of Civil Guards came around the corner and
spoke to her husband. She heard the Count telling the Captain: "I am the Bavarian Ambassador en route on urgent business for His Majesty in the Kingdom of Naples. This is my
chaplain and my doctor." The soldiers examined the passports
and returned them. Then they sauntered over and inspected

the carriage. The Countess lived through a moment of absolute terror. If the Pope had only kept his glasses on!

Now, she could no longer restrain herself. "Doctor!" she fairly shouted, "hurry and get into the carriage. I don't like this waiting here alone at night." In accord with his character the Pope fulfilled the shouted command, getting into the carriage on the side away from the soldiers. As he did so the Countess heard one of the soldiers say, "Except for his white hair the doctor looks much like our Pope." She scarcely breathed until the carriage was once more rolling down the road.

In those hours of terror their minds outraced the coach to the border of Naples. The miles seemed endless in the jolting carriage. Then they saw in the distance the town of Fondi like a cluster of shadows in the silvery night. At last they were over the border of Naples. The flight was accomplished. The Holy Father was safe.

The plunging horses were brought to a jolting stop. They all got out of the coach shivering with the cold and nerves, crying a little with joy. They stood by the side of the road with bent heads while the Pope and Father Liebel recited the superb strophes of the *Te Deum*.

At the edge of the great mole that juts out into the sea above Gaeta an attaché of the Spanish embassy and Cardinal Antonelli awaited the Pope's carriage. Antonelli was in lay dress with a three-cornered hat. He had a large red muffler wound about his neck and chin. The Pope laughed at Antonelli's appearance.

By nine-thirty in the morning the exhausted party had reached Gaeta where the Pope proposed to stop. A Swiss, Major Gross, in charge of the Guard at Gaeta, came over to examine the carriage. He was fussy and important, but after considerable questioning seemed satisfied with the good faith of everyone but the doctor and the figure in the red scarf. To test them Gross asked several questions in German. The Holy Father, not knowing the language, couldn't reply and the Major was on the point of arresting the whole party until Count Spaur's indignant promise of the severe punishment he would suffer moved the Major to allow them to proceed to the little Albergo del Giardinetto.

Count Spaur went on in the coach to Naples with a letter from the Pope apprising King Ferdinand of the Pope's unexpected and unannounced arrival in the Kingdom of Naples. The Pope offered to leave the kingdom at once if his presence there were to embarrass the King in any way.

The Pope was in a joyful mood. He would have to maintain his incognito until he discovered what attitude the King might take toward him. That, at least, would guarantee him a day of much needed rest before the uncertain encounter. Meanwhile the thick-headed Gross kept the party under watch. What kind of Germans were these that couldn't even speak the language?

A day later Major Gross was astounded by the sudden appearance of King Ferdinand in his command post. "Where is the Holy Father?" the King demanded without ceremony, obviously in the greatest excitement. "And Cardinal Antonelli?" The fat neck of the Major was crimson. Those two Italians who couldn't speak German. The two he had threatened—he who had prided himself on being such a good Catholic. Meek as a lamb he led the way to the Giardinetto. He saw the King embracing the doctor with exclamations of joy. He was too unhappy to ask to be presented, too embarrassed to ask forgiveness for his stupidity.

Chapter VIII

GAETA

THE quiet of Gaeta settled about Pius IX like a sunlit morning after a night of storm. From his quiet retreat the Pope was able to look back on the first years of his pontificate with clear vision. He had never expected to be Pope. He had never desired the office. He could still recall the evening of his election and the wave of terror that had engulfed him as his own voice told the mounting of votes in his favor. Behind that historical moment there was another, personal, and radiant with interior meaning. He had asked to be cured of epilepsy. He too had begged to lay down the cross of ill health that had been given him. He had promised to take up whatever cross the Lord would send him. That morning at Loreto, when the healing hand of Christ had touched him, it opened up the pathway to the realization of his dream of serving God in the priesthood. The cross given him in the place of the light one he had laid down was the heavy cross of his Master.

After the first moment of terror at the end of the conclave John Mary had assumed the cross without flinching. Those about him had wondered at his calm exterior during the years of political storms. He was calm and cheerful because he lived in the presence of Christ. His longing to make Christ known was the source of his kindliness in every sphere of activity.

The Pope was happy in Gaeta. Little by little his court

joined him, settling in and around the royal castle. The King and his family had received the Holy Father with such obvious reverence and affection that the Pope decided to remain in Gaeta instead of going out of the country. Both Antonelli and King Ferdinand played a considerable part in making the decision. By putting the Pope in his debt the King had hoped to get the Holy Father to concede his rights over Benevento which was actually part of the Kingdom of Naples. Cardinal Antonelli, a partizan of Austria, was anxious to prevent or moderate either a strong French or Spanish influence at the papal court. He was quick to point out to the Pope the disadvantages in leaving the Italian Peninsula.

In the quiet of Gaeta the Pope had time to look over the entire horizon of the Church. When he had assumed the papacy, John Mary with all his heart had longed to play a purely spiritual rôle that would touch all his children with inspiration and grace. Forces beyond his control had defeated his good aim: the days had been largely eaten away with purely physical tasks concerned with the government and discipline of the papal states. Most of these concerns the Pope now proposed to put in the hands of Antonelli. He was both subtle and imperturbable, something of a financial wizard; he seemed to have all those qualities the situation demanded.

Pius himself had tried to be a kindly ruler. That policy had largely failed through malice and intrigue. It was all well and good to talk of liberal policies, but it was obvious that the Italian people did not have the discipline that would insure the proper use of liberty. Democracy demands more of people than any other form of government. The people wanted a republic but it was still merely a name to them. They neither understood their own lack of necessary discipline, nor the limits to which a Pope could go in making concessions. One had only to look at unhappy Rome to realize that.

The revolutionary leaders had not discovered the Pope's

absence until mid-morning of November 25th, the day after his flight. Within a short time the whole city was in an uproar. The Pope had taken with him the great seal, no one had been appointed to rule in his absence. Even the revolutionary leaders were nonplused. This was the one thing they hadn't planned for. With the Pope in their power he could be blamed for wrong decisions; without him they were without their masks. They were strictly on their own now: the people of Italy and the world at large would hold them responsible for public order.

With the exception of the American minister to the Holy See, all the foreign representatives had joined the Pope in Gaeta. That was a fair indication that the Pope's position was a strong one.

Hiding their chagrin as best they could, the leaders sent several embassies to urge the Pope to return. Antonelli ignored them and countered with an order closing the Council of State. On December 4th, Antonelli appealed to the Catholic powers of Europe to restore the Pope to his kingdom. Again on the 14th of February he reiterated the appeal. The second appeal struck a responsive chord in the wily breast of Louis Napoleon, who was working toward his design of assuming the imperial purple.

France was at the time a strongly Catholic country. Shortly after the flight of the Pope to Gaeta, General Cavaignac, the President of France, had written the Pope the following letter:

Paris, Dec. 3.

Very Holy Father,—I address this dispatch and another from the Archbishop of Nicea, your Nuncio to the government of the Republic, to Your Holiness by one of my aides-de-camp.

The French nation, deeply afflicted by the troubles with which Your Holiness has been assailed within a short period, has been moreover profoundly affected at the sentiment of paternal confidence which induced Your Holiness to demand, temporarily, hospitality in France. France will be happy and proud to grant you that refuge which will be worthy of itself and of Your Holiness. I write you, therefore, in order that no feeling of uneasiness or unfounded apprehension may divert Your Holiness from your first resolution. The republic, the existence of which is already consecrated by the mature, persevering, and sovereign will of the French nation, will see with pride Your Holiness give to the world the spectacle of that exclusively religious consecration which your presence in the midst of it announces, and will receive you with the dignity and the religious respect which becomes this generous nation. I have felt the necessity of giving Your Holiness this assurance, and I heartily desire that your arrival may take place without much delay.

It is with those sentiments, Very Holy Father, that I am your respectful son,

GENERAL CAVAIGNAC

This epistle sums up the strong feeling of the French people for the Pope. In posing as the defender of the Pope, Louis Napoleon was currying favor with the French people and consolidating his position as future Emperor of France.

Meanwhile in Rome confusion multiplied. Those who call out the mob must be its masters. The republican leaders in Rome were not. Sacrilege and assassination became commonplace, especially in the provinces. The burden of taxes was enormously multiplied. Liberals who had, for so long, cried aloud for freedom of expression and action refused to tolerate the mildest expression of opinions among those who held contrary views. With the arrival of Mazzini, March 16, 1850, the republican government took definite shape. Saffi, Armellini, and Mazzini became the first triumvirs over a newly "elected" Constitutional Assembly prepared to legalize their decisions.

Among the most significant measures enacted was a law by which religious orders and ecclesiastical corporations were declared illegal. They were forbidden to own or inherit property: they had no longer any right before the law. In this fashion the way was opened for the looting of church treasures. Golden reliquaries that enshrined the revered bones of saints and martyrs, jeweled chalices that had held the Blood of Christ, copes, chasubles—these and a thousand other con secrated articles ornamented the counters and shelves of the pawn shops. Churches and shrines were looted, among them the Holy House at Loreto.

Yet the new rulers were uneasy at heart. The memories of Imperial Rome were pathetic remnants—walls and ruined columns centered mostly in the ancient Forum. Papal Rome was very much alive, not alone in soaring churches and arcaded galleries bearing coats of papal arms, but in the living hearts and consciousness of the Roman people. To placate this memory a renegade monk was persuaded to offer Mass at Saint Peter's at Easter time. Surrounded by unbelieving officials and deputies he offered the ancient Sacrifice on the altar reserved for the Pope alone. Then at the close of the Mass the monstrance enshrining the Host was taken out to the balcony above the entrance to the great church. The deluded people in the square were blessed by the rebellious monk in the name of the Roman Republic.

The great powers of Europe were not deceived by events. They refused recognition to the republic and kept their ministers with the Pope in Gaeta. France, Austria, and Spain, the Catholic powers, all offered to assist the Pope in regaining his throne, but Louis Napoleon who owed the Pope so much, perhaps even his life, took the first decisive action.

On the 25th of April, 1849, a small French force under the command of General Oudinot, landed at Città Vecchia, the port of Rome. It fell at once without resistance. This quick victory made Oudinot believe the capture of Rome would be equally easy. General Picard on April 30th tried to enter Rome by storming the gate of Saint Pancratius. The gate and

massive walls were manned by the legions of Garibaldi, strengthened by recruits from the provinces or legations. Picard was
rudely repulsed. He had to withdraw his forces in confusion,
leaving behind him at the scene of action the bodies of several
hundred dead and wounded.

The victory over the French led to a veritable reign of terror
in the Holy City. All those known to favor the Pope, or attempting to leave the city were thrown into prison. Suspected priests
and real ones were murdered in cold blood.

Louis Napoleon, in his capacity of President of the French
Republic, saw in the defeat of his troops a challenge to his prestige. Twenty thousand reinforcements were sent to strengthen
the forces in the field and a regular siege of Rome was begun.

The blockade of Rome was completed by the middle of
June. So acutely was it felt inside the Holy City that by the
first of July negotiations were begun, under the direction of
Ferdinand de Lesseps, for the capitulation of the Pope's capital.

The leaders all fled the city: Garibaldi retired with his legions, Ciceruacchio and his friends went into hiding in the
provinces to the east and the north. The French in superb
order marched into the ancient city: they were greeted in
silence for the most part. The rebellious smothered the hiss in
their throats; those who had suffered during the seven months
of terror and misrule restrained the joy that bubbled on their
lips.

The French placed a firm restraint on the press. All rights
of public assembly were revoked. Rome fell into an uneasy
silence, broken only by the lounging zouaves quartered in the
public square, and in sentries at attention before the churches
and public buildings.

Colonel Niel, who later became a field marshal and secretary of war under Louis Napoleon, galloped south to Gaeta.
He was received with quiet pomp by the Pope and his court.

With a dramatic gesture Niel bent his knee, kissed the Pope's slipper and presented the Holy Father the keys of Rome. John Mary received them with tear-dimmed eyes. His heart had been torn by the reports of sacrilege and murder. Now that was all over. He had prayed for his people, not forgetting his enemies and the misguided!

When the Holy Father spoke at last his voice was calm and resonant. He thanked General Niel and his troops; he paid homage to the French people who had restored him to his kingdom. The Pope conferred on the brilliant officer the collar of Gregory the Great, and presented Niel with an autographed letter of thanks. Everyone standing there looking at history was conscious of a significant lapse: the name of Louis Napoleon was not once mentioned.

There was a reason for this. During, and even before the siege of Rome, Louis Napoleon had attempted to instruct the Pope on the reconstruction of his government. The Holy Father, who knew vastly more about the character of his people than the noted French adventurer and opportunist, resented the interference. He saw clearly that any interference with the exercise of his temporal power at that juncture would be an interference and a hindrance to the full exercise of his spiritual power. The Pope was in fact to delay his return to Rome until he was assured that all danger of French interference in his government was past.

For the immediate present John Mary set about the business of forming a provisional government for the Papal States. Never had he demonstrated more heroically his forgiving character and love of all his children, including the rebellious ones led astray by wrong ideas or the heat of passion. Cardinals Altieri, Vannicelli-Casoni and della Genga-Sermattei headed the Council. Antonelli was continued in his office of Pro-Secretary of State. The Pope too appointed Council Chambers to take care of the necessary laws and finances. Courts of Justice were named. Commissions came into being to inquire into necessary improvements in the kingdom. One important commission was established to determine the losses suffered during the revolution by individuals and corporations.

The crown of the new dispensations was a second amnesty, issued later at Portici, a suburb of Naples, which was far more indicative of the Pope's fatherly concern for his people than the first amnesty had been. The Pope absolved of every penalty all those who had taken part in the late rebellion. The only exceptions were leaders, perjurers, and common criminals. For such as had led his children astray, broken their oath to him, murdered his people or plundered the churches, the Pope reserved the sword of justice.

No word was said about the constitution of 1848. Nor would it ever be mentioned again during the long reign of Pius IX. The Pope had tried a constitution. It had failed because of the envy of those who wished to destroy the Papal States, and the "good" people who lacked the wisdom and discipline to carry it out. In ignoring all mention of the constitution the Pope was demonstrating the realism of his outlook on the political situation in Italy. It takes sanctity to be both a realist and a kindly man, and Pius IX was both.

Having settled, for the moment, the outward affairs of the Papal States the Pope returned to his life of prayer and intuition. He was not one to linger in the past. His little lemonwood cross spoke to him of resurrection; his Mass and meditation gave daily news of Christ, hungry for souls hungry for Him. God had preserved His Vicar through terror and flight. Christ and His Mother had been with him all the way; now he felt the time was ripe to declare his thanks and to glorify God's Mother. In recent years the faithful of the world through their priests and Bishops had asked for the declaration of the dogma of the Immaculate Conception. In Spain and France, particularly, the glorification of Mary under this title had been especially loved.

In 1830, the miraculous medal of Catherine Labouré, shown to her in a dazzling series of visions, bore the prayer: "O Mary conceived without sin, pray for us who have recourse to thee." The Virgin herself had spoken.

Emigrants and ardent missionaries had long before carried this devotion to the Immaculate Virgin to the bounds of the earth. In India and Africa it was as well esteemed as it was in South America and in the little rosary of missions strung along the coast of upper and lower California and the Southwest.

To honor the Mother was to honor the Son, and John Mary loved the Mother from his first days when his childish eyes had looked up at her picture in the Cathedral of Senigallia: the grave Mother and the smiling Child.

After consulting his advisors the Pope was sure the time was ripe for the definition of the dogma. It was clear the world was going astray for things and names. The old truths, fundamental for men, were being forgotten or obscured.

On Candlemas Day, February 2, 1849, the Pope addressed an encyclical to the Bishops of the world concerning the promulgation of the dogma of the Immaculate Conception. This letter, *Ubi Primum,* asked all the Bishops to unite their prayers with the Pope's for enlightenment. It also requested them to make known the sentiments of the faithful. The Pope then designated a commission of theologians and Cardinals to examine the subject and formulate the doctrine. The Holy Father spoke of his many prayers to God and in touching phrases gave glory to Mary, "She who has crushed the head of the serpent; she who was placed between Christ and the Church; she who had always delivered Christian people from the most terrible calamities."

It was the Pope's orginal intention to condemn by name the

errors of the age as an introduction to the dogma. They were errors he had seen and rubbed elbows with in the early years of his reign. Some of them had been mentioned by name in his first encyclical. He knew the errors of the time at first hand and detested them with all his heart. The Pope's consultors deterred him from this design, however, and it was pointed out to him that the condemnation of error in conjunction with the dogma would dim the honor he wished to pay the Virgin.

It was also of some significance that the Pope chose as his chief collaborator in forwarding the dogma, Cardinal Lambruschini. In the end the Pope could say with affecting humility, "All the merit for the form of the definition belongs to poor Cardinal Lambruschini [he died before the promulgation] who really kept it moving toward a conclusion."

In the calm of Gaeta and later in Portici, where he lived for seven months, John Mary had an opportunity to look north on the continent, west to his children in the new world. Centers of persecution in England and the Low Countries had seemed to promise the total extinction of the Church in both places. But the blood of the martyrs and the providence of God had brought about a new planting. Famous converts and growing numbers of the faithful told a story more astonishing than the rebirth of the fabled phoenix. In hours of quiet prayer the Pope discerned the lightening horizon all about him: the faint flush in Europe, the pulsing glare in the Americas, north and south. He had been requested to restore the hierarchy in England and Holland during the recent years of storm and revolution. Now in his exile he began the actual work of bringing all these regions, the new and the old, under the life-giving order and discipline of the Church.

The grand, creative faculties of this Pope have been often misjudged or misrepresented. In his own day his enemies and detractors had the ear of the world; in our day historical writers too often see the Pontiff through "the pathos of distance": the strength of his manliness and the trueness of his vision have been lost in a forest of facts and misconceptions totally out of perspective with his own age.

John Mary Mastai was in the truest sense a citizen of the world. He had demonstrated qualities of serenity and at-home-ness in every period of his life. The easy way in which as a young student he slipped into the life of the papal court of Pius VII, his good-humored and intrepid adaptation to rough living in South America and the rebellious Sees of Spoleto and Imola, his benignity and charm in the first days of his reign, all these past triumphs were enlarged and duplicated during his sojourn in Gaeta and Portici.

King Ferdinand, his family, and the court of Naples were charmed and mystified by the unfailing good humor, the perpetual benevolence and wit of the Pope. Whether he spoke to prince or pauper he maintained a smiling attention that brought out the good qualities of people. The least sign of trouble evoked the Pope's ready charity and spiritual consolation. In both Gaeta and Portici he visited schools, churches, and orphanages; he received a constant stream of visitors.

All his life John Mary had shown an inquiring mind: this aspect of his personality led him to make excursions to Pompeii and Herculaneum. Of more spiritual import was a visit to the tomb of Gregory VII at Salerno. The Pope knelt before the vault of the great Hildebrand. He too had suffered much for the Church, but in the end he had purified it and his views had triumphed.

Early in March the Pope decided to take steps that would insure the end of his exile. It had begun in terror, but it had been a time of spiritual deepening and social pleasure. In Gaeta, unlike Rome, the Pope had been surrounded by courtesy and respect that flowed over into affection and love. The royal family had entertained the Holy Father and he had broken with precedent in receiving them in return at his own table. But the French were pressing him to return to Rome, and it was obvious that John Mary must leave the gracious south for his capital.

On March 9, 1850, the Pope called the Cardinals in Portici to a secret consistory. With them he set the date for his departure for home. Antonelli announced to the Catholic powers the imminent departure of the Pope and asked their help in maintaining the Holy Father in a position that would guarantee him the free government of the Universal Church.

In Portici the people had taken the Pope to their hearts. With more sorrow than joy they crowded about his carriage on the day of his departure. They remained on their knees until he had passed out of sight.

The Pope, too, was moved by the sorrow of departure. He stopped with his royal hosts at Caserta overnight. At dawn the next morning the Pope made his meditation and offered Mass. Then at five o'clock he entered his traveling carriage, after giving a special farewell blessing to the Queen and her children.

In the carriage with the Pope were King Ferdinand and his son Francis, heir to the throne of the Two Sicilies. The courtyard was clattering with coaches of the Sicilian and foreign nobility, the personages of the court and papal household. Some coaches would go as far as the borders of the Papal States, others would follow the Pope into Rome.

The Archbishop of Capua entertained the distinguished company at dinner. By evening of the next day the cavalcade had reached Gaeta. Here a banquet had been prepared. When it was over the Pope went out to give his special benediction to the troops of King Ferdinand massed upon the great mole and then proceeded to the border.

Chapter IX

RETURN TO ROME

PARTING from King Ferdinand moved the Pope beyond measure. "I bless you," the Holy Father said, "I bless your family, your kingdom and your people. I can't properly tell you how much I have appreciated your hospitality." King Ferdinand, on his knees, looked up at the handsome face bent above him. "I haven't done anything more than the duty of a Christian."

"Ah, yes you have, Majesty. Your loyal affection has been great and sincere." The Pope could say no more. He caught the hands of his royal host and drew him erect for a parting embrace.

At four o'clock on April 12, the Pope entered the city of Rome through Saint John's gate. The journey had taken eight days over roads that were quagmires, under variable skies. Once again the Pope's escort had been amazed at the tranquil way in which he endured both pleasure and discomfort. No hint of fatigue ever showed in his face or actions, he was always benign and graciously thoughtful of others. He had responded to the acclamations of the people along the way with unstudied eloquence. He had been deeply thoughtful on his knees in the cell where Saint Thomas had died, in the Abbey of Fossanova. At the receptions tendered him by Prince Doria at Valmontone and Prince Lancellotti at Velletri he had outshone his hosts in amiable princeliness. He had charmed General d'Hilliers, commandant of the French troops in Italy, who had come down to Velletri to present himself.

At Albano the Pope had given his parting benediction to the Neapolitan soldiers who had escorted him from Portici. From his carriage he watched with smiling eyes the maneuvers of the spirited French troop of African chasseurs who were to guard his entry into Rome.

Triumphal arches, the acclamation of the dense crowds watching his swiftly moving carriage, preceded and followed by galloping horsemen, all these reminded the Holy Father, once again, how closely interwoven were Palm Sunday and Calvary. He could still smell the burning tow held up on the silver stick the morning of his coronation. "Holy Father, thus pass the glories of the world!"

On the great steps before the classic entrance to Saint John Lateran the papal court and diplomats waited in their robes and uniforms of state. The Pope received the keys of his city from the commissioners of Rome, after a warm address of welcome. He then entered the great basilica, took his place on the throne and received the homage of his court and the attending diplomats who first kissed the cross on his slipper and then the ring of the fisherman. After Cardinal Barberini had exposed the Sacred Host, the ancient hymns of Benediction echoed in the high vaults. The Pope knelt like a marble statue, his eyes fixed on the monstrance.

Then he came out into the square. It was black with kneeling people. Shout after shout rose. *"Viva il Papa! Viva il Papa!"*

The carriage went whirling over the cobbled streets. Past houses wreathed in flowers, the arches of the Colosseum hung with priceless tapestries, the bridge of Sant' Angelo buried in yellow-and-white flags and flowers.

At Saint Peter's there was a second welcome, a second benediction by Cardinal Mattei. A way was cleared through the crowd. The Pope went on foot to the ancient black statue of Saint Peter under its canopy. He paused for a moment, bent and kissed the foot of the Apostle worn smooth by the reverent lips of pilgrims.

The Pope was pale as he entered the *sedia* for the journey to the apartments prepared for him in the Vatican palace which was to be his home to the end of his days.

The first days after the Pope's return were largely occupied with groups who came to congratulate him on his having come back to Rome. He gave solemn audience to the diplomatic corps on April 13th; on the 17th he received a large group of high French officers who were presented to him by General d'Hilliers. On both occasions the Pope expressed his cordial thanks to everyone who had helped him regain his kingdom. He expressed special regard for the Prince-President of France and for the young Emperor of Austria, Francis Joseph, whose troops had pacified Umbria and the Marches.

The Pope was equally energetic in thanking the aristocracy for the medal struck in his honor. He also visited the battlefield of the past year on the Janiculum Hill and was much affected by the ruin and destruction he observed.

All these receptions and excursions were official acts of the Pope: they provided an opportunity for a display of the graceful formality in which the Pope excelled. People said he was changed, a little more grave, a little less elastic and less quick to make hasty judgments. Certain acts, however, revealed how true he was to those golden lodes of character that had marked his entire life.

On the evening of the 13th, after the wearying reception of the diplomatic corps, the Pope with only a few attendants went to Santa Maria Maggiore. There on his knees before the relic of the crib and in Mary's chapel, he poured out his heart in thanksgiving. A few days later, attended by a chaplain, the

Pope suddenly appeared in the hospital of Saint Anthony on the Quirinal hill. There lay the wounded and maimed who had suffered for the Pope in the recent war. Nuns and nurses were stunned by the Pope's appearance. They watched him going from bed to bed asking the men questions about their homes and health. He had a rosary and medal for every man, a blessing and affectionate words of encouragement.

At one bed the Pope was moved to laughter. The young lad to whom he was speaking knew nothing about the proper forms of politeness used in addressing a Pope, but he did know the customs of the French army. To every question of the Pope he responded, "Yes, my Pope" or "No, my Pope." The Pope chuckled. A tender light came into his eyes.

Those first days of felicitations and praise were the prelude to significant developments for the Universal Church. One of the first acts of the Holy Father was the creation of new Cardinals. The most noted of these were Archbishop Pecci of Gubbio, brother of Leo XIII, and Nicholas Wiseman. Wiseman had lived for many years in Rome. As rector of the English College he had been loved for his amiable ways and revered for his scholarship. Pius IX knew him well and valued his wisdom and talents. Wiseman's novel, *Fabiola,* a story of the early Church and its martyrs, though it was wooden in its characterization and melodramatic in plot, had given him a currency in the field of popular letters.

It had been the intention of Pius IX to attach Wiseman to the Roman *Curia* but English Catholics had prevailed upon the Pope to place the English Cardinal at the head of the new English hierarchy, reestablished on the day Wiseman received his red hat.

The Cardinal, it now appears, had too wide a confidence in the English people and their native sense of fair play. On September 7, Wiseman unwisely issued his first pastoral letter titled "From the Flaminian Gate." Its grandiose phrases and tone of exaltation provided the necessary punch that brought out every shade of bigoted feeling in England. The old malicious phrase "scratch an Englishman and find a barbarian," appeared to be exemplified. Bands of zealots rioted in the streets of London. Pulpit and press thundered "no popery" and almost a century of good feeling went up in a blaze of fury.

This reaction must have surprised Wiseman as much as it did the Pope. Lord Minto, the British envoy, had been in Rome during the winter of 1847. He had lingered into the spring of the revolution of 1848. During this period he had explored the subject of the revival of the hierarchy with the Holy Father and Cardinal Barnabó, affectionately called Cardinal "Bo" by all who knew and loved him. Minto had reassured the Pope that Her Majesty's government would put no difficulties in the way of the revival of the Catholic Hierarchy. Between 1848 and 1850 the revolution had run its course and the Italian revolutionaries had caught the fancy and the ear of the English liberals, including the poets and, more important still, the English public. In spite of this change of mind about the policies and character of Pius IX, the English would have reacted far less violently had Wiseman not issued his somewhat dramatically conceived pastoral.

That Wiseman recognized this fact is shown in his succeeding actions. He was en route to take possession of his see of Westminster, but he lingered on in Austria until the storm had spent itself. Then in plain and unrhetorical terms he proceeded to explain by letter what the revival of the hierarchy meant for the Church and England. The explanation was accepted by most men of good will in England. Having shown a fury inconsistent with the English code of good manners, they were quick to make amends for the lapse. Wiseman took possession of his see without undue incident.

Parliament debated the affair for nearly nine months. Two laws were passed. One in 1851, made the new titles assumed by the Catholic bishops illegal. The second, in 1852, forbade public processions and the wearing of the ecclesiastical habit in the streets. These laws were designed as a stop to unreasoning bigotry. They remained largely inoperative. The "second spring" had begun. Though it was a slow spring, like most in England, it warmed to beauty long before the century had drawn to a close.

The revival of the hierarchy in Holland was attended with equal difficulties, though they were not as prolonged as they had been in England. The vicars apostolic who ruled the Church in Holland were in no hurry to change the favorable position of the Church or to challenge latent bigotry. The Pope agreed with his vicars. The experience in England had taught the Holy Father wisdom.

Dutch Catholics were about a third of the population of Holland. They had fought for their rights with shrewd stolidity that went well with Dutch character and democratic processes.

The actual revival of the Catholic hierarchy in 1853 came at the insistence of Thorbecke, the Premier of Holland. The public response was just as violent as it had been in England. The papal Bull of March 4th, restoring the hierarchy and establishing an archbishop at Utrecht, a city saturated with Calvinist tradition, brought about a month of distilled bitterness. Thorbecke and his cabinet fell. The situation seemed full of menace. The Pope met it with mildness and practical good sense. He asked for the prayers of the people as he had in England, and he required the newly appointed bishops to take an oath of loyalty to the king. The emphasis on the spiritual aspects of the case appealed to all men of spiritual knowledge; the oath of loyalty removed the major fears of papal encroachment on the liberties of Protestants.

The Pope had reason to be proud of himself. He had given Catholics public standing in two of the oldest Protestant strongholds. In the true style of his Master he had turned the other cheek in order that men might learn toleration and Catholics might have freedom before the law.

Only too often those who read history think of kings and Popes in a vacuum. Observing on paper only the good or great things achieved they, in a sense, lose sight of the most human and endearing qualities of their heroes.

John Mary had many great spiritual triumphs because he was deeply religious. In the midst of world affairs and important decisions he went his spiritual way. He was smiling and debonair. Those quiet hours in the morning spent at meditation and Mass and the hours before the Blessed Sacrament provided all the strength he needed for a tranquil day. Between tremendous decisions there were audiences with prelates, priests, and pilgrims in which the Pope ever demonstrated his sympathy, magnetism and charm. Always he gave a little unrehearsed homily that drew men back to spiritual concerns, or offered witty observations that were telling remedies for pride or slovenliness.

On one occasion the Pope was listening to a long drawn out request from an Italian priest—a certain Father Gallo. The Pope's face kindled with growing amusement for he could see that Father Gallo, though at base kindly and good, was ambitious to a degree in seeking advancement and honors. When the priest had finished his long and involved story he waited for the Pope's comment. John Mary cocked his head to one side, as he always did, and then observed: "When you become a monsignor you will be Monsignor Gallo. When you become a bishop you'll be Bishop Gallo and then no doubt Cardinal Gallo. But when you become Pope you'll be Papa Gallo" (parrot).

The Pope was always spotlessly clean in his person and dress. His doctors were somewhat scandalized when he told them that he bathed every day. John Mary disliked untidiness of any sort. When a priest came to an audience unshaven and requested that the Pope sign a document confirming him in a benifice, the Holy Father at once signed as requested. Then he wrote on the document, "I have granted this request because, from now on, the reverend gentleman has decided to shave."

The Pope enjoyed the company of writers and they equally enjoyed talking with him. On one occasion a noted author brought for the Pope's approval the life of a saint he had written. The Holy Father leafed through it. In his swift scrutiny he came on this sentence: "Our saint triumphed over all temptations but fell into a trap and married." John Mary's eyes crinkled with laughter. "Oh no!" he said. "This simply cannot be. As Pope I can't admit there are six sacraments in the Church and one trap."

A country curate once asked the Pope's permission to use the Paris Breviary because it was shorter than the Roman. "Why do you want this favor?" the Pope asked.

"Holy Father, it's because I'm so busy with the care of souls."

"And how many souls have you?"

"Three hundred, Your Holiness."

"Three hundred. Then I can't grant your request to use the shorter Breviary. You see, I have the care of three hundred million souls and I still have to say the long one."

However grave were the concerns of the papacy, however crowded his day, the Pope usually went for a walk in the city outside its walls. He loved vigorous exercise, yet he was never too concerned with himself to stop for a moment to console or help those who chanced to cross his path. He always carried money and medals which he freely distributed.

Usually the Pope drove in his carriage to the spot he had selected. Having reached it, he got out and walked. In one of these saunters the Pope was just alighting from his carriage when a fishmonger spied his white cassock and erect form.

The man had made a good living for himself and his little family by frying fish and selling them to passing people. Some of the dwellers in the crowded district had objected to the perpetual frying, and the Roman authorities had given the fishmonger an order to stop.

Seeing the Holy Father, the man rushed over to the Pope and fell on his knees in the dust. The Pope was just about to give the man a medal and a blessing when he fairly sobbed, "Holy Father, I'm ruined! I'm ruined!"

"What is wrong, my son?"

The man poured out his story. At its conclusion the Pope said. "Get up, my son, and bring me a pencil and a piece of paper." Half distracted, the man jumped up. All he could find in the little box at the back of his grill was the stub of a thick butcher's pencil. Taking this up he snatched a sheet of the coarse paper he used to wrap the fried fish. Presenting these to the Pope he peered over the Holy Father's shoulder while his Holiness made a brief order:

"Fry well! Don't stop frying! Fry wherever you like.

P. P. IX."

Most of the Pope's walks eventually led him to some church or other. The Holy Father's white cassock was usually well concealed by his long cloak, but people were quick to note the vigorous priest kneeling in the Blessed Sacrament chapel. At the close of one walk, the Pope went into the Church of the Twelve Apostles near the Piazza Venezia. He had almost finished his rosary, kneeling on the step of the Sacrament Altar, when his quick eye noticed that the top of the altar was heavy with dust. The Pope completed his contemplation of the last mystery, kissed the cross on his rosary, and tucked it into his belt. Then rising, he went up to the altar and wrote in the dust. He wiped his finger on a spotless handkerchief, threw back the enveloping cloak over his shoulders, and went into the sacristy. The monk on duty was too surprised to kneel down. "I have left a monument on the top of the Blessed Sacrament Altar," the Holy Father announced. He turned and went away with the long, swinging stride that always marked his progress.

The monk rushed out to the altar. At first he saw nothing, then his eyes were drawn to the altar top. Written in the thick dust were the words:

Pius IX, Pontifex Maximus

Chapter X

THE DOGMA OF THE IMMACULATE CONCEPTION

THE year 1854 was declared a Year of Jubilee. Wide indulgences were granted those making a pilgrimage to Rome. The people of the world and their bishops were quick to take advantage of the occasion. Over seas and mountains they came. Rome witnessed, as she had so many times, men of varying colors and customs sharing their love of the Savior in the affecting amity and impressive unity of belief and purpose. Once again footsore and weary pilgrims washed their faces and feet in the bubbling fountains that fill Rome with their sibilant music. The Pope multiplied his audiences and homilies. He seemed to be everywhere, taking his people to his heart. Once again the domes of the churches were lighted at night, the holy city was gay with hymns and flowers. It seemed quite like the old days before the revolution. Only the omnipresent red pantaloons of the French soldiers indicated there was a difference.

The heart of the Pope had been overjoyed at the response of his letters to the bishops asking for their prayers and advice in defining the dogma of the Immaculate Conception. The replies had all come in. Something over nine-tenths of the bishops were in favor of the definition. Of the tenth who were against definition, Archbishop Sibour of Paris and a few others said the doctrine could not be defined because it was not in the Scriptures. The other negative replies were mostly from Protestant countries. They maintained the time was not yet ripe for the definition.

The commission established by the Pope at Gaeta had been hard at work in searching out the history of the dogma and in establishing the precise form in which it was to be defined. This work was largely under the direction of the Jesuit Fathers Perrone and Passaglia. Perrone was the first theologian of Rome at this time. Passaglia was a brilliant but erratic man of great literary talent. It was their work on the dogma that prompted the enemies of Pius IX and all those who hated Mary to declare that the dogma was the "invention of the Jesuits."

Both Scripture and history threw the lie in the teeth of Mary's enemies and the Pope's detractors. The angel Gabriel had said to Mary in greeting, "Hail, full of grace!" Had she been stained with original sin at the time of the angel's appearance the greeting would have been untruthful and vain. It remained for theology to establish in what manner it was truthful.

Certainly the doctrine of Mary's freedom from original sin had been widely accepted in the first ages of the Church. The Church Fathers at Ephesus had hailed her Mother of God and the Oriental Church very early established the Feast of her Immaculate Conception. By the eleventh century the Feast had moved west. It was celebrated in England with the warm encouragement of Saint Anselm of Canterbury. The Council of Basle in 1439 prepared a decree on the subject but it remained unpublished. Sixtus IV approved the Feast and encouraged its celebration for the Universal Church.

The Franciscan Order had played a large part in making the devotion popular throughout the world. Among the great saints and doctors who spoke out in favor of the doctrine were Saint Irenaeus, Saint Ambrose, and Saint Augustine. Those against the concession of the privilege to Mary were hardly less eminent, though they came much later in time: Saint Bernard, Saint Albert the Great, Saint Bonaventure, and Saint Thomas Aquinas.

Saint Thomas expressed the great argument on the negative side. If the Virgin had been exempt from original sin she would not have been in need of the Redemption bought by the sacrifice of Christ.

It remained for Duns Scotus, the "Subtle Doctor," to find a way out of this difficulty with the assertion that the Virgin, by the will of her Son, was preserved in advance from the stain of original sin. In this way she could be said to have participated more perfectly in the Redemption than any other human being. The privilege accorded her went with her eminence and the rôle she had been selected to play for humanity. That was why the angel's salutation was the truth and not an idle compliment.

For the "common sense of the faithful" the world over, it could be said that like John Mary Mastai, they had taken the belief and devotion to their hearts.

Now toward the end of the Year of Jubilee in 1854, the work on the promulgation of the dogma was practically over. The glories of the Holy Year were working up to a glorious climax that was to begin a new dawn for the Church and Mary. All the bishops of the world had been invited to Rome for the occasion. They came by ship and stagecoach, by camel track and along the rails of that latest and wildly acclaimed invention that huffed along on iron rails at a terrific speed of twenty miles an hour.

By the end of November the bishops were all assembled in Rome. At the invitation of the Pope they met in consistory. There were four sessions under the presidency of Cardinals Caterini, Brunelli, and Santucci. Very slight changes were inserted in the actual formula that narrowed its application and made the doctrine more precise. The Pope "suffered" the changes.

The 1st of December in secret consistory the Holy Father reviewed the history of the dogma and asked the Cardinals' advice regarding the wisdom and opportuneness of promulgating the definition. A veritable acclamation moved the Pope to thank the Sacred College with words of praise.

In spite of the great events impending and the press of official business, John Mary somehow found time to show his old thoughtfulness.

Among the bishops who had come to Rome was Monsignor Bouvier, the Bishop of Mans in France. Shortly after his arrival the bishop fell seriously ill. In a roundabout way the news of Bishop Bouvier's illness came to the Pope's ears. "I must go and pay a visit to my son," the Pope said to his chamberlains.

"But would that be wise?" one chamberlain made bold to reply. "Bishop Bouvier is very ill. He couldn't possibly receive Your Holiness. Such a visit might disturb and upset him. It may even make him worse than he now is."

John Mary looked at the man with amazement. "Who speaks of receiving the Pope?" he queried. "I'm not talking of that at all. But how can the visit of a father harm a dear son?"

The Pope's view was well taken. In the evening, attended by his chaplain, John Mary went to visit the sick bishop. The bishop greeted the Pope with delight. He sat up against his pillows. His face was lit with encouragement. He kissed the Pope's hands murmuring softly, "Holy Father! Holy Father!" Then he said, after receiving the blessing of the Pope, "This is a great day for me. This morning I received my God; this evening I receive my father. What joy!" Everyone spoke of the tonic effect of the visit and John Mary's fatherly encouragement.

The morning of the 8th of December, 1854 was clear and beautiful. The blue of the Queen of Heaven was stretched like a great tent of light from horizon to horizon. At dawn, and even before the first light, crowds of people had come to Saint Peter's piazza where they were camped in their thousands. Those fortunate enough to have tickets of admission crowded into the great basilica glowing with the lights of thousands of candles suspended in crystal chandeliers from the brilliant arches of the great temple. Kings or their representatives were there in full dress uniform. The rain of light glanced from a sea of medals and gold braid; it was refracted in rainbows from the jeweled heads and fingers of beautiful and distinguished women sitting in the tapestried tribunes. Between the rosy walls were packed the devotees of Mary from the world over.

The black lace mantillas of the women and the sober full dress of the men told nothing of the exaltation in their hearts to see the joy of this morning. Hymns in praise of Mary, poured out in many languages from fifty thousand throats, were a poem of sound to her name. The litanies were sung asking the communion of saints to stand witness.

Silence fell. Then a burst of song from the Vatican choir announced the arrival of the Pope's procession. Soldiers and their commanders, the great officers of the realm, the officials of Rome, aristocrats and members of the Pope's household succeeded each other in deepening waves of color banded with the shrilling blue and orange of the Swiss Guard.

At last the *sedia* of the Pope came in sight ringed with the golden helmets of his Noble Guard. A roar of greeting welcomed the Holy Father. The tall feathered fans of gleaming white framed his magnetic face with the purity of snow. The long papal mantle was folded like beaten silver about his feet.

When the Pope had reached his throne he descended from the carrying chair and seated himself for the homage of the Cardinals, bishops, patriarchs and archbishops. At its close, the Office of *Terce* was chanted and the slow robing of the

Pope began. Sound, color, and the loveliest flowers of praise
culled from the Scriptures provided a radiant frame for the
Sacrifice offered in honor of the Mother of God.

After the Gospel, chanted in both Greek and Latin, Cardinal
Macchi, dean of the Sacred College, went in procession to the
Pope's throne. With him there were two bishops, one of the
Greek, one of the Armenian rite. Cardinal Macchi begged
the Pope, by virtue of his infallible teaching power, to define
the dogma of the Immaculate Conception. Pius IX knelt at
his prie-dieu and intoned the hymn "Come, Holy Spirit." The
Vatican choir and voices in every known language took up
alternate strophes of the song.

Then the Holy Father rose in the midst of a silence like
stone, put on his precious mitre, and began the reading of the
Bull *Ineffabilis* in which the doctrine of Mary's special privilege was explained and precisely defined. The Pope's voice,
so warm and musically impressive seemed at first smothered
by his emotions. Tears rained down his face. Then at the precise moment of defining the doctrine that Mary had been exempt from original sin from the very moment of her conception, power came to him, and the ringing tones of his voice
were heard in every corner of the tremendous fabric.

The Pope himself has left us a memorial of the morning in
a conversation with Mother Mary Macchi, a personal friend
of the Holy Father. She was a nun of Santa Trinità dei Monti,
a convent the Pope loved to visit. Once after dinner at the convent, the nuns asked the Holy Father to tell them what he had
felt in defining the dogma of the Immaculate Conception.
After a moment or two of recollection, the Pope replied:

"What I experienced and felt in defining the dogma cannot
be fully expressed. When I began the promulgation I felt that
my voice was too weak to be heard by the immense crowd [at
least fifty thousand people] in the Vatican Basilica. But when I
came to the formula of definition God gave His Vicar such

power and strength that his voice filled the whole basilica. I was so moved by this, that I was forced to stop speaking for a moment while tears rained down my cheeks. While God proclaimed the dogma through the mouth of His Vicar He made me see so clearly and fully the incomparable purity of the Blessed Virgin that deep down in my spirit my soul was overwhelmed with joy beyond this earth. . . . I do not fear to assert that the Vicar of God had need of a special grace or else he would have died of love through his knowledge and the tremendous flood of exalted feeling."

Like Saint Paul lifted up to the seventh heaven, the Pope was carried through the remainder of the Mass on a wave of exaltation. It was the greatest moment of his life.

Twenty-four years of reign still stretched before him. The assembling of the Vatican Council was in the midst of that future, two notable jubilees, and the uttering of the dogma of papal infallibility; yet to the mystical heart of John Mary the honor paid his heavenly Mother on this morning outshone in radiant beauty all the other triumphs of his reign.

His voice had a joyous ring as he proclaimed the plenary indulgence at the end of Mass; his face was luminous as he felicitated the throng of bishops who had gathered about his throne.

The manner used in proclaiming the doctrine paved the way for the dogma of the Pope's infallibility. Everyone noted a difference on this morning that was pregnant with meaning for the Church. The Holy Father had consulted the bishops of the world in preparing to define the dogma. But he had not associated the bishops with him in defining it, but had spoken by virtue of the supreme teaching power given him by Christ. It was to set a precedent for all time, a precedent followed by Pius XII in defining the dogma of Mary's Assumption.

That evening Rome was noisy with joy. The streets were filled with happy people and the carriages of the nobility. All

the houses and churches were outlined in garlands of light.
The dome of Saint Peter's sparkled like a perfect diamond set
against the deep blue velvet of sky.

Three years later, on the Feast of the Immaculate Conception, the Pope came to the Piazza de Spagna surrounded by
the full majesty of his court. In the center of the square was
a lofty column of cipolin marble with an inscription forever
calling to mind the promulgation of the dogma of the Immaculate Conception. The Holy Father blessed the monument
and unveiled the statue of Mary standing on top of the column.
It was the marble figure of God's Mother as Catherine Labouré
had seen in her vision, radiant of face, with outstretched hands.
"O Mary, conceived without sin, pray for us who have recourse
to thee."

The money necessary for the erection of the monument had
come to the Pope in a manner connected with his exile in the
kingdom of the Two Sicilies. While he was there King Ferdinand had urged Pius IX to cede to Naples his rights over
Benevento. The Pope had not concurred at the time, but in
1847, during a visit of the king's sons in Rome, the Holy Father
had signed an agreement granting to Naples his rights in the
ancient colony. In recognition of the grant the king's sons had
given the Pope a gift of forty thousand scudi. It was this gift
that had defrayed the cost of the beautiful monument that tells
Mary's glory to all pilgrims and signalizes forever the dogma
of her Immaculate Conception.

Chapter XI

LIGHT AND SHADOW

THE Pope was particularly interested in the Church in the United States. He was also indulgent and kind. In 1850, he raised the Sees of New York, New Orleans, St. Louis, and Cincinnati to the rank of archbishoprics. Bishops Hughes, Blanc, Purcell and Kendrick became archbishops. In 1853, San Francisco also became a metropolitan see.

Until the reign of Pius IX the American Church had been under the control of the Propagation of the Faith. It had the status of a missionary country with all the disadvantages such a situation implies. Pius IX prepared the way for bringing it under the authority of the regular Congregations.

But the Pope did far more than this for the American Church. Among his many benefactions was the American College in Rome which has had such influence on the Church in our country, and has given us a long line of distinguished Cardinals and bishops.

Piux IX bought the building for the American College with a gift of thirty thousand dollars. The property was on Humility Street. Its beginnings were humble. A second gift of thirty thousand dollars was sufficient to remodel the building which had been an old Visitation convent. The Pope watched the growth of the college with the eye of a kind father.

By the end of his reign in 1878, the Pope had raised Archbishop McCloskey of New York to the rank of Cardinal, and in his treatment of American bishops and pilgrims he showed a special fondness for America. His official portrait was painted by an American artist, Healy, in an atmosphere of gaiety and good humor. The Pope was himself simple and unaffected. He dearly loved a joke or witticism, and his optimism was attractive to a people who loved grandiose dreams, had great expectations, were ebullient and quickly humorous like himself.

After the Pope's death, when the family of Mastai-Ferretti lost their money for a time, the family house in which John Mary had been born was put on the market for sale. Cardinal Farley, of New York, immediately came forward with a gift of ten thousand dollars. This gift preserved the house for posterity and made possible its use in the work of furthering the Cause of Pius IX. It is still, however, the property of the Archdiocese of New York and has become an amazing museum of a significant and holy Pope. The winter parlor, the rose-and-gold drawing rooms, the little, rather dark, chapel with its picture of the Madonna of Sassoferrato, which John Mary loved, and where he celebrated his Mass so many times, have been kept as they were in John Mary's childhood. This house in Senigallia is in a sense an American shrine in which the unstinting love poured out on a new land has taken the perennial luster of living remembrance.

The entire world was very much in the Pope's mind. He enlarged and honored the Canadian hierarchy; regularized and reestablished church life in Central and South America by concordats wherever possible, spoke out boldly against the persecution of the Church in Mexico and Colombia.

Pius IX's tremendous achievements abroad were a true reflection of his achievements in Italy and on the continent of Europe. At his accession Pius IX found the Papal States backwards and unprogressive. When they were filched from him by the House of Savoy, over a period of some ten years, the

thieves found a kingdom in which a complete change had
taken place. Bad roads had been replaced by new ones, magnificent bridges and aqueducts had come into being, railroads
had been laid, gas had been brought to light public buildings
and squares. A comprehensive system of re-forestation was begun, the cultivation of silk, and other industries had been
generously encouraged.

Shortly after the Pope's return to Rome the Queen of Spain
sent the Holy Father a massive chalice heavily encrusted with
precious stones. The Pope thanked the Queen for the gift.
The chalice was then sold for fifty thousand scudi. With this
sum the Pope opened six bakeries in the poorer section of
Rome. In these bakeries bread was sold to the poor at a low
price. This act of the Pope did much to relieve the hardship of
the very poor. It also helped in keeping down the price of bread
in Rome at a time when there had been several scanty crops
of grain throughout Europe.

This was not the only instance of the Holy Father's perpetual
care of his people. His first-hand experiences in the social field
at Tata Giovanni and Saint Michael's had made the Pope one
of the foremost experts in the field, without lessening his humanity or humility. John Mary was the only crowned head of
a government with such background and experience, and he
inestimably excelled all in the depth of his sympathy and the
width of his charity. The Pope's orphan asylums, hospitals,
prisons, madhouses and refuges for the aged were far in advance of those maintained by any other government in Europe.

In addition to his interest in social progress, John Mary was
very much alive to individuals and their needs. Children particularly evoked in him an immediate response of kindliness
that has come down to us in a group of stories.

In the days before he fled to Naples, the Pope without attendants walked out through the gate of the Quirinal. He had
gone only a short distance when he saw a small girl sitting on

the curb at the edge of the footpath. Her curly head was bent in dejection, and she was crying bitterly. The Pope bent down and caught her grimy hand. The child, her face smudged with tears, looked up.

"Why are you crying, my daughter?"

The sobbing slowly halted for her reply. "I was coming home with a flask of wine and I fell. See!" She pointed to the fragments on the pavement. "I not only spilt the wine, but I broke the flask too."

"But surely you can't be blamed for an accident. Just tell your mother how it happened."

"You don't know my mother. She's sure to beat me."

"Well, that alters the case." John Mary reached into the pocket of his cape and brought forth a new-minted crown. "Now I'll tell you what to do. Go buy a new flask and fill it with the best Orvieto. Then instead of beating you, your mother will give you a kiss."

"But I'll have to tell her how it all happened."

"That's all right, just say a priest who lives in the Quirinal helped you."

On another morning, the Pope, who always opened his own mail, found a letter in a painfully-written childish hand. It was short:

> Dear Holy Father,
>   My mother is ill and can't buy medicine. We need thirty-three paoli. I will be glad to come and get the money if you will give it to me.

The Holy Father sent a messenger to summon the boy. When he was ushered into the Pope's study the Holy Father called the fine-looking boy to his desk without even the ceremony of a blessing.

"How many paoli did you say your mother needed for her medicine?" the Pope asked as a test.

The answer came without a moment's hesitation. "Thirty-three paoli."

"Very well." The Holy Father put into the boy's hand two gold pieces worth about thirty-six paoli. The Pope was reaching for a third gold piece, but the boy interrupted. "No, that's enough! This will make my mother well. My father is dead; that's why we are so poor. My mother and I are grateful to you and to God, dear Holy Father."

By this time the child and the Pope were almost in tears. John Mary laughed to break the tension. "Kneel down, now, and I'll give you a blessing for yourself and your mother. And remember you must come back and tell me how your mother gets on."

The boy dutifully complied with John Mary's request. "My mother is better," he told the Pope.

"I'll tell you what I'll do," John Mary said. "I'll send you to school and pay for all your expenses."

"I wish I could do that. But I can't leave my mother. I'm the only one she has to help her."

"Ah, wonderful, my son! Since your mother is so poor and you are so good, I'm going to look after both of you."

The Pope was equally forward-looking in simplifying the working of his government, and in improving the seminaries and colleges throughout his realm. It was he who began the revival that took place in the fields of Scripture study and Thomistic philosophy. In art, architecture, and poetry the Pope's influence began and furthered the Catholic revival that today is playing such a noted rôle in every country and every sphere of the fine arts.

Some idea of John Mary's readiness to accept and further scientific works is seen in his relationship with John B. De Rossi, a veritable genius in the field of archeology. De Rossi was in love with Roman antiquity, both Christian and pagan. It was chiefly through De Rossi's intuition and work that amazing discoveries were made in the ancient Christian catacombs. At first, the Pope could scarcely credit the magnificence of the work. One of the Cardinals came to Pius IX with the astonishing news that the catacomb of Saint Calixtus had yielded extraordinary and astonishing discoveries: "Hmm!" commented the Pope. "These are the imaginings of archeologists."

Later, when John Mary discovered that De Rossi had actually found what he claimed, the Pope went with his suite to inspect the work in progress.

As he came into the dimly-lighted gallery where De Rossi and his men were working, De Rossi dusted off his hands carefully and bent to kiss the Pope's ring. Then, looking up, eyes atwinkle, he said, "Welcome to the imaginings of archeologists, Your Holiness."

The Holy Father laughed heartily at the sally. He examined everything. His suite grew restless while the Pope poked about in corners and listened to the involved explanations of the archeologist.

The two men became great friends. Pius IX assisted the progress of discovery with generous funds and delighted to honor De Rossi in every possible way. Now De Rossi was urged to go forward vigorously in uncovering the antiquities of the pagan Forum and all those other places sacred to the worship of the early Christians.

On the morning of April 12, 1855 a message was brought to the Holy Father that De Rossi had discovered the tombs of Pope Alexander and the martyrs Eventius and Theodulus. The Pope was excited by the news. He was in conference with a distinguished group of archbishops from Lisbon, Dublin, Sydney, and Vienna. The Holy Father, who dearly loved excursions, invited his guests and a group of Cardinals, among them Antonelli, to go with him for an inspection of the exciting find. The party went by carriage through the Porta Pia, a short distance beyond the church and convent of Saint Agnes, into

the spring glory of the Roman countryside. The vines were
beginning to twinkle their variegated planes along the trellises.
Blossoming trees seemed to dance in the golden distance. The
green fields were flaming with great swaths of scarlet poppies.
Many noted groups from Rome had preceded the Pope and his
guests to the scene. He dismounted from his carriage in a flurry
of *vivas*.

The Pope, surrounded by his court, went into the catacombs
and prayed. Then taking from De Rossi a proffered ham-
mer, he gave the first stroke on the cement that held one of the
marble slabs on the tombs of the martyrs.

Taking his guests with him, the Holy Father went on foot
a short distance to visit the ruins of a Roman villa in which
there had been found several patches of mosaic floor of great
beauty.

The morning had warmed to noon by the time the party returned to the convent of Saint Agnes. As was his invariable
custom, the Pope first entered the chapel for a visit to the
Blessed Sacrament. Everyone was in a happy mood when he
finally came out into the refectory where a collation had been
prepared.

After the meal was over, the entire company went into the
large reception room of the ancient convent, that extended
beyond the walls over the stables. The Holy Father was in a
merry mood, and his guests were enchanted with his repartee
and the lively conversation it engendered. Each moment the
crowd in the room grew more dense. Every monk, and the
large groups of sightseers from the newly discovered tombs,
wanted to listen to the animated conversation and have a look
at the Holy Father.

At this point the prefects of the College of Propaganda came
to the door of the reception room and begged the Pope to receive the eighty students who had greeted him that morning
with an address of welcome. The Pope readily complied. Pius

IX seated himself in a great thronelike chair under a canopy of tapestry. Slowly the students of the college filed into the already crowded room.

There was a sudden sound of sagging and snapping timbers —a great babble of screaming voices. With a noise like thunder the whole floor gave way and the entire crowd, including the Pope, went plunging down twenty feet into the stables below. A dense cloud of plaster dust rose to the ceiling. The hysterical pandemonium that ensued may well be imagined. Those elsewhere in the house, servants and monks, Cardinal Schwartzenberg and Monsignor Hohenlohe who were chatting in the next room, rushed down to the first floor. Everyone was crying the Pope's name.

With torn fingers they gradually pulled aside the bricks and jagged beams. Some of the students and visitors were bruised and injured. The Pope, though shaken, was totally unhurt. He had lost his *zucchetto*. His white cassock was stained with dirt and dust. The scarfing folds of the canopy had protected his head in the fall.

Once he had been helped to his feet, the Holy Father took charge of the situation. He calmed the excitement, superintended the removal of bruised and injured in his own suite of carriages. Then the Pope wiped his smudged face with a damp towel and washed his hands in a proffered basin. All the while the Bishop of Burlington, Vermont, with customary American energy, was brushing great clouds of dust from the Holy Father's cassock. The Pope said to him at last, "You are making this a veritable Ash Wednesday."

John Mary finally led the way back to the chapel and intoned the *Te Deum*. He prayed a long time in thanksgiving and for all those injured in the terrible fall. Though several of the students had been seriously injured, no one in the accident was killed or suffered permanent injuries. The Pope himself ascribed this happy ending to the watchful care of the Mother of God.

The Pope's excursions did not always end in such drama and excitement. Most of them were quiet times in which he identified himself with his people by entering into their lives and affections with a thoroughness that few Popes have ever achieved. The atmosphere of these encounters is drenched with tenderness and a spirit of good fellowship worthy of a fairy tale. As a usual thing the Pope proceeded on his excursions entirely unannounced. The resulting situations were a spontaneous challenge to his spiritual magnificence and sense of fun.

One day the Pope went to the Church of Saint Francis a Ripa, in order that John Mary, like any other pilgrim, might gain the Portiuncula indulgence.

The Holy Father sat enthroned during the conventual Mass. He was the very picture of amiable kindness. The sweet chanting of the Mass on this summer morning was a tribute to his presence among the Franciscan friars.

After the Mass, the Father Guardian asked permission of the Pope to present the brothers to him in the sacristy.

"Of course, I want to meet them all," John Mary said. "But I'm not here to disturb the routine of the house. Isn't this the time at which the brothers usually sing the Office?"

"Oh, yes, Your Holiness."

"Very well then, we'll all go to the choir."

The Holy Father re-seated himself for the singing of the Office. An excited young novice placed in his hands a copy of the Book of Hours. The Pope, on opening it, discovered it was more than a little stained with use, and with the thumbprints of novices hurrying to choir after their breakfast.

When the Office was finished the Pope carried the book with him to the sacristy. An armchair was placed for his reception of the brothers, and a cushion for his feet.

Before he sat down, the Pope, assuming a face of false severity, said to the Father Guardian, "Haven't you a better Office book to give the Holy Father when he comes to visit?"

The Father Guardian was horrified at the sight of the book the Pope showed him. "Yes, Holy Father. Yes, we have a better book! The novices must have quite lost their heads to give you that volume."

"Ah! The novices! Very well, I'll deal with them." After receiving the older members of the community with kindly words, the novices came forward. They were obviously nervous. The whole community was, too, while they wondered what the Holy Father would do.

The first novice bent down to kiss the Pope's slipper. As he did so the Holy Father gave him a soft rap on his shaven crown.

"Ah, little brother," he said, "is this the way to treat the Pope by giving him a dirty book?" Each succeeding novice got the same rap and the same sort of raillery. The reception ended in peals of laughter, and the Holy Father departed in an atmosphere of genuine affection.

From the Vatican came a messenger with a superb Book of Hours. In it the Pope had written in his own hand, *"Ad usum Papae,"* which could be interpreted "for use of the Pope" or "for the way in which the Pope was used."

Pius IX had a genius for breaking through formality and making people at home with him. He loved to go out to Castelgandolfo, the Pope's summer villa, which he repaired and ornamented. The peasants of the countryside enjoyed these visits. The Pope was thoroughly at home with them, because they treated him with homely courtesy he much enjoyed in his casual walks through the lovely countryside.

Stopping in a small village one day, the Holy Father was soon surrounded with enthusiastic peasants. It was the time of the harvest festival. The grain was in, the grapes had been trodden out. Everyone was in a merry mood. They surrounded the figure of the Pope and serenaded him with country songs while they played on violins and pipes. So great was the crowd that those nearest to the Holy Father pressed him, touching his sleeves and fingering the stuff of his cassock and white silk sash. Then at last John Mary said in an amused voice *"Basta! Basta!"* ("Enough! Enough!"). Those nearest to the Pope repeated the command and relayed it to those behind him. The music and singing suddenly stopped. Then a complaining man's voice was heard from the back of the crowd.

"Why do you say 'enough'? You have had the good fortune to touch the Pope. You think that's enough for you. But what of us?"

"You're right," the Holy Father said laughing. John Mary stayed until he had touched every head in the crowd and had given them an individual blessing.

On another occasion the Pope was taking a walk through the fields near the villa. Observing his erect figure, a large group of peasants came running across the fields to greet him. The Pope gave them his blessing and then said: "You are fortunate, my children, to be able to live in such a beautiful countryside and breathe such pure air."

A bold peasant, much to John Mary's amusement, replied: "Yes, we are fortunate, Holy Father. But why don't you come out here more often? You'd be much better off with us instead of staying down there in that dirty Rome all the time."

It was the guileless merriment of a child that taught the Pope to enjoy these occasions. Often enough the plain speaking of the peasants shocked the Holy Father's entourage, but John Mary enjoyed the encounters. Like a genuine nobleman he thought nothing of himself, but he realized that his office was something to be shared with all men in that simplicity of manner employed by Our Lord in His walks through the teeming villages of Palestine.

The Pope's quickness of manner was often of extreme advantage in saving from embarrassment the simple souls who applied to him for help. Each year on the Feast of Saint Louis of France the Pope went in state to the church of the saint, accompanied by the entire diplomatic corps. There, surrounded by French officers and simple soldiers, he paid a tribute to the high holiness that is the soul of France.

After the Mass there was usually a simple collation, followed by a reception of the French nobility, officers' wives, and servants. On one of these occasions a scrupulous old cook of a high French officer came with the gentry to pay her respects to the Holy Father. When the old lady knelt at the Pope's feet for his blessing she surprised everyone by starting at once to confess in a penetrating voice her sins and supposed temptations against the sixth commandment. What she had to say was rather of a delicate nature. Ambassadors and high officers grew first red with embarrassment and then went into tortures of surpressed laughter.

The Pope, completely surprised for the moment, finally broke in on the old woman's recital. His face was gravely compassionate. He touched her head with the sign of blessing. "Very good, my daughter. I can see you are greatly troubled. Behind you there is a group of Sisters of Compassion from Lyons. You have special need of compassion. Speak to these sisters a little later, and I'm sure you'll be satisfied."

A charming picture of the Pope's love of people comes to us from the Jubilee Year of 1854. On the 17th of May the French corvette *Meteor* came along the coast of Italy on a scientific cruise. The corvette stopped at the port of Anzio, where the Pope had come to get a breath of cool sea air. The sailors, hearing that the Holy Father was in town, asked to be presented to him. Permission was granted, and the entire group in sparkling white uniforms and polished to the ears had a wonderful visit with the Pope. At the end of the audience the Holy Father told the group he would bless their ship the next morning.

The day dawned calm and beautiful. Sharp at 8:30 the Pope,

with a small group of attendants, came on board the *Meteor*
that sparkled like its name. Every piece of brass glittered above
the decks, white as the Holy Father's cassock. Flags and pen-
nants were everywhere, not only the colors of France but the
cheerful white and yellow of the papal flag.

An armchair was placed on the deck. Scientists, officers and
crew came singly before the Pope. To each he spoke a little
and then gave his blessing. When the ceremony was over, the
Holy Father was invited to go on a day's cruise to San Felice
and back. He agreed at once, and the ship put out to sea. The
Pope examined every part of the vessel. He insisted on seeing
the working of the scientific instruments, asking intelligent
questions meanwhile. His own lack of ceremony and his ready
wit soon had every man at his ease.

Hearing there was one sailor ill in the infirmary John Mary
said, "Fever or not, I must see him. Poor boy, he must be
lonely: so young and so far away from home."

John Mary, in his ready French, questioned the sufferer,
asked a hundred questions about the boy's home life and then
gave him his blessing. "I'm sure you will soon be well, my son,"
he said in parting.

At the sailors' dinner hour John Mary insisted on going into
the mess-room. Instead of sitting at the head of the table he
commanded the servers to sit down. Then, setting the example,
the Holy Father, assisted by the ship's officers, began to serve
the men. For years after in the little villages of France the story
went round. "And who served me? Our Holy Father himself,
making jokes all the while. You would never believe it. How
good he is! How charming! It was one meal I know I shall never
forget!"

The ship halted at San Felice. John Mary was rowed ashore
in the big launch. As it came in close to the shining strand it
was discovered that the boat drew too much water to permit it
to be drawn up on the beach. With cries of delight the sailors

jumped into the water and formed a chair of linked arms. On this human chair the Pope was conveyed safe and dry to the beach.

In the summer of 1857, John Mary decided to make a tour through the eastern and northern sections of the Papal States. The Pope had originally planned this journey because he wanted to make a pilgrimage to the Holy House at Loreto. Like Jack's beanstalk, the journey grew and grew.

The tour in its final form had two purposes: the Holy Father wanted to see at first hand the improvements he had planned and made and those still needed. But most of all he wanted to show himself in those parts of the kingdom that had long been most disaffected. John Mary was far shrewder than many of his critics. He well knew that most of his people were simple peasants. Left to themselves, without being worked on by liberals and fanatic revolutionaries, they were loyal to the Holy Father and loved him in their simple, humble way as he loved them.

The childlike heart of the Pope took real joy in the prospective excursion. Antonelli, and John Mary's advisors among the Cardinals, disliked the idea. They warned the Holy Father against the danger of assassination and insults of all kinds. The Pope merely laughed at these cautions. "Which of my sons would kill his father?" he asked. "And which of my sons would fail to welcome me?"

Above all, John Mary looked forward to a visit with his family. How good it would be to sit down in the gracious old house in Senigallia saturated with the loves of his childhood. His mother and father were both dead, but Aunt Vicki would be there and his always affectionate brothers. How wonderful, too, it would be to kneel in the Holy House at Loreto where the healing hand of God had touched him.

On May 4th the Pope offered Mass in Saint Peter's. He took

a light breakfast, said farewell to his court, and entered the basilica again to kiss the foot of Saint Peter's statue. The piazza was gay with the uniforms of the papal troops. The Holy Father blessed them and the enormous crowd that had come to wish him a happy journey. Then entering the heavy berlin, drawn by six horses, the Pope took the road for Civita Castellana which was to be his first stop. A cortege of traveling carriages followed the Holy Father, carrying some of the chief personages of the papal court.

The Pope's expectations were more than realized. Everywhere along his route, at crossroads and villages, in small towns and large, his sons from the lands and shops greeted him with unaffected joy. Tapestries and banners, age-old, came out of hiding; there were masques and floats, gorgeous costumes and towers of burning incense and perfume. Shouting peasants and workmen in their holiday dress lined the way.

Always, the Pope turned their minds toward God. He went first to the cathedral for Benediction of the Blessed Sacrament. Then John Mary received the elected or appointed representatives of the people and spoke to the crowd thanking them for their love, telling them of God's love for them.

The ancient aristocracy of Italy showered gifts on John Mary and flattering attention. He was gracious to the rich or noble but quick to see through anything that was phony or pretentious.

At one wealthy house, not noted for its Catholicity, the Pope's hostess was loud in her praise. "What an honor it is to have you here, Holy Father; how marvellous, how wonderful!" So she went on and on. Finally she brought out her gold-covered guest book. "Do sign, Holy Father. Such an honor. Even one word will be enough!"

"One word? But I can do better than that." The Pope took the gold-and-ivory pen, dipped it in the gold ink-well and wrote:

"Remember, man, that thou art dust and unto dust thou shalt return." With a great flourish he signed his name, "Pius IX, Pontifex Maximus."

At Bologna, the supposed hotbed of disaffection, the Pope was received in a riot of acclaim. John Mary exercised his charm and spiritual talents, gave generous alms to the poor and one hundred thousand dollars to repair the cathedral. The climax of his visit was the crowning of the statue of Our Lady of Protection, very old, and like many others in Italy, ascribed to the artistry of Saint Luke. For the crowning ceremony the fabled statue was carried in procession through the streets to the cathedral. There the Holy Father placed a massive gold crown on the head of the Virgin.

At Bologna a delegation came from Ravenna to ask the Holy Father to pay a visit of state to the city of ancient shrines and inimitable mosaics. Antonelli had cautioned the Pope not to go to Ravenna because it was the stronghold of the Carbonari who dealt in assassination with the bland ease of those who sold French pastries.

Against the advice of his officers and the Austrian generals, John Mary boldly accepted the invitation. The warmth of his reception staggered everyone. The ancient town was jammed with bright peasant costumes. The Pope was acclaimed in a spontaneous burst of joy that made the cautious thoughtful. Perhaps after all the Holy Father knew his people better than those who so readily offered advice.

Most memorable to John Mary's sensitive heart were the welcomes accorded him at Spoleto, Senigallia, Imola, and Loreto. There he was intimately known for his goodness and love. In a delirium of joy the people pressed around him. Protocol was forgotten: his sons and daughters kissed his hands, fingered the fine wool of his cassock. Neighbors, friends—he was at home.

In Loreto the young men of the village wanted to unhitch the six horses from his carriage and draw him up the hill. The Pope smilingly dissuaded them. He barely made his way through the shouting thousands to the Holy House. Then he went through the lofty door into the noble church thronged with nobility and clergy, past the gorgeous marble screen into the little room of sun-baked brick. He fell on his knees and placed a splendid gold chalice on the altar steps, his gift to Mary's shrine.

Here he had laid down the cross of illness for the heavier cross of great affairs. But his heart had remained young. In the years of fury and storm it had danced ever before the Lord like the flickering ruby lamps hanging from the modest roof above him.

In Senigallia people from the entire town and countryside packed the squares and streets wall to wall. They pelted the Pope with flowers and shouted his name. They were all proud of him, glad to welcome him home. John Mary dismounted from his carriage in the wide square with its rows of plane trees outside the cathedral. He was moved to tears. Here it had all begun, his human life and his life with God. A cooling breeze blew in from the Adriatic; the air was fresh and fragrant.

After Benediction the Pope went home to the family house. The Bishop of Senigallia had offered John Mary the use of his palace. The Pope thanked him. "I will rest better in my father's house. I want to see again all the things I love so much."

The bishop and the people respected John Mary's wish. They escorted him to the wide square doors and left him with his family. After affectionate greetings John Mary went through the rooms. His hands smoothed the damask of the chairs and couches. He knelt in the dark chapel to pray; he knelt in the room where he had first seen the light of day and where his father and mother had died.

The family crowded about him while he talked and opened the gifts he had brought them. Beautiful rosaries for his brothers and nephews, fine cameos for the women and girls of the family. Aunt Vicki's was the most beautiful of the lot, but there was no envy over that. After all, she was the companion of John Mary's childhood and had prepared him for his first Communion.

In the church of the Magdalen John Mary offered Mass at the family altar. The vaults of his father and mother were there in the floor beyond the railing. How much he owed his parents! How lovingly he remembered them in this atmosphere!

There was still time in the short three days for the visits of old friends. They came and found John Mary unchanged. He had the same lack of ceremony, the same charm of manner and grace of speech. One friend whose nickname was "Stu," a name he hated, had spent an hour with John Mary. As the man was leaving the Pope's presence John Mary suddenly remembered the nickname. "Goodbye, 'Stu'!" he called after the departing figure. The man turned. His face was quite red— he hadn't heard that odious name for years. At last he smiled, "I'm forgetting for the moment you're the Pope. Shut up!" he said.

The three days at Senigallia, all too short, had rested the Holy Father in mind and body. He felt renewed in spirit and courage for the endless rounds of banquets, speeches and receptions that lay before him. When someone showed him a paper of the day in which the Pope was caricatured as a big turtle John Mary laughed heartily. "It's good," he said. "And quite true. I do move slowly, but I always move forward. And I have no vulnerable points."

As he always did, John Mary maintained his close touch with people. They brought him their simple problems and he did his courteous best to solve them.

In Florence one man asked to speak with the Holy Father

during his private tour through the art monuments of the city. John Mary stopped in the city street and gave the petitioner ready access to his person.

"I can see you are troubled," the Pope said. "What is wrong?"

The man was weeping. "I'm a horrible sinner, Holy Father. Horrible! Horrible! I came to see you out of curiosity. Suddenly I was overcome with shame and repentance. I wish to confess to you, Holy Father, for you are the only priest that can absolve me from my terrible sins."

"Come with me, child," the Pope commanded. Followed by his escorts of dukes and princes the Holy Father went into a neighboring church, heard the man's confession and absolved him.

It was little things like this John Mary remembered best when he was back in Rome. They reminded him how spiritual was the true life of a Pope, how all the power and the glory of his position was swallowed up in the radiance of his priesthood.

Everyone in Rome said the tour had been a great success. Taxes were down and everyone in the Holy City was filled with cheerfulness and warm regard for the Pope. No prince or emperor of the time had ever received more spontaneous or thrilling acclaim. Even Antonelli was pleased about it. But John Mary himself saw behind the bright façade of the present with sorrowful directness.

During the tour he had probed the hearts of his old friends Minghetti and Count Pasolini. They had gone forward in their liberalism and now were at odds with John Mary and his policies. For his part, the Pope found them unrealists. They were in love with the parliamentary freedom of the English and the French. They wanted the same freedom in the Papal States and Italy. But behind them lurked the sinister figures of Cavour, Mazzini, and Garibaldi. Minghetti and Pasolini were, without knowing it, playing the game of those who meant to take Italy for themselves in a fashion that meant the end of freedom for the Church and the abolition of the contemplative life that was the glory of the church. Atheism, naturalism, communism and materialism—John Mary had brushed shoulders with them everywhere on his tour. These were the real enemies of an age run mad for novelty. These were the only enemies he had always hated.

Chapter XII

THIEVERY FROM THE NORTH

B EFORE the Pope could speak out against the false ideas of
the day he saw the results of them in the assaults made on
his little kingdom of the Papal States. The work of stealing the
outlying sections, piece by piece, actually began in July, 1858.
The Emperor of France, the man John Mary had saved from
certain imprisonment and possible death was at Plombières in
the Jura Mountains. Ostensibly Napoleon was there to drink
the healing waters and enjoy a rest. Visiting with him was Count
Cavour, the chief minister of Piedmont, who had come to
power in 1852.

Charles Albert, the former King of Piedmont, had been
forced to abdicate after the disastrous defeat of his troops by
the Austrians at Novara in 1849. Charles Albert's son Victor
Emmanuel was the new king. He was a rather loutish young
man who loved hunting. As a politician he was a cypher, and
during his long reign remained securely in the pocket of his
chiefs of state, among whom Cavour was the most notable.

Cavour was both clever and ruthless. He had been moulded
by the liberal principles of the French Revolution, but the
engrossing idea of his life was the unification of Italy under the
King of Piedmont. For this he slaved, sweated, and plotted
with remarkable astuteness and complete success. He took
cynical advantage of Mazzini and Garibaldi who were waging

173

a wordy and often theatrical struggle for a republican Italy. Cavour used them or abused them, as it suited his purposes. In the end he made them do exactly what would serve his ends, and the king's.

In order to achieve world-wide recognition for Piedmont as the voice of Italy, Cavour sent a force of fifteen thousand to join the allies, England, France, and Turkey, who were fighting the Crimean war against Russia in the defense of the Sultan and the Dardanelles. At the peace treaty that closed the war Napoleon failed to do anything for Piedmont. Now, however, at Plombières, he was on the verge of starting war against Austria. His most natural and important ally would be the king of Piedmont.

Napoleon III respected Cavour. Both were cynical, both were opportunists. But how was Piedmont to be rewarded for her past services in the Crimea and in the new war against Austria? The interview between Cavour and Napoleon, amply documented in Cavour's astonishing letter to Victor Emmanuel, gives us the answer.

It is not a pleasant picture. Here in a noble room, ornamented with every resource of art and civilization, two men of liberal ideas and Christian education sat down together in the hope of finding a cause for war against Austria. Their plotting would lead to the death of thousands of the best soldiers of France and Piedmont; thousands of Austrian young men as well. Homes would be ruined, farms laid waste. The scene might well have served as a rehearsal for our times: the plotter of Berchtesgaden, or the sinister planners in the Kremlin.

Cavour and Napoleon decided, after some discussion, that a cause for war against Austria had to be created. This was the plan. The Italian population of Modena would appeal to the King of Piedmont asking him to protect and annex the duchy to his kingdom. The king would send a threatening note to the Duke of Modena. He, resting secure in the knowledge of

Austrian help, would reply with equal effrontery. The French would then invade the territory of the Duke. Austria would come to his aid and the war would be on.

Napoleon's reward would be twofold. Austrian influence in Italy would be curtailed or nullified. Piedmont would cede to France Savoy and Nice. In exchange for the ceded territories Piedmont would be given Lombardy and Parma and a free hand in preparing the way for the ultimate rape of Romagna from the Papal States. At the war's end, Napoleon either designed or pretended, Italy was to be divided into a northern kingdom embracing the richest and best half of Italy, with Victor Emmanuel as king, a central kingdom under the Duke of Tuscany, a southern kingdom of the Two Sicilies. The Pope would be left with Rome and its coastal environs. To console the Pope for the loss of his territory the kingdoms of Italy would be united in a confederation under the presidency of the Pope.

The war against Austria was declared in April, 1859. It was fought with a terrible slaughter of men at Magenta and Solferino. It ended with the Armistic of Villafranca and a stunning defeat for Austria. The Pope, who had been reassured of the safety of his States by a weasel letter from Napoleon and the double talk of Napoleon's ambassador in Rome, remained neutral. He did, however, beg and pray for an early peace.

During the course of the war the agents of Cavour completely upset all possibility of a confederation for Italy. The revolutionaries in Tuscany, Parma, and Modena threw over their ducal rulers. Revolt also flared in Ancona and Perugia in the Papal States. How artificial it was may be judged from the fact that it was easily put down by a force of only two thousand of the Pope's guards under General Schmidt.

In the armistice agreement Piedmont appeared to get far less than she had been promised. Napoleon seemed to have thrown over his ally.

Piedmont still held the trump card in that she had not ceded to France either Nice or Savoy. For a year the comedy proceeded while Napoleon seemed to blow hot and cold on the ambitions of Cavour and Piedmont. Before the final act could take place the Pope, who had watched the developing situation with anguish, played an unexpected card.

Since 1850, Monsignor de Mérode had been one of his most trusted secretaries and friends. De Mérode had been a soldier in the French army. A visit to Rome turned his thoughts toward the priesthood and service of the Pope. De Mérode was the brother-in-law of Montalambert, one of the most prominent defenders of the Pope in France.

Early in 1860, de Mérode, who had been made minister of war against the wishes of Antonelli, persuaded the Pope to enlarge his army. This surprised no one. The manner of enlarging the army did. The Holy Father sent out an appeal to his faithful sons all over the world, asking them to enlist in the papal forces. The first response was immediate and enthusiastic. From France and Austria, from Ireland, England, and Spain and far off America, young men came to enroll under the yellow and white flag. They came at their own expense. The wage they received, about a nickel a day, was not enough to support them. But they began their service with an *esprit de corps* entirely enviable. Many of them were of noble or ancient blood.

Pius IX, much to the annoyance of Cardinal Antonelli, threw himself into the new project with his accustomed vigor. He received all the zouaves in audience, visited their austere encampments, watched them drill and parade. In all, the little army numbered some ten thousand effectives. With their slanted caps and baggy trousers they were a romantic looking crowd, and they had something of the spirit of crusaders.

The general of the papal forces, selected by de Mérode, was Lamoricière. He had made a famous name for himself under King Louis Philippe, fighting the Arabs in North Africa. When

Napoleon III became Emperor, Lamoricière retired to Belgium as a protest against the imperial regime.

The appointment of Lamoricière was considered a good joke on Napoleon. The emperor was at first deeply offended. A protest by his ambassador in Rome brought silken assurances from Antonelli. The Pope's new army was to be used against the raids of Garibaldi and the revolutionaries. It had no other purpose.

Napoleon gave his grudging consent to the employment of Lamoricière, but the presence on the general's staff of many young French officers who were the enemies of Napoleon did little to allay the emperor's suspicions. Besides, it interfered with the private arrangement he had made with Cavour for taking over a great part of the papal kingdom.

The details of the final act of the drama were arranged with Napoleon at Chambéry, August 28, 1860. It is reported on good authority that Napoleon said farewell to Victor Emmanuel's agents with the words, "Good luck, and work swiftly."

With Hitler-like precision, raids and disorders were engineered throughout the Papal States. Garibaldi with his Red Shirts started up from the south. Lamoricière went out to meet the multiple threat. He placed his hastily armed zouaves at strategic points: Spoleto, Terni, Perugia and Ancona. From these strong centers they could sally out and put down rebellion.

The artfully planned disorders in the Papal States were played up large in the opposition papers in Piedmont, and in the liberal press in France and England. The scene was thus set for the invasion of the Papal States by the armies of Piedmont who were said to be stepping in for the innocent purpose of restoring order.

From Chambéry Napoleon went on a two weeks' cruise to Algiers. No one could reach him. General Goyon, Commandant of the French troops in Rome, was on a convenient leave in Brittany. Thouvenel, the French secretary of state, went on a holiday in the country immediately after the first shock of the developing crisis.

On September 7, Cavour dispatched, by messenger, an ultimatum to Antonelli. It did not reach the Cardinal-Secretary until the 10th. Before a reply could be drafted General Cialdini invaded the Papal States with an army of seventeen thousand men. General Lamoricière had expected attack from everywhere except Piedmont. Now, by forced marches, he tried to get his army of six thousand zouaves to the safety of Ancona, the fortress town on the Adriatic. He was caught by the army of Cialdini at Castlefidardo. After a brave defense against vastly superior numbers the papal army was defeated and scattered. Lamoricière and a small group of men managed to get to Ancona. The last resistance there ceased on September 28th, when the lighthouse on the mole was shattered by the gunboats of Piedmont.

During the days of storm John Mary practically lived in his chapel. He aged visibly. Illness whitened his face and hair. For himself he did not mind the heavy crosses that came one after another. It was an honor to participate in the sufferings of Christ. In hours, long, lonely and bitter, Christ had shown him the mystery and the glory of suffering. But for those young hearts of his zouaves, those bright faces and strong hands gone early to the dust—he could weep for these. He could weep and sorrow too for the seamless robe of the Patrimony of Peter torn asunder by robbers and a deceiving prince who owed his life to the Pope.

In an allocution on the day Ancona fell the Pope in scathing words denounced both the Piedmontese and the French government.

The French foreign minister through his ambassador threatened Antonelli with a "terrible persecution" of the Church in France. Antonelli reminded the minister that the Church had always been able to thrive on persecution.

The Pope himself was urged to leave Rome by various med-
dling governments, including Great Britain. But John Mary
had enough of flight. His own people wanted him to stay among
them, and he was willing to endure the hazard of capture or
death.

A plebiscite was taken in the territories stolen from the
Pope. The public vote was all in favor of the aggressors whose
troops controlled the land. It was a precedent our own age now
knows so well.

In the midst of his great sadness Pius IX, in 1861, was approached secretly by Cavour with a proposed settlement. The
real purpose of the proposal was to permit Piedmont to remove
her capital from Turin to Rome. Had Cavour succeeded in his
maneuver Rome would have fallen into his hands without firing
a shot. It would have been the capstone of Cavour's triumphant career already coming swiftly toward the twilight of
death.

A memorandum was drawn up by Diomede Pantaleoni, a
liberal of sorts and a close friend of the ex-Jesuit Passaglia.
The memorandum offered certain guarantees to the papacy in
exchange for the complete loss of the temporal power. The
Pope would remain an independent ruler in the midst of the
Italian state. He would have complete civil immunity and un-
disputed ownership of all those palaces, churches and other
buildings that had long been the property of the Popes. An
assured income would be set aside for the Pontiff, his court, the
Sacred College, bishops and clergy. The Pope would have complete right to nominate bishops. The Church would be allowed
her own press, her schools, and societies; her ministers would
be free to preach as they wished.

These were the main points of the memorandum, acceptable
to Cavour. Through Cardinal Santucci the proposed settlement
was shown to Pius IX and discussed by the Pope with Cardinal

Antonelli. The settlement was largely the same as that accepted by Pius XI, in 1929. Why did Pius IX refuse it?

The answer is very plain. The theft of most of the Papal States was only about a year old. To make a settlement with the thieves was against moral principle. As Pius IX had said many times, he could not give away or alienate what he had been elected to preserve. For the Pope, complete freedom of movement and action was necessary if he was to fulfill his high office. That the memorandum seemed to guarantee. But how could John Mary accept the word of men who had so often said one thing and done another? Men who had so often reassured him and then betrayed him.

Piedmont could promise fine things to the Pope and the Church. From his Spartan study in the Vatican, simple as the cell of the poorest monk, the Pope could examine the record of Piedmont spread out on the desk before him. Vile laws against the Church and religion. Public abuse of the Church in books and magazines. The abolition of contemplative life, the arrest and persecution of bishops and priests, the theft of sacred gifts from shrines and churches. Now the robbers were asking him to put himself in their hands. They wanted him to trust their good faith. Once before he had put himself in the hands of such men. They had driven him from Rome to Gaeta; they had threatened his life and had since made attempts to kill him.

John Mary had always been kindly with men, whatever their persuasion. He had worked with liberals like Minghetti and Pasolini. Day after day he prayed for those who hated him and the Church. It was quite another thing to deliver the Church into the hands of Pilate and these new high priests of irreligious progress.

Cavour was bitterly disappointed that the settlement was refused. By the end of May he had other things to think about. On May 29, he was seized with an intestinal infection which brought on a fever.

With the darkening curtain of death being pulled swiftly about him the religious side of Cavour took command. He was a traditional Catholic, whatever else he had been in passing. Now, in the face of death, he asked for and received the last Sacraments of the Church. Fra Giacomo, an amiable Franciscan, and a friend of the Cavour family, came to give the last rites of the Church. Cavour died the next day.

In bringing the Sacraments to an excommunicated man without first asking for a formal retraction of error, Father Giacomo had disobeyed the law of the Church. As a punishment he was removed from his pastorship of Our Lady of the Angels. But though Church law made his punishment mandatory, the Pope on hearing the news of the minister's death exclaimed, "O God, be merciful to the soul of this unfortunate man!" The Holy Father hastened to offer Mass for the repose of Cavour's soul.

John Mary could see through all the braidings of that skein of life the scarlet thread of magnificence. Had a man of like talent loved him and the Church, as Cavour loved his king and country, then Rome would not now be threatened on every side.

The death of Cavour slowed down for a while, but did not halt, the drive to take over the last remnant of the Papal States. During the year 1861, Naples had fallen to the revolutionaries under the command of Garibaldi. King Francis, the son of John Mary's old host, King Ferdinand, escaped from Gaeta. The King brought with him the entire royal family. John Mary received them with great tenderness. The whole papal court turned out for the official welcome. The Quirinal was refurbished and thrown open to house the princely refugees.

With personal affection and every art of hospitality the Holy Father tried to make them at home in the Eternal City.

The revolt against the Bourbons, and the ensuing vacuum and confusion in the government of Naples soon made it possible for Piedmont to inherit the rule of the Two Sicilies.

It is quite probable that the southern *coup* gave Napoleon some food for thought. Things in Italy were moving much too fast. The security of his regime at home in France depended on the good will of the great mass of ardent French Catholics. To alienate them would endanger his rule as emperor. It was increasingly clear that Piedmont had her own plan for Italy and her own timetable. Once Piedmont had depended on his will. Now that she had waxed mighty and the unification of Italy was an accomplished fact recognized by France and England, the Emperor's power to control his child was growing less and less. That posed a dilemma.

The great cry in Turin was "On to Rome!" If Napoleon permitted that slogan to become a reality he would lose the support of his Catholic majority. If he did not permit it he would expose himself to the displeasure of Piedmont and Great Britain.

French Catholic opinion had kept French troops in Rome since 1849. Their pressure was a guarantee that Piedmont would not be allowed to take over the Eternal City. With his feverish and fertile imagination Napoleon came up with a proposed solution to the dilemma. If the capital of Piedmont were to be moved to Florence from Turin, and Piedmont would guarantee the Holy City and the Pope's remaining territory, it would be possible to withdraw the French garrison from Rome. Piedmont and Great Britain would be pleased; the Pope and Antonelli would be relieved of further anxiety.

It took some time and considerable plotting before Napoleon's idea could be put into effect. There were several changes of prime ministers in Turin, and Victor Emmanuel did not wish to leave his own city for any other than Rome. In Turin it was hoped that by drawing out negotiations Napoleon might change his mind. But Napoleon was adamant. "I only wish to get out of Rome," he told Victor Emmanuel's ambassador, Nigra. "But I will permit no one to enter—neither the king nor Garibaldi. Give me the assurance that nothing will happen, and I'll remove my troops."

Victor Emmanuel made a last attempt to change Napoleon's mind. The king dispatched a special envoy, Menabrea, to plead the case of Piedmont. The king wanted the French troops out of Italy, that is certain; but he did not wish to pay the price Napoleon demanded. Seeing that Napoleon refused to move, Piedmont gave in. The accord between Napoleon and Victor Emmanuel, called the "September Convention," was signed at Paris on the fifteenth of September, 1864.

During the delicate negotiations Antonelli and the Pope had been kept entirely in the dark. The Emperor dispatched a long message to the Count de Sartiges, French ambassador to the papal court, instructing him to inform Antonelli of the accord reached in Paris. The most important points of the "September Convention" were the following:

1. Italy (Piedmont) promised not to attack the territory of the Holy See.

2. France undertook to retire her forces from Rome gradually, over a period of two years, as the army permitted the Pope was expanded and strengthened.

3. The government of Italy withdrew all opposition to the forming of the Pope's army—composed of volunteers from all countries. The new army was to be only large enough to defend the Papal States and *not* large enough to threaten the Italian army.

4. Italy agreed to pay a just part of the debts of the old Papal States.

De Sartiges went to Antonelli with his well-planned explanations. For once the *sang-froid* of the Cardinal-Secretary was completely shattered. In a vitriolic torrent of words he poured out on the unhappy ambassador all his pent up fury against the whole nest of lies and perjured acts.

"The Holy Father will be only too happy to see the French troops leave Rome. They have been stupid—and hated by everyone. France herself has meddled and lied and betrayed the Holy See!" There was a great deal more than this expressed in blunt peasant terms, spiced with lurid adjectives.

De Sartiges, stood there in the great room hung with pale blue silk, enduring the storm with widened eyes. He had expected anger, but Antonelli was known for his correctness of form and feline propriety, his coolness and urbanity of phrase. Now his eyes blazed, his hands shook with fury. The French envoy saw in the scene merely the end of a long period of fluctuating good feeling. But to the heart of Antonelli it was the utter ruin of a policy that had been the bulwark of the Holy See for over twenty years.

Chapter XIII

THE SYLLABUS OF ERRORS

WITH a still more interior anguish Pius IX accepted a new and heavy cross as he watched the aftermath of the theft of Romagna, Umbria and the Marches. Most of the religious orders were disbanded. Some five thousand monks and nuns lost their rights before the law. Church property was confiscated. A flood of furious anticlericalism was unleashed in Italian newspapers, in broadsheets, and on the floor of the chamber of deputies. King Victor Emmanuel still wrote the Pope obedient and affectionate letters, but all about him grew a rich crop of errors that led men astray into eternal darkness. Each morning the Pope himself could read the whole story in the newspapers and dispatches piled on the table in his study.

The "liberals," the French, English, and even the American government, were always telling the world that the Pope's dominions were badly ruled and needed reform. Actually, the Pope's benevolent theocracy, though out of style when judged by liberal political standards, was far in advance of the government of its time. The social evils pilloried in the novels of Dickens were not to be found in the Pope's kingdom. The form of his government might seem old-fashioned to men who mouthed shibboleths and forgot the pity and tenderness of Christ toward the young, the poor, the aged, and insane.

John Mary had desired to condemn the errors of the age as

185

a preamble to the dogma of the Immaculate Conception. He had been dissuaded from that. But he had not been idle in waging vigorous war against error in thought and action.

For almost twenty years, from the first encyclical of his reign, *Qui Pluribus,* Pius IX had reacted violently against impiety and irreligion. In encyclicals, briefs, allocutions and papal letters he had denounced the multiple errors of the time as they appeared or seemed to wax bold in snatching up the souls of men. Between 1842 and 1864 over thirty important acts of Pius IX had been issued in warning or condemnation of false doctrines that threatened the truths of religion, the family, marriage, and the rights of the Church in the state and society.

It is incorrect to imagine that the situation in Italy and the theft of the Papal States brought about the condemnation expressed in the encyclical *Quanta Cura* and the *Syllabus.* A careful analysis of the two documents shows vividly that they refer to conditions in Austria, Germany, France, Colombia, Mexico, Spain, Peru, and Switzerland, as well as Italy.

From the time of Clement XII the Popes had been fighting the false ideas of the eighteenth century "enlightenment." Pius IX had taken up the battle with renewed vigor. It had been enough to see the havoc created by false ideas in the unbelieving world at large. That was only part of the story. Within the Church itself there were a great many liberal politicians like Minghetti, Cavour, and Pasolini who had given up their religious practise for the sake of liberal ideas. There were Cardinals and bishops who went along with the tide of nationalism and progress. Even such a superb servant of the Holy See as Montalambert was half in love with ideas that could only lead in the end to the exaltation of the civil power and the destruction of religious life.

Now John Mary felt, as never before, that the time was ripe for a massive condemnation that would strike at the very roots of error, and would shine a blinding light on the old truths and principles of the Faith. The axe must be laid to the root of the tree. Such a reasoned condemnation taken from his own encyclicals might also demonstrate to the world that the Pope lived by principle and not by changing fashions, that he was not at one time liberal and then anti-liberal. His policies were the same, some of his methods had changed. The chief alteration could be seen among those liberals who had once worked with Pius IX for the wide unification of Italy and had now gone into the narrower service of Piedmont. In Italy Pius IX had lived in the midst of the aberrations in their rawest state. Atheism, communism, naturalism, indifferentism—these he had seen at close range. There were bishops all over the world who had not had the Pope's experience and knowledge. In consequence they were slow in detecting, and even slower in opposing, evils that were giving birth to an age of horror and bloodshed under an omnipotent state.

Liberty, freedom—these concepts in the western world, John Mary saw only too clearly, depended upon ethics and religion for their strength and fertility.

In scoffing at ethics and religion, in trying to abolish both by word and law, the nineteenth century prepared the way for national crookedness, mass murder, and the hell-bomb of the twentieth century.

The encyclical *Quanta Cura* and the *Syllabus* were actually promulgated on December 8, 1864. Their publication was delayed until December 21st, in order that the Pope's Nuncio in Paris might publish them on the same day that marked their appearance in Rome.

The encyclical *Quanta Cura* explained the Holy Father's purpose in publishing it and the *Syllabus*. In glowing words the Pope referred to the work of his predecessors in returning the sheep to the fold "from poisoned pastures." Pius IX has continued their work in the many acts of his reign issued against the errors of the age. The Pope enumerates some of the chief errors of the time. He lashes out at the malign will of those who attempt to withdraw society from the influence of the Church. It is such men who are trying to do away with family life through the propagation of communism and socialism. From their action, all over the world, comes the unjust persecution of the clergy and religious orders. The Pope next denounces those who attempt to bow the Church under the civil authority, or try to deny the rights of the Church and the Holy See in the proper ordering of society.

These are the reasons that the Holy Father must raise his voice to put the faithful on guard against the pernicious influence of the enemies of religion who through poisoned books, magazines, and papers carry their impious doctrines to the four corners of the world.

The Pope exhorts the bishops to root out these evil plants and begs them to redouble their zeal in teaching the truths and practice of religion, for "Happy is that people who have Our Savior as their ruler."

The encyclical concludes with the granting of a plenary indulgence which could be gained during the space of any set month of the year 1865.

The *Syllabus*, appended to the *Quanta Cura*, lists eighty errors condemned by Pius IX in various papal documents over a period of twenty years. For the convenience of the bishops the Pope has cited the particular document from which each condemnation is taken. In this way the condemnation may be seen in its proper context.

The *Syllabus* caused a tremendous storm over the entire world. It was said the Pope had condemned all liberal government, all liberalism of thought and freedom of opinion. Ignorant commentators who neglected to read *Quanta Cura* called the Pope obscurantist and anti-liberal. The revolutionaries referred to him in such mild terms as a "vampire," and spoke of the papal rule as the "cancer of Italy."

In the lodges of Freemasonry all over the world a campaign of abuse and misrepresentation was stepped up against Antonelli and the Holy Father. Accusations without a shred of reality were trotted out. The Pope bore the mounting abuse with something more than heroic patience. The beauty of his face was untroubled. His heart too had no shade of rancor.

John Mary had been ill, once seriously, just before the "September Convention" was in the making. To the chagrin of his enemies he got well, took up again the burdens of the papacy, recovered his sparkling good humor. All this—when the world he had known seemed to be falling into ruin.

A foreign journalist, much in the modern manner, tried to pry behind the Pope's tranquil façade. In speaking about the theft of the Papal States to the Pope the journalist asked a leading question.

"Your Holiness, when will these wretched things come to an end?"

With an electric quickness the Pope replied: "I can't really say. I'm the Vicar of Our Lord, not His secretary."

In his own city of Rome the Pope said vigorous words that touched the reception of *Quanta Cura* and the *Syllabus,* vigorous words in keeping with his own faith and complete emotional balance. He addressed them to the Lenten preachers selected to give courses of sermons in the great basilicas and churches.

"The war against religion is being waged with 'poisoned-tipped weapons.' And the war is not really over. We have perfect confidence that the Church will triumph in the end. God permits this persecution in order to weed out the good from the wicked, like the winnower in the Gospel who separates the grain from the chaff. Preach then, announce the word of God with zeal and charity. You must fight unbelief and irreligion

with all your might. For here in Italy it is not the heresy of
Luther or Calvin that gains ground. It is the denial of faith and
the contempt for all belief that evil men desire to spread among
the crowd."

To a distinguished visitor, who during an audience with the
Pope spoke words of sympathy for his many difficulties, John
Mary made another statement that gives us a clew to the source
of his inner peace.

"If the cabinets of Europe have their politics I have mine."

"Perhaps it would help the situation if you could tell me
what they are, Holy Father?"

"I'm quite willing to do that." The Pope's beautiful voice
was warm with emotion. "Our Father, who art in Heaven. Hal-
lowed be Thy Name. Thy kingdom come. Thy will be done
on earth as it is in heaven." The Pope paused and then lifted
his head. "Now you know my policy. And you may be sure
it will triumph."

The Pope had lost much of his revenue from the Papal States.
Except for the Peter's Pence, offered him largely from Belgium
and France, he was the poorest sovereign in Europe. But however poor, however harassed, however weary, he had time to
notice and sympathize with the sorrows of those who made up
his intimate household.

For several days he noted that one of his chief secretaries
was gloomy and oppressed. The Holy Father queried him.
"What's wrong, Monsignor?"

"I hate to speak about it, Holy Father. Your Holiness has
too many burdens as it is. My little troubles are a mere shadow."

"Not to me, Monsignor. Tell me what's wrong?"

"It's my father, Holiness. He has debts, he's failing in business."

"Is the amount great? As much as a million lire?"

"Oh no, Holy Father, not that great. But it is two hundred
thousand."

"Don't worry then, my son. Pray to the Madonna tonight and I'm sure she will help you."

Out of the wreck of his own private fortune John Mary managed to squeeze the required loan.

There were other luminous examples of John Mary's thought of others and forgetfulness of self.

Among these was the case of a poor man arrested by the Roman police for boldly hawking an anonymous pamphlet against the Pope.

The man was thrown into jail. When the Holy Father heard what had happened he had the man brought before him. The man stood there near the Pope's desk. His mouth was sullen, his eyes downcast, his hands were trembling.

"You needn't be afraid," the Pope said. "After all it isn't your fault that people attack me in pamphlets. You were merely trying to make a living. So I pardon you completely."

The man was amazed. Now he was gazing into the kindly face before him. Tears sprang from his eyes. He fell on his knees.

"Forgive me, Holy Father. I didn't know how good you were. But I can make amends. And I can tell you the names of the men who wrote the pamphlet."

"No!" said the Pope, "don't tell me their names. Let them keep their fault in silence. Perhaps God will touch their hearts with repentance."

On one of his long walks the Pope went to visit Santa Trinità dei Monti. He stayed for Benediction and a modest supper, and then spoke to the girls of the school who had just returned from their summer vacation.

The Pope prefaced his remarks with joking references that caused waves of laughter under the rows of white veils worn by the girls in the chapel.

"Don't be downcast, my daughters, that you are here to work

again. Laugh! Be happy! Gaiety is the daughter of innocence.

"Play hard. Then, remember that you must alternate between hard work and innocence. You know the old saw, 'the bow that's always drawn tight breaks.' Some of you would like the bow never to be drawn tight, but that can't be. The bow must be drawn tight in study and prayer. It is slack during vacation when you are free and at play. Now the end of slackness is mostly finished. You must work, study and pray."

It was the same sort of childlike innocence that led the Holy Father on his round of visits to churches, schools, and hospitals.

When the cholera raged in the Holy City, the poor, its chief victims, were carried off to the great hospitals of Rome. Many of them died there, and a rumor went running about the city that the doctors were poisoning the poorest patients.

The Pope caused something of a scandal in the papal court by going to visit the two largest cholera hospitals, Santo Spirito for men and Saint John Lateran for women. John Mary's sagest advisors, including Antonelli, were horrified that the Pope should expose himself to the disease. John Mary brushed their objections aside. "If it's God's will that I die, I shall die, and that's an end of it."

Both hospitals had their chaplains who were assisted by a corps of volunteer priests from various religious orders. It was not necessary for the Holy Father to endanger himself in any way. But such was the breadth of his love for all his people who suffered that John Mary felt impelled to do what he could in bringing comfort and inspiration to his sick and frightened children.

It was no formal visit the Pope made. He did not merely condescend to walk down the central aisles of the vast wards with a mask over his face. From bed to bed he went consoling the dying, hearing confessions, anointing hopeless cases, giving each patient his blessing, asking about their families. Jew or gentile, the Holy Father treated each one with tender courtesy.

Then he went to the convalescent wards with words of encouragement and gifts of medals and rosaries.

Confidence was restored; rumor died with the progress of the fearless white figure walking through the haunts of terror and death.

People are inclined to picture this Pope always in strokes of pious light. The strength of his manhood flashes out from his journey on the *Meteor,* and there are hundreds of other stories that spotlight John Mary's manliness, especially on those occasions when he visited his zouaves, ate at their mess and fraternized with them in their rough encampments.

After the odious "September Convention" the Pope's army was reorganized under General Kanzler. John Mary put himself to all sorts of inconvenience in welcoming the new recruits at every hour of the day.

On one occasion the Pope was working in his study after an exceptionally busy day of audiences and consultations. A considerable group of zouaves came to see him unexpectedly in the early part of the evening. John Mary had them brought to his study. They were a fine lot, John Mary thought. Strong, tanned, vigorous. "Welcome, my sons," he said, rising from his desk. He went among them giving each a blessing, chatting intimately, making jokes.

"You must have a remembrance of our meeting," the Pope said at last. He walked to the desk and searched through several drawers. There wasn't a single medal or rosary left. He had forgotten to have the supply renewed.

The Pope smiled to himself. Well, he had received many gifts that day. With his own hands John Mary opened several boxes of the finest Havana cigars. A fragrance of superb tobacco filled the whole room. The Holy Father himself passed the cigars to the men. "You're not robbing me, because I don't smoke. And since you do, just think of me while you're enjoying yourself."

It was the same sort of jovial simplicity that made John Mary enjoy another encounter he had.

The day was shot with sunshine. The Pope and Cardinal Santucci had driven to the Pincian gardens where they had enjoyed a brisk walk under the shadows of the immemorial trees. Returning toward the place at which the carriage waited, the Holy Father noted a sturdy peasant youth standing at the side of the road. The peasant boy had a big chunk of bread in both hands and was taking great bites of it with the most obvious relish.

The Pope, whose white cassock was covered with a dark cloak, was pleased with the picture. "Good morning, my son," he cried out in a merry voice. The peasant, his mouth filled with bread, and not recognizing the Pope, said nothing in reply. The boy turned idly; his eyes followed the two figures. Then he saw the carriage with its rich gilding. "It must be the Pope who spoke to me," the peasant said to himself. Quickly he spat out the mouthful of bread. "Pst! Pst!" he called out. "If you *are* the Holy Father, a blessing! A blessing!"

John Mary was so amused with the young man's ingenuous boldness that he turned about, spoke at some length with the peasant and then gave him his blessing.

At Castel Gandolfo, the same year, the Pope had another experience that moved him to laughter and gave him an insight into the need of instruction most country priests seemed to forget.

The Holy Father, with a chaplain, was moving briskly along a country road getting his daily exercise. Near the side of the road was a young peasant boy watching over a flock of goats. The Pope paused and approached the lad. They fell into conversation and the shepherd gave bright answers to John Mary's questions. Finally the Pope said, "Do you know your prayers?"

"Yes, Holy Father, I know the *Pater Noster*."

"Can you say it for me?"

"Yes, Holy Father. Do you want me to say the long or the short one?"

John Mary was amazed. Even a Pope could learn, and he didn't know there was a short form of the ancient prayer.

"Say the short one."

"All right, Holy Father." The boy dropped his stick and folded his hands. *"Pater Noster, et ne nos inducas in tentatione, amen."* The Pope was shaking with laughter as he gave the boy a gold piece and continued his walk.

When there were so many good people in the world John Mary had little time to think evil of men. All over the world he was being abused by apostles of the new liberty, but there was consolation in the morning face of his Lord and the simple hearts who loved Him and revered the Pope.

The children of this world were so sure of themselves and the knowledge behind their hooded eyes. Even among the Cardinals and bishops and priests, in Italy and out of it, there were many who preferred error to truth, nationalism to statesmanship and the love of God.

A certain foreign visitor, wishing to console the Pope for the theft of the Papal States and the abuse directed against Antonelli and the Holy Father, observed: "One thing is sure, Holy Father. Whatever the storms and massive waves, the bark of Peter can never be overwhelmed, can never be sunk."

"What about the crew?" the Holy Father inquired in a mild voice.

Chapter XIV

THE VATICAN COUNCIL

THE climax of the year 1862 was the canonization of twenty-six Japanese martyrs. They had given their lives in protest against an all-powerful state; they had died for freedom of a religion in a state that permitted no deviation from emperor-worship. In a sense, this canonization pointed up many of the truths expressed in the *Quanta Cura* and the errors condemned in the *Syllabus*. Several governments saw the connection. In France and Victor Emmanuel's Italy the authorities tried to stop the bishops from attending. The attempt was largely unsuccessful, for when the day dawned at last three hundred and twenty-three bishops, a hundred thousand of the faithful and over four hundred priests attended the splendid ceremonies in Saint Peter's and listened to the decree of the Holy Father elevating to the altars of the Church the names of twenty-six saints.

The air was full of rumors that spoke of a Church council to be convened in Rome. Since the Council of Trent in the sixteenth century there had been no massive codification of dogma and Church discipline. Yet, in the interval, a host of errors and heresies had sprung up which, taking a long view of world affairs, were to threaten the Church more severely than the Reformation had done.

Many of the visitors coming to Rome for the canonization

of the Japanese martyrs expected to find the Holy Father crushed or intimidated by the recent tragedies in Europe and the Papal States. They found a vigorous Pope in whom the flame of the spirit burned bright. He was deep, he was active, he was charming. But he was more. There was something magnetic about him that had come from the long hours spent on his knees in his chapel with sorrow for his bedesman. There he had learned to leave all vexations in the hands of God. There too he had found the radiance implicit in his charity, his humorous outlook, and the tranquil sentiments that flowed from his lips.

At seventy the Pope's face looked young for his age. That youth was accentuated and illuminated with flashes of good humor and intuition that made conversation with the Holy Father a perpetual joy. Sciatica had come to plague him. He suffered excruciating pain from varicose veins in his legs; his working day with its endless conferences, audiences, and affairs of state would have tired a horse. But John Mary had monumental reserves that steeled him against the revelation of his private sufferings or personal sorrow.

The threats against the existence of the last remnant of the Papal States, that had been given the Popes by King Pepin of the Franks in 757, were both private and public. The year 1862 offers us a private example that is an astonishing revelation of the Pope's powers and personality.

Before John Mary's reign the Popes of modern times had been more or less distant figures. They were seen in the distance enthroned in majesty. Kings and important personalities might have audiences with the Holy Father, but the common people were kept at a distance.

John Mary changed all of that. Before his flight to Gaeta he had walked among his people as casually as Harun-al-Raschid. Twice a week he had received many guests at evening receptions in his gardens.

After Gaeta, audiences were more carefully organized. The Pope saw great throngs of people of all classes, but admission was usually by ticket. Only the Pope himself or the highest functionaries could make an exception to the rule.

One day in May, 1862, a middle-aged man presented himself for an audience with the Holy Father. He wore the customary evening dress but had no ticket of admission. One of the chamberlains asked him several questions that seemed to establish the visitor's good faith. The chamberlain, Monsignor Racca, seated the man in the anteroom and entered the Pope's private chapel. John Mary was kneeling there completely absorbed in prayer. "There is a middle-aged man outside in the anteroom who says he must see you, Holy Father!" The Pope answered nothing. The secretary repeated his words.

Then the Pope without raising his head answered, "Let the dead bury their dead."

The secretary didn't know what to make of the Holy Father's reply. John Mary added, "How can I give audience to a dead man?" The monsignor hurriedly went out of the chapel into the anteroom. He found a crowd gathered about the body of the visitor stretched out on the marble floor. He had died from an attack of apoplexy. Inside the pocket of his tail-coat was a loaded pistol and a dagger, razor-sharp.

Such threats left no stain of regret on John Mary's consciousness. The Lord had been hated, and how could the Pope expect less in an age filled with revolutionary fury and hatred of God?

The Pope was more than unafraid; he was unperturbed by any of the sound or fury. The edge of his humor remained keen as ever.

One evening in Saint Peter's during the May devotions which John Mary celebrated with great magnificence and his personal presence, the Pope noted a man who had several times crossed before the Blessed Sacrament exposed, without making the customary genuflection. The Pope turned to the

Cardinal-Dean kneeling beside him and whispered, "See that man? He must be either the devil or a sacristan!"

In 1864, during the heat of the summer at Castel Gandolfo, Monsignor de Mérode, the Pope's friend and counselor, was struck down with a sudden terrible fever. So contagious was the disease that no doctor from the district was willing to attend the sick man.

Finally Doctor Castano, the chief surgeon of the French army, hurried out from Rome. By the time he arrived Monsignor de Mérode seemed to be unconscious. His face was purple and he tossed incessantly.

Suddenly Pius IX entered the sickroom.

The sight of the white figure produced an instant effect on de Mérode. He stopped tossing, half rose, and tried to kneel upright in his bed.

John Mary put his arm about the sick man's shoulders. "No, my son," he said. "Lie there quietly. God will not take you away from our service. Remain with us! Hope! And all will be well."

Within a few days the monsignor was on the mend. Everyone said the Pope had cured him.

Equally strange was the story of the Austro-Belgian nun, a visitor at Santa Trinità dei Monti. She had come for the Japanese canonizations but had been struck down by an attack of paralysis. Her right arm was completely paralyzed. It looked gray and dead.

When the Holy Father paid one of his many visits to Santa Trinità he heard of the case and went into the infirmary to see the sick woman. She had already been paralyzed for ten months.

The Pope had a teasing sort of gaiety that was infectious. Soon he had the sick woman laughing. Then he asked her. "With which hand do you make the sign of the cross?"

"With my left hand, Holy Father. I can't use my right."

"You're a poor sort of Catholic!" The Pope's eyes were smiling, magnetic. "Try to make the sign of the cross with your right hand." There was a gasp from the group about the Holy Father as the sick nun slowly and painfully made the sign of the cross with her right hand.

"Why are you wearing your ring on the left hand?" the Pope continued. "You must move it to the ring finger of your right hand." The nun tried hard but was unable to execute the Pope's command. John Mary smiling broadly now, took the ring from the left hand and moved it to the other hand. The nun, with surprise, felt a tingling in her hand. She bent and unbent her fingers in a kind of ecstacy. "I'm cured! I'm cured!" she cried.

The Pope's interest in people never slackened. Striding along the sanded walks of the Pincian Gardens one day John Mary saw two pretty English nurses watching the fluttering and strutting doves. John Mary stopped and spoke to the two girls. After some conversation the Holy Father said. "I'd like to give you my blessing for yourselves and your families."

"But we're not Catholics, Holy Father."

"Does that make a difference to you? It doesn't to me."

"Oh no, Holy Father."

The two girls knelt for the blessing. So enchanted were they with the personality of the Pope that both nurses started to attend every religious occasion graced by the Holy Father's presence. In a short time they both joined the Catholic Church.

In 1866, on the Feast of the Immaculate Conception, the Pope issued a new invitation to the bishops and the faithful. They were invited to come to Rome for the feast of Saint Peter and Paul in 1867, which would be the 1800th anniversary of the death of the two Apostles.

There was particular gaiety in Rome with the advent of Christmas. The last of Napoleon's troops were leaving the city. They were being replaced by the Pope's police and the zouaves of General Kanzler, the new Commander-in-Chief of the Papal

Army. The presence of the French troops, like all foreign occupations, had been resented by many Romans.

After seventeen years of occupation the objections no longer seemed important. But the people found it good to see the foreigners leaving. The government of the new Italy at Florence made no false move. Confidence was increasing that the "September Convention" had settled the Roman question for some time to come.

The crisis was far from over. Garibaldi was growing more intemperate than ever in his denunciations of the Pope and the papal government. The revolutionaries were becoming violently active in the remaining territory of the Pope. In Florence and Rome there were many important officials who boasted openly that Rome should and would be the capital of a finally United Italy.

The centenary of Saint Peter and Paul was celebrated with unexampled splendor.

Beginning on Corpus Christi, June 20, 1867, the celebrations were inaugurated with a royal procession composed of twenty-eight Cardinals and over three hundred bishops. At the end of the glittering train came the Holy Father carried on a high platform, borne on the strong shoulders of the Swiss Guard. But on this occasion the Pope wore neither mitre or crown, nor was he enthroned. Instead he knelt on the platform. The long papal mantle was folded about him and his hands raised high the monstrance with the Sacred Host.

The following day was the anniversary of John Mary's coronation. On that day he received the bishops of the world in intimate audience and welcomed distinguished guests. At a consistory, on the same day, the Pope announced his intention of convoking a world-wide council. In the evening the entire city glowed with light. The seven hills were ringed with them; the valleys were seas of fire.

Each day of the celebration seemed more splendid than the last. On June 28th, the eve of Saint Peter's feast, the Holy Father ordered that the chair of Saint Peter, enshrined in the "gloria of Bernini," should be revealed for veneration. The glorious golden coffer was opened. Bishops and royal guests came forward to venerate the ancient relic and then escorted it to the Chapel of the Virgin where the Swiss Guard began their perpetual watch.

On the morning of June 29th, pilgrims found Saint Peter's decorated with solemn splendor. The Pope read the decree of canonization for a large number of new saints. After the Gospel had been chanted in Greek and Latin, the Holy Father delivered a homily that glorified the memory of Saints Peter and Paul and extolled the virtues of the saints just raised to the altars of the Church. He finished his address with an ardent prayer, asking God's protection for the city of Rome. His pleading tones rose like a fountain in the electric silence.

This drama was intensified at the end of the Mass when the Pope's carrying chair reached the center of the nave. It paused there. The shouted *vivas* died. Then the Holy Father in firm tones renewed his excommunication against all those who had despoiled the Papal States.

From Saint Peter's the Pope went to Saint Paul's Outside the Walls in his most precious carriage of state. The ancient basilica had burned in 1823. Almost immediately the work of rebuilding had started, but Pius IX had played the chief rôle in making the new Saint Paul's one of the most gorgeous churches in Christendom. And this at a time when there was the greatest strain on the economy of the Papal States.

The Holy Father, despite the long ceremonies at Saint Peter's, blessed the vast temple and assisted at the solemn Mass in honor of the Apostle of the Gentiles. Everyone was amazed at the Pope's tireless energy and high spirits.

Earlier in the year, at Easter time, John Mary had given the

Romans a telling example of his vigor and wit. The famous Dominican preacher Cocozza was giving a series of sermons at the Minerva. Cocozza was noted for his flamboyant rhetoric and wire-drawn drama. The sermons attracted such a tremendous crowd that the Jesuit Church, the Gesù, was practically deserted. This led witty Romans to coin a saying: "At the Gesù they convert you; at the Minerva they divert you!"

Cocozza's series was so popular that people sat everywhere on steps and railings. Some men climbed to the top of the confessionals. They sat there dangling their feet and applauding every telling point the preacher made.

On the evening of March 25th, the expectant audience was electrified at the sudden appearance of the Pope. With characteristic grace he mounted the pulpit. In his talk he forbade in future all excessive drama and overblown rhetoric in the churches of Rome. "What we want," the Pope said in conclusion, "is preachers who make people enter the confessional, not those who make men jump on top of them."

The celebrations in honor of the centenary of the Apostles ended on the evening of July 1st, with a large pilgrimage from a hundred of the chief Italian cities. Leading the pilgrims was the young Count Boschetti of Modena. The Holy Father received the huge crowd in the great Hall of Consistories. Count Boschetti presented the Holy Father with a number of expensive gifts and a splendid illuminated album. The book contained an address of loyalty and the endless signatures of the Pope's faithful sons in the chief cities of Italy.

The tribute moved John Mary to tears. Pointing to the angel that surmounts the Castle of Sant' Angelo, the Pope recalled that it is Saint Michael himself who protects the city of Rome. The words that followed were a cry from the Holy Father's inmost heart. His voice trembled. There were tears in his eyes.

"People say I hate Italy. No! It isn't true. I never was her enemy. Always have I loved her! Always have I blessed her and

sought her happiness. And God alone knows how with tears
I have prayed for her always!"

The pilgrims cried out at the Pope's words, then fell into a
frenzy of shouts and cheers. So great was the uproar of enthusiasm that it fairly shook the walls.

When the Holy Father was leaving the room, pilgrims broke
through the ranked guards and chamberlains. They tried to
kiss the Pope's hands; they snatched bits from his robes, as
souvenirs of the occasion.

The series of celebrations in Rome infuriated Garibaldi.
Once again with the help of the Piedmontese he began to muster
his red-shirted legions on the southern border of the Pope's
dominions. The cry among the revolutionaries was *"Rome or
death!"*

The menace was obvious. The Pope referred to it in a consistory, September 20, 1867. In October, the Holy Father
issued an encyclical on the state of the Holy See in which he
spoke of "calamitous days" and condemned those who govern
Italy and "permit the Commandments of God and the laws of
the Church to be soiled under the trampling feet of the impious."

Napoleon III was closely watching the Roman crisis. He had
signed the "September Convention" that guaranteed Rome and
the remaining papal territory. For once, he meant to keep his
word, perhaps less from conviction than his need of Catholic
support in launching his new "liberal" empire. In any event,
a force of fourteen thousand troops of the line was poised at
Toulon. The emperor threatened to embark these troops at
once if Rome were to be attacked.

The Piedmontese from their temporary capital in Florence
made every attempt to prevent Napoleon from executing his
threat. At the same time, behind the scenes, they encouraged
Garibaldi to continue his march on Rome.

The plan of attack called for a meeting of Garibaldi's legions at Nerola. From this town the various groups were to proceed toward Monte Maggiore, Monte Libretti, and Monte Rotondo, and thence march on Rome.

General Kanzler recognized the multiple threat. He did not make the mistake of dividing his small army as Lamoricière had done. The zouaves were sent to man the massive walls of the capital. The reserves were placed in strategic positions from which they could bolster the defenses at any given point.

Within the Holy City a state of siege prevailed. Barricades were erected in the streets. The evening Angelus was the signal for the curfew hour. After dark, bands of armed citizens patroled the streets and assisted the police in keeping order.

Many well-known revolutionaries had long been active in Rome. They now formed themselves into a special committee of action. Their first thought was to smuggle arms into the city. Several sharp clashes resulted in which the zouaves were victorious, but later events proved that the revolutionaries had been partly successful in arming their fifth column.

Of all the bombs thrown and outrages perpetrated the most sensational was the exploding of a mine under the Serristori Barracks of the papal zouaves, not far from the Vatican Palace. This outrage was the work of two young hotheads, Giuseppe Monti and Gaetano Tognetti, and several accomplices.

The explosion rattled windows all over Rome. When the smoke cleared, twenty dead zouaves were found in the ruins and many wounded soldiers were carried to various hospitals.

Monti and Tognetti were caught, tried, and put to death in November, 1868. Both young men came back to the Church before they died.

There was panic in Rome among the highest authorities. It was doubtful whether or not the small papal army would be able to withstand the red-shirted legions. There could be no doubt at all what the result would be if the Piedmontese troops assisted the legionaries. What would Napoleon do?

Pius IX, on the 27th of October, kept vigil in his chapel. He remained there all day praying and fasting. His only nourishment was a single glass of water. Late in the evening, through Antonelli, assurances came that Napoleon's troops had arrived at Civita Vecchia and were moving into Rome.

At Florence, a last minute face-saving maneuver was attempted. The king and his ministers issued a proclamation condemning Garibaldi and his march on Rome. A copy of the document was dispatched to Napoleon by General Cialdini.

In the light of these events, Garibaldi saw the game was up. He gathered all his troops at Monte Rotondo and Tivoli in preparation for getting them back to the borders of the Papal States.

At a war conference in Antonelli's cabinet, Kanzler and de Failly, the French commander, decided to sally out of Rome for the purpose of driving the Red Shirts completely out of the papal territory.

The papal zouaves and the French soldiers of the line made contact with Garibaldi's legionaries at Monte Rotondo and Tivoli, November 3rd. The battle ran its uneven course the whole day. Both sides fought with notable bravery. As evening was falling in its thickening mists a third column of French fell upon the soldiers of Garibaldi. The French were armed with a new repeating rifle firing twelve rounds a minute. Their appearance decided the battle. Garibaldi ignominiously hustled away toward Florence. The Piedmontese arrested him en route and took him to the fortress of Varignano. He remained there only a few days and was released, which points up his true relation with Piedmont.

The red-shirted army broke and fled, leaving behind them a thousand dead on the field of battle. Over five hundred Red Shirts were prisoners. The following day the Garibaldians asked for an armistice. They were allowed to retire in peace beyond the papal frontiers.

The victory at Mentana led to a round of celebrations in Rome at which the victors were praised and fêted. Most affecting of the ceremonies growing out of the battle was the requiem Mass for the dead zouaves celebrated in the Sistine Chapel. Cardinal Panebianco, the Grand Penitentiary, officiated; the Pope himself gave the absolution. He was so deeply moved that when he came to sing the Oration he broke into audible sobs.

The Roman hospitals were opened to the wounded of both armies. The Pope went in person to see all the wounded. He gave them his blessing and distributed medals among them.

Following these visits, John Mary went to the Castle of Sant' Angelo where the prisoners were. The Pope came into the great room as dusk was falling. A deadly silence fell among the prisoners. The Holy Father gave a short speech.

"Your leader has told you I am the vampire of Italy. For this you fought against me. But here I am among you. But what do you find? Nothing but a poor old man!"

A great many prisoners were deeply affected by the Pope's words. Many of them rushed forward, begged the Holy Father's forgiveness and kissed his hands.

"You will be released soon," the Pope promised the prisoners. "There is only one thing I ask in return. Before you leave Rome make a short retreat and return to God."

The victory at Mentana and the ensuing quiet in Rome opened the way for summoning the Vatican Council. Invitations were sent to every bishop and vicar apostolic in the world. The opening day was set for December 8, 1869. In April of that year, many bishops came on in advance in order to celebrate with the Holy Father the fiftieth anniversary of his ordination to the priesthood.

Gifts poured in from every country. The Empress Eugénie, who loved and admired the Pope, sent twenty-five thousand gold napoleons. There were paintings by famous masters, gold chalices of all sorts, monstrances, exquisite silk vestments, and beautiful spun albs and surplices, so delicate they seemed made out of fluted cobwebs. There were great mounds of cheese and wine bottles from the Pope's humbler children, home-cured hams, and hand-carved, gilded boxes.

The Holy Father took the bishops on a tour through the vast rooms where the gifts were assembled. Before one gift he paused a little longer than usual. It was a simple coral necklace and earrings sent by some poor woman who had no other gift to offer. The Pope touched the necklace with appreciative fingers. A warm smile played about his lips.

John Mary celebrated the morning of his anniversary with a low Mass in Saint Peter's. It seemed like yesterday that he had offered his first public Mass in the Church of Saint Anne of the Carpenters. The children of his heart from Tata Giovanni had sung the Mass: a clear rush of children's voices praising God. Now his children were from the world over; a superb choir chanted the praises of the Eternal Fisherman he had become.

Fifty years in the priesthood had given him strong shoulders to bear the cross. Often his heart had been wrung by evil, and sorrow. Those occasions had served to identify John Mary ever more closely with his Master. In that union was a joy so intense that it made all suffering of small account, a poor gift to offer Christ who had borne the sins of all humankind, good Popes and bad Popes included.

Fifty years of union! It gave John Mary's face a particular radiance this morning of his jubilee.

In the afternoon the light still shone in the Pope's countenance when he came into the Vatican Gardens. The orange trees in their prim tubs seemed to be offering a special tribute of delicious gold in his honor. A reception had been arranged for all his brother bishops who had journeyed across the world to spend this day at his side.

The moment the bishops saw the graceful white figure, the benign and radiant face, a shout went up from the assembled prelates. They crowded close to him, like schoolboys, calling his name and kissing his hands as once long ago his boys had done on that memorable evening at Tata Giovanni before he went to South America. It was a spontaneous demonstration that John Mary would never forget.

By the end of November most of the bishops had gathered in Rome from the four corners of the earth. In numbers they outranked those who had assembled for any Church council and it could also be justly maintained that this council represented every continent.

A great many vicars apostolic and missionary bishops were too poor to pay their own expenses. John Mary found places for them and gave them money to pay their bills. He wasn't at all smug about his princely generosity. "I don't know whether I'll come out of this council fallible or infallible," he remarked to a visiting writer. "But one thing I am sure of—I'll come out bankrupt."

The right wing of Saint Peter's Basilica had been carefully prepared for the council by the Pope's architect, Vespignani. The form of Saint Peter's has the shape of a Latin cross. The right arm of this cross was shut off from the remainder of the church by gigantic movable partitions that could be rolled into place. Inside the vast council chamber, along the walls, tapestry tribunes had been erected for royal guests and heads of governments who might wish to follow the deliberations of the council.

The Pope's throne was elevated at the far end of the room. It was flanked on both side by benches for the College of Cardinals. Before the papal throne a fine altar was erected facing the body of the hall that contained the tapestry-covered seats of the other Fathers. There was also a raised lectern near the altar from which speakers could address the assembly. In the early deliberations of the Fathers the hall was found to be too vast for most speakers. Curtains were stretched across the ceiling, and along the walls. These lowered the height of the hall and improved the acoustics.

The machinery of the council had been arranged with great care. Five presidents had been appointed to preside over the sessions of the bishops. The chief of these was Cardinal Reisach of Munich. He was assisted by four Italian Cardinals of the *Curia*. When Cardinal Reisach died, in late December, Cardinal de Angelis took his place.

The Russian government had unleashed a furious persecution of the Church in Poland. No Polish bishop was allowed to attend the Vatican Council. Most of them were in prison or under house arrest. The Pope, in one of his heart-warming gestures native to him, allowed Father Sosnowski, an escaped priest from Lublin, to sit with the bishops.

The Holy Father's appeal to Protestants and the Greek Orthodox Church for reunion with Rome and a part in the council went unanswered. Yet among thoughtful Protestants and the enlightened members of the Orthodox hierarchy there were many who sympathized with the council and the work it proposed to do.

Unlike Mary's usual blue weather, the morning of December 8, 1869, was heavy with rain. Grey clouds hung over the seven hills; water gurgled in the gutters and swelled the yellow crest of the Tiber. Some eighty thousand people ignored the storm and crowded into Saint Peter's basilica. Outside in the square, other thousands huddled under the forest of black umbrellas or sheltered beneath the monumental colonnades. By 8:30 the procession of bishops and Cardinals got under way after the Pope had intoned the hymn "Come Holy Spirit" in the Sistine Chapel.

Seven hundred silver-coped and white-mitred bishops filed

down the grand staircase into Saint Peter's. Last of all came the carrying-chair holding the Holy Father aloft. Those who realized that the Pope was seventy-seven years old were amazed at his youthful look. Under the thick grey hair his face showed unwrinkled and tranquil. His graceful hand flashed in continual blessing.

The procession filed before the ancient statue of Saint Peter, superbly clothed and mitred, and then paused before the central altar where the Blessed Sacrament stood exposed. The Holy Father alighted from his chair, took off his mitre and bowed in prayer before his Lord. When the Pope had finished his devotions, the procession re-formed and went slowly into the council chamber. There was a gravity in every face, for they all knew they were playing an important rôle in a history that went back through the ages to the first council in Jerusalem, in the lifetime of the Apostles.

This, the twentieth world council of the Universal Church, faced all the Fathers with grave decisions that were to shape the course of the Church for a century. The Pope himself had said, "Councils go through three phases. That of the devil, then of man, and finally of God." Yet this morning in an atmosphere electric the Fathers seemed to feel they were all under the wings of the Holy Spirit.

The prayers and litanies were sung in preparation for the solemn Mass offered by Cardinal Patrizi, Vice-Dean of the Sacred College. After Mass an opening address was made by Monsignor Puecher-Pasalli, instead of the slow rite of the bishops offering their personal obedience to the Holy Father. The Pope intoned the oration to the Holy Spirit, "Come to our help, O God!" When the Litany of the Saints had been sung and the Gospel containing Christ's commission to His Apostles, the Holy Father addressed the assembly of Fathers. He thanked them all for their union with the Holy See and commented on the work before them.

The Pope's discourse was followed by the *Veni, Creator.* Then Cardinal Fessler of Austria, secretary of the assembly, read from the height of the lectern the decree prescribing the holding of world-wide councils. The Fathers all voted to observe the rules. The Pope by virtue of his apostolic authority declared the twentieth ecumenical council opened.

All this while, by the Holy Father's command, the doors of the chamber remained open. The enormous crowds in the outer parts of Saint Peter's enthusiastically followed every step of the proceedings. Now they all joined thunderously in singing the *Te Deum.* The opening session of the council had lasted from nine in the morning until three in the afternoon.

The Holy Father appeared only at the public sessions of the council. He left to the many famous theologians and Fathers the hard task of formulating the doctrines that were to be defined, and the disciplinary measures necessary for the proper ordering of affairs in dioceses, the *Curia,* and the priesthood.

Meanwhile, John Mary was busier than ever. Large groups of tourists invaded Rome from every country. They wanted to see the Pope first and then the Fathers, going in procession to the private sessions of the council.

The Holy Father welcomed the crowds with open arms. He was almost eighty years old, but he had lost little or none of his radiant charm, or his taste for hard work. There was a kind of teasing tenderness about him that enchanted people. Usually he entered the audience room in state and walked through the crowds, talking to the people intimately. Then, ascending the steps to his throne glittering at the far end of the room, he would gather the wandering attention to himself as he did in one French audience. "You have come to see the Pope and to receive his blessing. The Pope you have seen and you will soon receive his blessing." At this point John Mary launched into a simple address that was usually an appeal to piety or the love of Christ and Our Lady. The Pope loved both with childlike simplicity and he tried to kindle his own love in the hearts of his children who had come from the farthest corners of the world.

The presence of a large part of the hierarchy also enabled the Pope to see the bishops of every nation. He received them in their groups and spent hours with them discussing problems and complaints. In this fashion Pius IX accumulated a tremendous knowledge of the needs of Catholicism all over the world. Increased missionary activity, the reconciliation of the Oriental Church, and a thousand other splendid results flowered from these tiring meetings.

Somehow, between the Pope's audience-crowded day, he managed to find time for his long visits to the Blessed Sacrament and the vigorous walks that delighted him, kept him well, and brought him into close relationships with the Roman people.

One day, going down to his carriage, John Mary saw the guards trying to chase away two elderly peasants, obviously man and wife. The Holy Father rebuked the guards and spoke to the two people, who knelt for his blessing. The woman was carrying a large package which she offered to the Pope.

"What is it?" John Mary asked.

"It's a ham, Holy Father, we cooked it for you ourselves. It's a fine one you may be sure. And we want you to eat it today."

"Thank you, my children." The Pope gave them each a medal. "You are very kind to think of me," the Holy Father said, conveying the heavy package to one of the guards. "But you know, even though I'm Pope, I can't eat it today, because it's Friday. However, I'll begin to eat it tomorrow."

During one of these casual saunters the Pope passed the Church of Saint Chrysogonous. His quick eye noted a group of Trinitarian Fathers enjoying the sun and gossiping. In passing the group, the Holy Father said in a casual voice, "Why do you stand here all the day idle?" This comment so upset the group that it led them to do a little heart-searching which in turn led to the establishment of the Trinitarian missions in Africa.

Such chance encounters spurred John Mary to some of his best efforts during the Vatican Council. One of these concerned the episcopal appointment of a very humble Franciscan.

The good friar did not want to be a bishop, and he explained his reasons bluntly.

"But, Holy Father, I have such a limited intelligence. A bad memory, too. I can never be an efficient bishop."

"Don't worry about that, my son. You'll be a *good* bishop, that's all that matters. And you won't have to put up with that proud nonsense they inscribe on the tombs of most bishops, 'Of glorious and happy memory.' "

Simple people taught John Mary to see through more complex souls, or those who were proud or arrogant. A group of Church of England clerics, who were at least technically heretics, *insisted* to the Pope that there must be some form of blessing that he could properly give them. "There is," replied the Holy Father, and he used the words of the celebrant at high Mass when he blesses the incense: *"Ab illo benedicaris in cujus honore cremaberis."* (May you be blessed by Him in whose honor you will be burned.)

It was also witty of the Pope to say, as he did of the Puseyites in England, "They are like the church bells that summon people to church but never go in."

John Mary was equally droll with those of the household of the faith. An old nun brought to the Vatican a picture of Pius IX. She asked him to autograph it for her with a quotation from Scripture. The Pope took the picture in his hands. When he looked at it he could hardly restrain his laughter. It was such a frightful likeness that John Mary could hardly recognize himself. Carefully the Pope inscribed it with the words Our

Lord spoke when He walked to meet the Apostles on the troubled sea. "It is I, be not afraid."

The Pope's high spirits during the council, were so contagious that they swept even the reserved Manning along with him into a wintry jest or two. At the time the council was in the midst of the heated debate on infallibility, John Mary said to Manning, "I wish your Queen would come to Rome for a visit. She and I are colleagues, you know. Over here I'm Pope-King but she's the *papessa* of England." Such sallies probably inspired Manning's comment to the press. "We are busy here at the council and we do our work. But if we want to know what we are doing we read the *London Times*."

The work of the Vatican Council proceeded with dispatch. Its committees of fifteen worked out the doctrinal and disciplinary outlines that were later presented for the consideration and agreement of the Fathers in full session.

Pius IX made no attempt to influence the council. Like any "private doctor" of the Church, as the Pope chose to call himself, he was open to consultation and ready to give his opinion but he was unwilling to do more than that. It was quite unnecessary.

Of the Fathers who had assembled in the world-wide council the great majority were of the center or the right. On the extreme right were the so-called ultramontanes who were said to be "more Catholic than the Pope." Chief of these was Archbishop Manning of England. A distinguished convert from Anglicanism, Manning had demonstrated very early in his career a remarkable talent for affairs. He quickly rose to the rank of bishop and maintained the closest liaison with the Holy See through his friend Monsignor Talbot, rector of the English College. Talbot was one of the Pope's intimate circle.

Upon the death of Cardinal Wiseman, several years after the Vatican Council Pius IX himself, after months of prayer and Masses offered to the Holy Spirit, passed over candidates more acceptable to the English bishops in appointing Manning Cardinal of Westminster.

Manning's character has received far less than a just appraisal. His work at the Vatican Council has also been largely misinterpreted. The formal exterior and frigidly correct manner of the prelate masked a heart that was warm and loyal. Like Cardinal Gibbons and Bishop von Ketteler of Germany he was a pioneer in labor movements that benefited working people all over the world. Manning was not merely loyal to the Pope because of his swift advance in rank, however thoroughly he may have appreciated the honors showered upon him. His wide experience in the Church of England had taught him to appreciate the necessity of discipline and a supreme, divinely-inspired authority that could be invoked when necessary.

Manning also loved the continental forms of piety and devotion. They were warmer, more expressive, nearer to his own heart. These ideas and sentiments are well expressed in Manning's book, *The Eternal Priesthood*.

In consequence of his conservatism and Roman piety, Manning was anxious to do everything he could to strengthen the central authority of the Church. In the sharp struggle over the doctrine of the Pope's infallibility Manning must have seen with clarity that a failure to formulate and proclaim the dogma would be a defeat for the Universal Church and an encouragement to national churches all over the world. Manning had grown up in a national church. All its defects in form, doctrine, and discipline he knew at first hand.

The great majority of the bishops, led by Manning, were opposed by a minority of so-called "liberal" bishops and Fathers. Their leader was Monsignor Dupanloup, Bishop of Orlèans. Superbly lucid in thought, but often too subtle for his own good, Dupanloup had been of great service to the Church in France. He had also served the Pope well, notably after the outcry against the *Syllabus*. Dupanloup hoped that the Church would adapt itself to liberal ways and policies. Unlike Manning, Dupanloup had his growth and development in the French Church which prided itself on its orthodoxy, but was equally jealous of its independence and often arrogant in its nationalism. Dupanloup was stained with the Gallican purple.

The French bishop had one advantage over Manning. The policies that Dupanloup pursued were the popular ones of the age. They could be sure of a good press in the liberal world. That was, publicity-wise, the only world that counted at the time. Allied with Dupanloup were writers of first eminence like Montalambert and Lord Acton. Newman, in a general sense, was also on their side. The influence these men exercised went far beyond their writings to ministers in control of Europe's destiny.

Despite the coming battle over infallibility, which everyone saw darkening the horizon like a menacing thundercloud, the first work of the council went on smoothly, session after session. The discipline of the Church was strengthened. The doctrinal position in regard to the Faith was precisely formulated.

The first draft of the schema, that dealt with the fundamental doctrines in regard to God, revelation, and the Faith, was not acceptable to a number of bishops. This led to several sharp clashes of opinion between noted groups of Fathers. The schema had been drawn up by Father Franzelin, the famous Jesuit theologian. With the help of Bishops Pie, Deschamps and Martin, the tract was amended. In its new form it pleased all the Fathers who accepted it by acclamation.

On Sunday, April 24, 1870, after a Mass celebrated by the beloved theologian, Cardinal Bilio, the Fathers gave their formal consent to the schema. Pius IX solemnly promulgated it, gave an allocution to the assembled Fathers, and intoned the *Te Deum*.

Behind the scenes there was continued acrimony and inflamed discussion over the question of the Pope's infallibility.

The question had not originally been submitted to the Fathers. After the tract on Faith, the next subject for revision and definition was the constitution of the Church. In the normal course of things this would have included sections dealing with the powers of the Pope.

But in the minds of Dupanloup and the minority, among all the Fathers in fact, the one burning question was the Pope's infallibility. It had been generally held in the Church from its very beginning, but the doctrine had not been defined as an article of faith to which all Christians must give credence.

The minority Fathers were determined to prevent a definition of the doctrine. Dupanloup and his friends were not content to work alone among the Fathers. The council itself, free, democratic, and unfettered should have been the accepted battleground of professed liberals who believed in majority rule. But like all professional liberals they considered their own conviction the *only* conviction. They were bent on forcing their minority will on the vast majority of the Fathers who did not agree with the minority opinion.

Seeing that their efforts among the Fathers won them insufficient adherents, Dupanloup, Acton, Montalambert, and their cohorts wrote against the definition to their friends in the press and government. They came within an inch of getting the great powers to intervene with a protest which would have made the definition impossible. Providence thought otherwise. Only Napoleon made an actual protest, and it was firmly rejected by Antonelli.

The unorthodox conduct of the few "liberal" bishops in stirring up world opinion against the doctrine outside the council spurred John Mary, as a "private doctor" to the expression of his own opinions. These were in favor of infallibility. He expressed them clearly but with some asperity. These expressions were much criticised by the "liberal" bishops who had done far more of the same thing.

In April, two hundred bishops petitioned that the tract on the powers of the Pope be considered at once, out of its proper order. The presidents of the council denied the request. Then Manning and his friends appealed to the Pope. Dupanloup countered the appeal with a letter of warning to the Holy Father telling him that the question of the infallibility had already set Europe afire, and a consideration of it out of its proper order would fan the flame to a European disaster.

The Pope weighed both the requests and on April 19 ordered that the schema be debated at once.

The schema *De Ecclesia* had originally contained two chapters on the Pope's primacy, none on his infallibility. On March 6th, a new draft was circulated with three chapters on the primacy, one on the infallibility.

The drafted chapters on the papacy were brought before the entire council on May 13th. For two months a furious debate raged among the Fathers. The minority Fathers were by far the most intemperate. There were some, perhaps many, among the minority, who thought a definition would only anger the governments of the world and keep Protestants from coming into the Church. On the first vote in the council the minority were able to muster one hundred and forty votes against a definition of the Pope's infallibility. The unreasonable attitude of the minority leaders and the gradual clarification of the doctrine by amendments whittled down the minority to a final eighty-eight.

During the last days of the debate the intransigeant party, led by Archbishop Darboy of Paris, went to the Pope and offered a compromise which would have done much to make the dogma vague. The Pope refused to intervene. To him it was the work of the council to formulate and amend the original draft. The council refused Darboy's amendments.

Recognizing their defeat, most of the minority Fathers agreed to leave Rome and abstain from the final voting. There was a shadow of excuse for their departure in the obscure European situation. France and Germany appeared to be on the verge of war.

The 18th of July was the day of the final vote on infallibility: five hundred and thirty-three Fathers gave their consent to the doctrine as we know it today: The Pope is infallible when he speaks *ex cathedra* to the Universal Church, that is, when exercising his office as pastor and teacher of all Christians he defines with his supreme apostolic authority a doctrine concerning faith or morals to be held by the Universal Church. The Fathers settled the vexing question once and for all in concluding: "Such definitions of the Roman Pontiff are irreformable of themselves and not from the consent of the Church."

Two bishops voted *no:* Bishop Fitzgerald of Little Rock, Arkansas, and Bishop Riccio of Cajazzo, in southern Italy.

The stifling heat of the Roman summer had pressed down on the city for days. All through the final voting torrential gusts of rain lashed the roof and windows of the vast church. Between the steady drum of rain the lightning flashed over the grave faces of the Fathers and the Pope, sitting enthroned in the midst of the Sacred College. Roll upon roll of thunder followed.

The final result of the voting was carried up to the Holy Father. The council room had grown pitch dark from the storm pressing down outside. An attending Cardinal lighted a huge taper and brought it to the Pope's throne. The dim spear of light enabled John Mary to read the decree ratifying and promulgating his infallibility. In a short allocution the Pope spoke of those things that troubled his heart.

The Holy Father pointed out that "the authority of the Sovereign Pontiff is great. It does not destroy; it constructs. It sustains and will be found defending the rights of our brothers, that is to say, the rights of the bishops." The Pope recalled that some of the bishops had voted against him. He warmly invited them to return to their unity with the See of Peter and begged God to enlighten their minds and hearts. Then the dissenting bishops would be able to say with Saint Augustine, "My God, You have given me Your admirable light! And now I see." To which the Pope added, "Ah! Yes, that they may indeed see!"

Many were moved to tears by his words.

Having come to the end of his appeal, the Holy Father intoned the *Te Deum*. At the precise moment when his resonant voice sang the first phrase, a path opened in the heavens outside. A piercing shaft of light came through one of the great windows and completely lit up the face and silvery hair of the Pontiff. The Fathers were tremendously moved by the portent. They broke into shouts of joy which were taken up by the crowds in Saint Peter's. The voices of the Sistine Choir were completely drowned in enormous waves of sound.

The appeal of the Pope in the morning's allocution was soon fulfilled. One by one the minority bishops made their submission to the decision of the Council. Maret in October, 1870, Dupanloup in February, 1871, Archbishop Darboy of Paris, shortly before his murder by the communists the same year. The other minority bishops soon followed suit.

An interesting glimpse into John Mary's character comes to us from his attitude toward one of the minority bishops, de Mérode, a member of the Pope's intimate household.

De Mérode, like the other minority bishops, had not been present at the formal voting. In the evening of July 18, de Mérode was on duty as a chamberlain in the Pope's apartments. He went in to say good night to the Holy Father when his tour of duty was over.

De Mérode knelt to kiss the Pope's ring, awaiting his dismissal for the night. He had been warned by many of the opposition that the Holy Father would probably be gravely displeased.

"Have you nothing to say to me, *Monsignore?*" the Pope inquired.

"Most Holy Father, please tell me if I have been slack in my duty here in any way, and I will hurry to do anything I have omitted."

De Mérode looked up at the Pope. John Mary was smiling that radiant smile his face had worn through all the terrible years in which de Mérode had served him well.

"No, no, my son! Everything has been well done. I only wanted to know if you might have anything to say to me. You may retire. Good night!"

Novelists would end the scene here, but more is demanded of the biographer.

Pius IX was heroically forgiving but he was something of a tease, especially with his good friends. Shortly after the above episode which convinced de Mérode that John Mary was holy in an extraordinary way, the bishop was again on duty in the Pope's study.

He laid on the Holy Father's desk a bundle of important papers. The Pope flicked through them, noting their headings. Then he looked up and said brightly, "That's funny; shouldn't there be another paper here?"

The Holy Father was laughing. De Mérode joined him. The next bundle of papers contained his written submission.

Chapter XV

THE FALL OF ROME

FRANCE declared war on Germany, July 18. The Prussian army proved far more powerful than Napoleon had fancied. As commander of the French army Napoleon was only an ersatz Bonaparte. The military genius was all on the side of von Moltke who maneuvered the French into the disaster at Sedan. Napoleon, and some seventy thousand of his troops were captured by the swift-moving Germans.

Napoleon had expected help from Victor Emmanuel, but none came. Piedmont had nothing to gain from the war if France won; everything to gain if France lost. It was a sort of poetic justice that Napoleon's opportunism had been surpassed by that of his former friends.

The early German victories before the Sedan debacle forced Napoleon to recall the French troops in Rome. They began to embark at Civita Vecchia, August 4. On her own authority as regent of France, the Empress Eugénie sent the cruiser *Orenoque* to carry the Pope to France if he wished to escape from Rome.

The departure of the French forces meant only one thing to the Pope and Antonelli—the end of the temporal power, at least for a time. The small papal army of thirteen thousand men could not hope to fight against four times their number enrolled in the armies of Piedmont.

The defeat at Sedan in early September caused real joy in Florence. At last the way was open to Rome. On the 8th, with indecent haste, Victor Emmanuel dispatched to Rome his envoy, Count San Martino. Pius IX received the king's messenger in formal audience. The Holy Father's face was stern as he read the letter from Victor Emmanuel:

Most Holy Father—With the affection of a son, with the faith of a Catholic, with the loyalty of a king, with the sentiment of an Italian, I address myself again, as I have done formerly, to the heart of Your Holiness. A storm full of perils threatens Europe. Favored by the war which desolates the center of the continent, the party of world revolution increases in courage and audacity, and is preparing to strike in Italy and in the provinces governed by Your Holiness, the last blows at the *Monarchy* and the *Papacy*. I know, Most Holy Father, that the greatness of your soul would not fall below the greatness of events; but for me, a Catholic King, and an Italian King, and as such guardian . . . by the dispensation of Divine Providence, and by the will of the nation of the destinies of all Italians, I feel the duty of taking, in the face of Europe and Catholicity, the responsibility of maintaining order in the peninsula *and the security of the Holy See.* Now, Most Holy Father, the state of mind of the population governed by Your Holiness and the presence among them of foreign troops, coming from different places with different intentions, are a source of agitation and of perils evident to all. Chance, or the effervescence of passions, may lead to violence and effusion of blood, which it is my duty and yours, Most Holy Father, to avoid and prevent. It is necessary for the security of Italy and the Holy See that my troops already guarding the frontiers, should advance and occupy the position which will be indispensable to the security of Your Holiness and to the maintenance of order. Your Holiness will not see a hostile act in this measure of precaution. My government and my forces will restrict themselves to an action conservative and tutelary of the rights, easily reconcilable, of the Roman population, with the independence of the Sovereign Pontiff, and of his spiritual authority, and with the independence of the Holy See. If Your Holiness, as I do not doubt, and as your sacred character and the goodness of your soul give me the right to hope, is inspired with a wish equal to mine of avoiding all contact, and of escaping the danger of violence, you will be able to take, with Count Ponza di San Martino, who presents you with this letter, and who is furnished with the necessary instructions by my government, to take those steps which will best lead to the desired end. Will Your Holiness permit me to hope still that the present moment, as solemn for Italy as for the Church and the papacy, will give occasion to the exercise of that spirit of benevolence which has never been extinguished in your heart toward this land, which is also your own country, and of those sentiments of concilation which I have always studied with an indefatigable perseverance to translate into acts, in order that, while satisfying the national aspirations, the Chief of Catholicity, surrounded by the devotion of the Italian population, might preserve on the banks of the Tiber a glorious seat, independent of all human sovereignty. Your Holiness, in delivering Rome from the foreign troops, in freeing it from the continual peril of being the battleground of subversive parties, will have accomplished a marvelous work, given peace to the Church, and shown to Europe, shocked by the horrors of war, how great battles can be won and immortal victories achieved by an act of justice and a single word of affection. *I beg Your Holiness to bestow upon me your apostolic benediction, and I renew to Your Holiness the expression of my profound respect. Your Holiness' most humble, most obedient, and most devoted son.*

Florence, September 8, 1870   VICTOR EMMANUEL.

The raw hypocrisy of the request caused John Mary to burn with righteous indignation. The remaining Papal States formed one of the most peaceful kingdoms of the world. The zouaves and police found it easy to keep perfect order with a minimum of effort. The only troublemakers were the revolutionary followers of Mazzini and Garibaldi smuggled into the Papal States with money and passports provided in Florence. "Be angry and sin not," the Scripture said.

Now the time had come. The warm voice of the Pope grew heated with indignation. He told the astonished count one by one the crimes of Piedmont: the lies, the hypocrisy, the persecution of the Church by evil laws, the abuse of the Pope and the Cardinals in newspapers and books, the dispossession of monks and nuns, the sacrilegious theft of church property. The King, the ministers of the crown, deputies and senators were no more than "whited sepulchers filled with dead men's bones."

The Holy Father's voice shook with wrath, his words were terrifying. San Martino was so entirely overcome at the furious outburst that in going out of the audience room he couldn't find the door. Fumbling about, the unhappy and surprised envoy tried to go through one of the long windows!

The Pope's reply to the king's letter was short and magnificently ironic. It had a touching quality far beyond anything the Pope had said to the king's envoy.

Your Majesty, the Count Ponza di San Martino has put into my hands a letter which Your Majesty has been pleased to address to me: but it is not a letter worthy of an affectionate son who glories in the profession of the Catholic religion, and who prides himself on due observance of kindly faith. I do not enter into the details of the letter itself, because I would not renew the grief which its first perusal caused me. I thank my God, who has suffered Your Majesty to add to the bitterness of the latter days of my life.

In conclusion, I cannot admit the demands advanced in your letter, nor can I give any adhesion to the principles contained in it. I once more pray to the Lord, and I place

my cause in His hands, because it is wholly His. I ask Him
that He may deliver you from all dangers, and bestow upon
you those favors of which you have need.

From the Vatican, September 11, 1870.

Pius, Papa IX.

Of one thing the Pope felt sure; he would not much longer
be free to take the vigorous walks he loved so much. He went
often through the city during the menacing days, visiting the
churches and places of which he had been most fond. His face
wore a look of nostalgic sadness like one who looks at a beloved face never to be seen again.

Moving through the Pincian Gardens the Holy Father was
approached by an old policeman with a complaint.

"Holy Father, I've been on the force for twenty-five years.
But they won't let me retire and they won't give me my pension."

"Now isn't that just like the world, my son. Here I am with
less than twenty-five years' service, yet they're trying to *force*
me to retire and *with* a pension, too."

Events proved that neither words nor principles meant anything to the Piedmontese. On September 11th, the Pope's dominions were invaded by sixty thousand troops under the command of General Cadorna, a renegade monk. Along with the
regular army of Piedmont came a throng of Red Shirts, riffraff
and their camp followers, prostitutes, free-thinkers, atheists and
Carbonari.

John Mary agonized over the coming fall of Rome. At his
morning Mass he prayed as never before in his life. The
cruiser *Orenoque* still waited at Civita Vecchia but the Pope
had no intention of leaving Rome. He was determined to stand
or fall with his people.

Like the towering spiritual Popes who had preceded him,
John Mary prayed publicly for himself and his people. He

went to Mary's shrine in Santa Maria Maggiore; he invoked the aid of the miraculous Bambino in the Church of Ara Coeli.

Slowly the armies of Piedmont closed about Rome. As they came nearer, the advance columns of zouaves were drawn in from the suburbs to the dubious safety of the walls of the Eternal City.

On September 18th, John Mary went with two chamberlains to the Church of Saint John Lateran.

The papal army was drawn up for review in the huge square before the church. The soldiers were awaiting the Pope's coming with intense sadness, for they knew it might very well be the last time they would see him alive and free.

When the Holy Father's carriage arrived, the Pope alighted. A great chorus of men's voices greeted him. John Mary went first into the building that houses the Holy Stairs, across the street from Saint John's.

One by one, John Mary painfully ascended the stairs on his knees, praying silently with intense devotion. When he had reached the little chapel at the top, the Pope's eyes were heavy with tears, as he prayed aloud:

"O great God! My Lord and my Saviour! Thou, of whose servants, I am the servant and the unworthy representative, I implore Thee by the precious blood shed, of old, upon these very stones . . . by the anguish, by the sacrifice of Thy Divine Son, who willingly ascended these self-same stairs of opprobium to offer Himself as a holocaust for the people who insulted Him, who were about to slay Him. O have pity, I beseech Thee, for Thy people, for Thy Church, which is Thy well-beloved Spouse, and for me, Thy unworthy servant. If it be Thy holy will, hold back Thy chastising hand, turn away Thy just anger. Do not permit the sacrilegious feet of the enemy to desecrate Thy holy places. Spare my people, for they are also Thine. If there must be a victim, oh then, dear Lord, take me, but spare them. Sacrifice thy unworthy servant, thy undeserving representative. I am old; too long have I lived; let me be sacrificed. Mercy, O God, mercy! But come what may, let Thy holy will be done!"

The Pope finally came out into the sunlit square. Slowly he walked among the lines of his soldiers, bidding them goodbye and giving his blessing. Then he returned to the Vatican never again to leave it.

The morning set for the assault on Rome was sunny and warm. Seldom had the wide squares with their pulsing fountains looked lovelier. The warm stucco walls and the weathered stone threw back a salute to the light.

Sharp on the stroke of seven o'clock the Holy Father vested for Mass in his private chapel. John Mary's face was tranquil; his movements were majestic and unhurried.

"I will go to the altar of God, to God who gives joy to my youth!"

God had given John Mary many joys. The strength of joy had prepared him for the burden of the cross he had carried so long. The Pope waited in quiet for the will of Providence to declare itself. If this chalice could not pass, then God's will be done.

John Mary was grateful for the presence of the ambassadors of the great powers this morning. They had gathered around him during the days before the flight to Gaeta. Once more they had come to bolster his courage on this morning of destiny. They were ready to protect his person against the excesses of the revolutionaries should that be necessary. There had been several thwarted bomb plots against the Pope's life these last days. No one knew just how far the revolutionaries would be allowed to go before Cadorna put a stop to their excesses. The danger was real. Everyone knew it and they were all worried about John Mary's safety.

Many of the ambassadors grew more and more worried while the Mass went on. The violent thunder of guns rattled the windows of the chapel.

When the Holy Father's Mass was over he knelt at his prie-dieu and heard a second Mass offered by his chaplain. By this time the burst of shells had reached a peak of fury. Still unhurried, the Pope received the ambassadors in audience. He protested against the "sacrilegious force" that was being used against him and the Holy City. His face was heavy with grief while he continued.

"Once before the diplomatic corps gathered about me, to aid me in an hour of tribulation and sorrow. It was in 1848, not here, but in the Quirinal. . . . I have written to the King. I do not know whether my letter has reached him. But, whether it has or not, I have now no hope of touching his heart, or of arresting his ungracious proceedings. . . . Bixio, the notorious Bixio, is here at our doors, supported by the Italian army. He is now a royal general. Years ago, when he was a simple republican, he made a promise, that should he ever get within the walls of Rome, he would throw me into the Tiber. In an hour or two he may fulfill his promise. Were it not for the sin which would stain his unhappy soul, I would not make an effort to thwart him. May heaven forgive him. . . . Only yesterday I received a communication from the young gentlemen of the American College, begging, I should say demanding, permission to arm themselves and to constitute themselves the defenders of my person. Though there are few in Rome in whose hands I should feel more secure than in the hands of these fearless young Americans, I declined their generous offer with thanks and bade them devote their kind efforts to caring for my wounded soldiers.

"Yesterday, on my way to the chapel of the *Scala Santa,* I saw the flags of the different nations waving over their respective establishments throughout the city. I realized with

pain that these colors were flung to the breeze by these people
to save their property and lives from the invaders, to extort
from them the security and respect which my poor flag is no
longer able to afford. I would be glad, gentlemen, to say that I
rely upon you, and upon the countries which you have the
honor to represent, for deliverance from my difficulties and for
the restoration of the Church, as was the case in 1848. But
times are changed. The poor old Pope has no one on earth
upon whom he can rely. Relief must come from Heaven. Still,
gentlemen, remember that the Catholic Church is immortal."

By this time the Pope had begun to worry that Kanzler
had exceeded his orders for only a token resistance. A prolonged battle seemed to be in the making. John Mary's whole
concern was for the lives of his zouaves. Nothing could be
gained in sacrificing them in a cause so obviously hopeless.

The Holy Father's orders to General Kanzler had been brief
and precise.

General, at this moment, when a great sacrilege and the
most enormous injustice are about to be consummated, and
the troops of a Catholic king, without provocation, nay, without even the least appearance of any motive, surround and
besiege the capital of the Catholic world, I feel in the first
place the necessity of thanking you, General, and your entire
army for your generous conduct up to the present time, for the
affection which you have shown for the Holy See, and for
your willingness to consecrate yourselves entirely to the
defense of this metropolis. May these words be a solemn document to certify to the discipline, the loyalty, and the valor
of the army in the service of the Holy See.

*As regards the duration of the defense, I feel it my
duty to command that this shall only consist in such a protest
as shall testify to the violence done to us, and nothing more.
In other words, that negotiation for surrender shall be opened
as soon as a breach shall have been made.*

At a moment in which the whole of Europe is mourning over the numerous victims of the war now in progress between two great nations, never let it be said that the Vicar of Christ, however unjustly assailed, had to give his consent to a great shedding of blood. Our cause is the cause of God, and we put our whole defense in His hands. From my heart, General, I bless you and your whole army.

The Holy Father recognized that something had prevented Kanzler from the exact fulfillment of his written commands. That there might be no mistake as to what these had been the Pope now ordered a white flag hoisted to the lantern of Saint Peter's and the top of Sant' Angelo. Gradually the gunfire slackened. A sinister quiet fell on the city broken by the hoarse voice of triumph billowing in from the outskirts of the city and the Porta Pia where a great breach had been made.

The troops of Piedmont poured in, roaring drunk with triumph. Soldiers with hammers and axes broke through the gates and doors of the Quirinal Palace which Victor Emmanuel proposed to occupy. The Pope had been requested to hand over the keys.

"I'm sure they'll find a way to get in without keys," the Holy Father replied. "I have nothing more to say."

In the first rush of triumph there was rape and looting and the murder of a considerable number of zouaves. But Cadorna had strict orders from the king that every precaution must be taken to protect the lives of the Pope and cardinals. The king knew that the representative of the Powers would scrutinize the entire occupation. The prestige of the new Italy was at stake.

By nightfall most of the Pope's army had gathered in the old Leonine City centered around Saint Peter's and the Vatican. Under a sky heavy with stars the zouaves kindled their tiny fires between the wide shadows of Bernini's colonnade. With the morning the zouaves were drawn up in their companies. General Kanzler had settled with Cadorna that the Holy Father's troops were to lay down their arms with all the honors of war. The Piedmontese also held themselves responsible for the safety of the men and their return to the country of their origin.

The zouaves were all at rigid attention while their officers addressed them on the terms of the surrender. Suddenly one of the men caught sight of that well-known, white figure standing at one of the corner windows of the Vatican. The zouave gave a shout, "The Pope, the Pope!" The cry was taken up by thousands of voices. They threw their caps in the air, they fired their rifles and screamed at the top of their lungs. *"Long live the Pope-King! Long live Pius IX!"*

The fury of sound and emotion completely shattered John Mary's calm. He was weeping and his voice broke as he gave his blessing to those strong sons who had offered up their lives to him.

Then, John Mary, showing for the first time the sorrow that was in his heart, collapsed into the arms of his attendants.

Chapter XVI

TWILIGHT

PAPAL ROME was no more. A thousand years of history had come to an end. John Mary turned resolutely to the tasks before him.

He made an indignant protest against the treatment given his zouaves, after their formal surrender. For some days they had all been imprisoned on a diet of bread and water, before being sent home. The Piedmontese had often broken their word to John Mary in the past. This fresh example grieved the Pope more than all other lapses, and he did his best to shame his enemies into decency before the world. The excuse that came easiest to hand was trotted out. "The period of detention was necessary to protect the zouaves against the righteous anger of the Romans." How hollow this was can be easily determined. In his march into the outlying sections of Rome, before the city fell, General Cadorna had expected the Romans to rise up and join his armies. Instead of that he found the shutters up everywhere. The peasants and shopkeepers hid in their barns and houses. It was a humbling but indicative experience.

With characteristic kindness the Pope sent his blessing to all the soldiers of both armies injured in the battle for Rome. The Holy Father longed to visit them in their wards, but he was now King of Rome without a kingdom. Yet the Lord had said "forgive us our trespasses as we forgive those who trespass against us." John Mary sent the injured baskets of pastry and food from the Vatican kitchens.

It was obvious to the Pope that the sessions of the Vatican Council could not be continued in any forseeable future. Rome was filled with odious caricatures of the Pope and Cardinals, with blasphemous books and fly-by-night newspapers fetid with filth and hatred of God. Persecution of the contemplative orders had started; the streets were not safe for those who wore the religious habit.

In the decree *Postquam Dei Munere,* Pius IX suspended the Vatican Council for an indetermined period. It was a grievous disappointment to John Mary, because of the splendid things the council had already accomplished. The faith had been clearly defined against all the new heresies of the age; the powers of the Church and Pope had been precisely formulated.

The conquerors had offered the Pope a sop for the loss of his dominions in the "Law of Papal Guarantees," which assured the Pope an income and defined his status. Pius IX indignantly refused the settlement, pointing out that the thieves planned to reimburse him for a small part of the revenue from his own States. He also denounced them for the hypocrites they were, and asked how it was possible to trust the word of those who had so often broken it in the past, who were even then in the midst of a vicious campaign against the Pope, the Church and the cloistered orders.

The end of the temporal power brought Antonelli's influence to an abrupt end. The Cardinal-Secretary had assured John Mary that Rome would never fall into the hands of Piedmont. The cardinal was so sure he had all the answers and the worldly wisdom to bring them into being.

John Mary had been content to leave the general direction of political affairs in the hands of Antonelli. Now the political phase was over. Antonelli's worldliness and worldly wisdom were a handicap for this new age of the catacombs in which the Pope would have to kindle again the spiritual lights of Europe.

Antonelli was still fond of his large collection of precious stones, he still entertained lavishly in his salon hung with sky-blue silk, he still talked interminably without saying a great deal. The Cardinal lived in the past while a new age was being born.

Antonelli had been a good servant in a troubled time. For twenty years he had played government against government in keeping together some semblance of a Papal Kingdom. Both Austria and France had respected the Cardinal's talents and silken ways. They preferred to deal with him rather than the Pope; they constantly expressed to the Holy Father their approval of His Eminence. Now the opinions of France and Austria were no longer of importance: they had as little value for the Church as Antonelli's genius for finance.

The perfidy of their governments had not undermined John Mary's love of his children. It saddened him to watch the long drawn-out course of the Franco-Prussian war, the endless encounters with their holocaust of lives.

At his Masses in the morning John Mary prayed for peace. He used his influence with Kaiser Wilhelm I to end the war as speedily as possible. The Pope could see in Italy now, as he had seen all his life, how war produced little more than destruction and the debasement of the people.

In withdrawing himself from the world, in becoming in fact the "prisoner of the Vatican," John Mary had more time to meditate on the wisdom of the cross. The last eight years of his life were filled with sorrows that pierced him to the heart. Irreligion was rampant in the government of the new Italy and it led to irreligious laws that penalized the Church on every side.

The Church was also severely persecuted in France for a time. The "communards" of Paris even dared to shoot Archbishop Darboy. The archbishop had opposed John Mary bitterly during the struggle over the infallibility. Now the Pope envied his old opponent in his martyr's death.

The Carlist War in Spain brought John Mary new unhappiness along with the persecution of Catholics in Switzerland and elsewhere about the world. But these sorrows were small crosses compared with the developing struggle with Germany.

Bismarck, the German Chancellor, was filled with the wine of triumph. Europe seemed to be at the mercy of his machine-like arms. Austria was humbled, France had fallen. It was time to humble the Church. The Prussian mentality scorned all the soft teaching of Catholic schools and churches. It should be obvious to the world, the chancellor thought, that the papacy was a failure. It was something outmoded, out of the Middle Ages, pretty and quaint like the buildings in Nuremburg.

The Pope might fancy himself infallible, but the Catholic Church must be brought under the control of the omnipotent state and be forced to serve her purposes. The Falk Laws implemented Bismarck's thinking. Catholic schools were closed. Monks and nuns were thrown out of their convents. As usual in such struggles, the Jesuits lost everything and were forced to leave the country.

The German bishops reacted with German vigor. They boldly denounced the Falk Laws and organized both a spiritual and political opposition. The Pope, who had been cut to the heart, showed a flash of his old fire when someone sympathized with him over the developing tragedy. "Bismarck or Trismarck," the Holy Father said, "it will all be the same in the end; the Church will triumph!" John Mary's prophecy came true, but he did not live to see the Church triumph in this particular struggle.

But one prophecy John Mary made is being amply fulfilled in our own time. The prophecy was made to Louis Veuillot, the editor of the powerful French newspaper, *The Universe*.

Veuillot had fought in all the Pope's battles. His forceful articles had often caused Napoleon to wince, and he had been
largely responsible in making Catholic opinion respected and
articulate in France.

During Veuillot's first visit to Pius IX, after the "September
Convention," the Pope said,

"We are in a bold century, the century of the railroads. They
hurry on. They move fast, and they move badly. . . . The
times are evil.

"I have maintained the temporal power and I have defended
it in peril of my life because it is useful to the complete liberty
of the Church. And the complete freedom of the Church is
necessary to Catholic society and all humankind.

"If the Vicar of Jesus Christ must once again go down into
the catacombs, freedom will go with him. God and freedom will
no longer be on earth. Without doubt the order of freedom
will be re-established but after how much time and at what a
terrible cost! . . ."

Those without the Pope's vision had never seen what the
whole struggle was about. Atheism, materialism, communism,
secularism and overweening nationalism, they were preparing
the way for the all-powerful state and the slavery and denigra-
tion of men. The struggle with Bismarck's Germany was like a
dress rehearsal for the insanities of communism and fascism
that we today know so well.

John Mary's sorrows were lessened by the affection poured
out on him in thousands of national pilgrimages. The Holy
Father could no longer go to his people but they came to see
him, from France, Germany, Austria, Canada and the United
States—every island and continent of the world. However tired
or ill he was, the Pope always displayed toward the pilgrims
the warm heart of a welcoming father.

Audiences were at set hours, with admission by ticket. The

Pope usually walked up one side of the room and down the other, speaking intimately to the groups and individuals. Then from the dais he would address the pilgrims in a short speech and bless the religious articles the pilgrims carried.

On one occasion a peasant woman from France held up the blessing of religious articles while she fished about in the voluminous folds of her black sateen skirt trying to find the rosary in her pocket. The Holy Father waited for a time and then said in a merry voice, "Never mind, mother, the blessing goes into the pocket too."

Most of the pilgrims brought gifts of money to the Pope. The loss of his States had completely shut off his revenue. French, Belgians and Americans, who for the first time appeared in large organized groups, were generous in helping the Holy Father maintain his court and large-handed charities. Their kindness enabled the Pope to say; "Money means nothing to me. The more I give, the more I find. The providence of God is the inexhaustible source of all."

Catholic children all over the world were particularly sympathetic with John Mary's plight. They sent him artless little notes written in their childish scrawls.

One small boy wrote:

> Mama asked me what I want to be when I get big. I said "A soldier of the Pope!" Bless me, so I may grow strong enough to be your soldier,
> Charles Robert Rivanazzano

The boy enclosed a gift of sixty centimes. Little girls sent the Holy Father their small treasures: rings, medals, and prizes of money.

Sometimes the gifts were particularly affecting. A parish orphanage in France, without any prompting of the nuns, gave up their only holiday of the year in order to forward the small sum of money to the Pope. Deaf and blind children sent pennies and nickels, anything at all they considered of value.

Often in the evening the Holy Father could be seen pondering, with misted eyes, the piles of children's letters on his desk. Always he wrote tender replies in which were enclosed holy pictures and medals.

Outside his windows the black sky was like a thick curtain. John Mary could never go to Tata Giovanni through streets in which hatred and death waited. But his thoughts could go to his children. They, too, had been generous like the children the letters on his desk so beautifully pictured. Fuller than his treasury of gold was this treasure of unspoiled hearts.

John Mary's love of children moved him to help John Bosco with gifts and encouragement. They understood each other, these two. And they were like two boys themselves when they spoke of Don Bosco's work of rescue among the abandoned children.

Far across the peninsula, in Salzano, there was a young priest named Giuseppe Sarto. He too agonized over the sorrows of Pius IX. When Cardinal Sarto came to the Papacy against his will he showed his loving admiration for John Mary in choosing the name of Pius X.

Within three years of his coronation Pius X started the first interrogation of witnesses toward the establishment of the heroic sanctity of Pius IX. Saint Pius advanced the necessary money, about six thousand dollars, from his own meager income.

John Mary felt himself rich in both joys and sorrows, rich in friends, richest of all in love. In those riches there was a living reflection of the story of the tragedy and triumph of his Master.

Memorable days to Pius IX as a prisoner in the Vatican were those on which he went into Saint Peter's for the canonization of many new saints. John Mary had spoken vigorous words against the mental aberrations of the day. But that was not enough. Men ran after worldly learning. The Pope by decree raised to the rank of Doctor of the Church his own beloved patron, Saint Francis de Sales, and Saint Alphonsus Liguori that the world might see the attraction of heavenly wisdom. He canonized Benedict Joseph Labre who, despising the luxuries and soft things of life, lived in voluntary filth and went to his ecstatic death teeming with vermin.

The Pope's mystical vision and inward gaze, fanning into high flame his entire religious life, did not alter either his friendly ways, his wit, or his native charm, similar in its enchanting quality to that of Saint Francis de Sales. He was the same John Mary that charmed the children in the orphanage of Saint Michael or Tata Giovanni.

A certain vigorous priest from the Romagna got into an argument with some strangers in a Roman cafe over the loss of the temporal power. Fiery words led to blows. The priest finally picked up a chair and belabored his opponents.

John Mary, hearing of the incident, wrote a letter to the priest and enclosed a sum of money to be used in making a retreat. After the retreat was over the priest came back to thank the Pope.

They talked of many things. At the end of the audience the Pope said with a wide smile, "Make sure there are no more Romagna lightnings!"

"Don't worry, Holy Father, I've learned at my cost."

"No, no, my son," the Pope corrected, "at *my* cost!"

John Mary still loved to tease those religious whose ambitions outran either their talents or complete dedication to the religious life. There was a Benedictine monk, Dom Pescitelli by name, from the monastery of Saint Paul's Outside the Walls. Pescitelli very much wanted to be a Cardinal and often gave the Holy Father a hint to that effect.

Finally, during a private audience with the monk, the Pope said in a half musing way,

"You Benedictines should get your money ready, because I'm going to make a Benedictine Cardinal."

"It's a great honor for our order, Holy Father!" Pescitelli's voice was fervent.

"Yes, without doubt that's true! And I can give you a further hint, the fortunate man's name begins with the letter P." The Pope paused while his auditor fairly swelled with pride. "But," the Holy Father continued, "he's not an Italian." Dom Petra, a French Benedictine proved to be the lucky man.

The Pope's manly directness extended to the man who typified the opposition to him—Victor Emmanuel.

When the Emperor of Brazil came to visit the Pope after 1870, he told the Holy Father, "Victor Emmanuel is not really as black as he's painted. I'm sure I can bring him to the feet of Your Holiness. Then you will bless him and we shall have peace."

The Pope replied with deep gravity:

"If Your Majesty brings Victor Emmanuel to me I shall not tell my grooms to throw him down the stairs. But I will speak to him with such force that when he goes out of my study he'll be too stunned to find the stairs."

The Pope's blunt words were more than a clew to John Mary's entire outlook on the Italian King. It had puzzled some observers that Pius IX always treated Victor Emmanuel like a naughty son. The Pope corrected and admonished the king in friendly letters. In the various excommunications of all those who played a part in the theft of the Papal States the king was never mentioned by name.

Pius IX knew only too well, from his own experience before Gaeta, what it can mean for a ruler to be the actual prisoner of his ministers. Victor Emmanuel's affection was probably quite sincere. But he was vain and ambitious. His attitudes and even his moustaches aped the melodrama of Napoleon III. Victor Emmanuel fancied himself an autocrat, but he was controlled and steered in the direction determined by Cavour and his successors.

It was, very likely, the Pope's complete insight that prompted his kindly attitude toward the king.

When we remember the Holy Father's advanced age and many ailments during the last eight years of his life we are all the more astonished at the killing routine to which he held himself daily.

The Pope rose every morning at six o'clock in the winter, but in summer long before that hour. By six-thirty, shining and fresh, he was kneeling in his chapel. For meditation he generally used the two books his mother had given him long ago, or the works of Saint Francis de Sales.

It was a pleasure to watch him offering Mass. He read the sonorous Latin words with complete intelligence and was entirely absorbed in their inner meaning. In thanksgiving he heard another Mass offered by one of his chaplains. Breakfast followed, which meant a cup of coffee and a piece of bread.

Interviews with important functionaries started the hours of activity: the secretary of state, heads of Congregations, foreign ambassadors and bishops used up most of the morning. At mid-day and later in the afternoon the larger audiences took place. Between these, the Pope usually went for a walk in the Vatican gardens. If the weather was bad the Holy Father walked in the Sala Matilda.

His meals were very simple. John Mary had always liked plain food followed by a single glass of Burgundy wine, most of which came to him as gifts. If he felt hungry between meals, he took a glass of sugar water.

Visits to the Blessed Sacrament and the recitation of the Breviary filled the early evening hours, after which the Pope worked late at his letters and papers while Rome slept.

The American artist, G. P. A. Healy, was employed to paint the Holy Father's picture. John Mary went to the sittings with boyish enthusiasm. Healy was enchanted with the Pope's comments on history and people. During one sitting the conversation moved to the famous Carmelite preacher, Father Hyacinthe. Healy had often heard the noted speaker at the Cathedral of Notre Dame in Paris, and he was curious to know what the Holy Father's attitude would be toward the man who refused to accept the infallibility, left the Church, and married. The Pope's eyes were twinkling as Healy rambled on in an attempt to draw some comments from John Mary.

"Yes," the Pope said at last, and he was smiling. "They tell me Father Hyacinthe has married an American woman. Well, he has taken his punishment into his own hands!"

At one session Healy looked up in surprise to see John Mary peering over his shoulder at his unfinished portrait. "I beg Your Holiness to sit down," Healy said, somewhat abruptly.

The Pope laughed as he returned to his chair. "I usually give orders and do not take them, Mr. Healy, but you see I also know how to obey."

Healy's picture became the official portrait of John Mary, and when Pius IX had exceeded the length of Saint Peter's reign in Rome a copy of the portrait was placed high on the pier above the first Pope's statue in Saint Peter's Church. John Mary showed his appreciation by creating Healy a Knight of Saint Gregory.

January of the year 1877 found the Pope tired in mind and body. He was in the thirty-second year of his reign, seven years longer than the years of Peter, which legend said would never be exceeded. The world had made much of that, sending him gifts and coming to celebrate with him in 1877, the fiftieth anniversary of his consecration as a bishop.

Truth was, John Mary often felt old and ill. There had been so many deaths these last years, his brothers Joseph and Gabriel in 1858 and 1859, his brother Gaetano in 1871. Then Louis died in 1876. John Mary was the last son of his line. It grieved him to see Aunt Vicki so old and sorrowful. The Pope had lost three able coadjutors: Cardinal Barnabò and Cardinal de Mérode, and the noble Patrizi, Vicar-General of Rome.

Cardinal Antonelli died in 1876. When word of the secretary's serious illness was brought to the Pope he said, "Tell the Cardinal to make a good confession." The Holy Father's concern for the soul of his worldly Secretary of State revealed itself in John Mary's further comment after the death of Antonelli. The Pope was informed that the Cardinal had received the last rites of the Church with touching piety.

"Now I understand everything," John Mary said. "I shall say Mass for the repose of his soul."

Pius IX was criticized for not permitting the burial of Cardinal Antonelli with public pomp. In this circumstance the Pope showed his good sense and his correct reading of the revolutionary mind and temper. Antonelli's name was hated even more than John Mary's. The disgraceful scenes that took place at the final burial of Pius IX were proof that the revolutionists were looking for any occasion which could be used as a rallying point to stimulate public hatred of the papacy.

The Pope went often to pray at the foot of Saint Peter's statue, when the doors of Saint Peter's had been closed for the night. He prayed for strength and asked over and over, "How long, O Lord? How long?"

Rheumatism had cut off the walks he loved. Still the Pope went out to take the air in a sedan chair carried by relays of pages. It was painful trying to get in and out of the narrow space. An ulcer on the Pope's leg made movement more and more difficult.

In the middle of the night of January 9th, 1878, a messenger came in haste to the Vatican. Victor Emmanuel was dying. He had sent to beg the Pope's blessing for the hour of death, and asked the lifting of the censures imposed upon him. Pius IX never hesitated. At once he dispatched to the Quirinal Monsignor Marinelli with the necessary faculties for absolving the king, and the blessing for the hour of death. Marinelli arrived too late. The king was dead.

The Pope grieved for his wayward son, cut down in the vigor of life. The Pontiff showed the width of his charity in permitting the king to be buried in the Church of Saint Mary of the Martyrs, which we know as the Pantheon. The Holy Father imposed only one condition: all mention of the title, King of Italy, was to be excluded from the burial liturgy.

Toward the end of January the Pope had to say his Mass sitting in a chair. Movement was becoming increasingly difficult. The time of his death was obviously drawing near. "Whenever the Lord calls me I am ready to go," the Holy Father said with a smile.

One morning, being moved in his chair through the Mass, the Pope came to these words: "Thou [the Lord] knowest me in my sitting down and rising up." The thought of the resurrection like a trumpet call seemed to fill the sick Pope with immortal vigor. His chaplains were electrified to see the Holy Father standing erect.

For some time John Mary had gone to necessary audiences in a specially contrived bed. It looked like a chair from the front, but it was hinged at the back in such a fashion that the Pope would seem to be sitting erect.

On the Feast of the Purification, the Holy Father's last public appearance took place. He received the customary gift of candles from all the religious communities of Rome. In his memorable voice, that had lost nothing of its music, the Pope made his last speech:

"Before our day the people used to come to the priest. Now the priest must go to the people. And when you are with your people what will you say? Preach fine sermons? No! You will teach them there is one God in Three Persons, of whom the Second was made Man to save us. It is the one thing the people don't seem to remember. And the one thing they *need* to know."

On February 6th, propped up in his bed and obviously suffering, the Pope received all the Cardinals in Rome. Among them he singled out Manning for a special affectionate adieu, "Goodbye, dearest one," he said.

Manning had been in Rome for some time. During the long illness of the Holy Father the English Cardinal spent many hours at the Pope's bedside. Many biographers have wondered how the two prelates, so dissimilar in exterior gifts, could have passed the weary time. But those who ask the question know too little about the Pope's mystical side, or Manning's expressive piety.

The Pope's final charge to the Cardinals was simple, "Guard the Church that I have loved so well."

The night of February 6th was a restless one. John Mary's fever mounted, the congestion in his lungs increased. He was breathing with difficulty, long rasping breaths.

Doctor Ceccarelli, the Pope's physician, came at nine o'clock for the morning examination of his illustrious patient. John Mary greeted the physician with a smile. "Good morning, my dear Doctor. This time it's the end."

The Cardinal-Vicar gave the order for the exposition of the Blessed Sacrament in all the churches of Rome, and the prescribed prayer for a Pope in his last agony.

The square before Saint Peter's was peppered with praying people. Their eyes were fixed on the blank windows of the Pope's apartment. Every minute carriages arrived at the guarded gates. The oldest aristocracy of Europe was gathered in the salons surrounding the Pope's rooms. Many of the noble women had brought their children with them to witness the dying agony of the great Pope they considered a saint.

During the slow hours John Mary's breathing became more and more harsh. It echoed in the silent room where Cardinals and princes knelt on the tile floor. The Holy Father was perfectly clear in mind. In his hand was the lemonwood cross of his childhood. He raised it in blessing from time to time, or kissed it with tenderness. All John Mary's great crosses were falling from his shoulders.

Toward five o'clock in the afternoon Doctor Ceccarelli asked Cardinal Bilio to recite again the splendid prayer *Proficiscere* (Go forth, Christian soul!). The dying Pope roused himself and said in a firm voice. "Yes, go forth!" The prayer was said, and then amid tears the Sorrowful Mysteries of the rosary were begun. The gasping breath of the dying man could be heard above the steady drone of prayer.

With the beginning of the Fourth Mystery the hard breathing slowed. Doctor Ceccarelli leaned over the bed and wiped one pearly tear from the Holy Father's cheek. The Lord had finally called John Mary.

Never in the history of Rome had there been such an outpouring of grief at the death of a Pope. The echo of the tears and sobs about his deathbed went out over the entire city. Peasants, shopkeepers, workmen, nobles, they all cried with unashamed tears.

The old revolutionaries gnashed their teeth with rage as they watched the surging crowds filing through the door of Saint Peter's to pay their last respects to Pius IX.

A phony Roman plebiscite had seemed to guarantee the theft of the Holy City, but many in the long file of people in Saint Peter's square made the comment, "This is the true plebiscite we are watching now."

The Pope's body lay in state in the Blessed Sacrament Chapel in Saint Peter's. Only one door was opened to permit the entry

of the slow moving stream of human beings. They passed between a double file of soldiers, the soldiers of the new and alien
state. The winter light was hardly more than dusk, except in the
Sacrament Chapel where torches flamed against the rosy walls
and six massive candles threw their beams on the serene face
and glittering robes of the dead Pontiff. The ornate gates of the
chapel were closed, but the Pope's slippered feet protruded
through the bronze grill. Almost everyone kissed the reliquary
cross on the Pope's slipper; many touched to his feet rosaries,
medals, and religious articles of all kinds.

Three noble guards in their golden helmets and splendid
trappings guarded the bier with drawn swords. No one had
more than a glance for their splendor. All eyes were memoriz-
ing that beautiful marble-like mask with its kindly smile, out-
shining the radiance of the torchlight.

Four days later the temporary entombment took place. It
was in the evening. The great spaces of Saint Peter's Church
were empty. In the Sacrament Chapel and the Chapel of the
Choir the amber light of many candles glowed. A triple coffin
waited the Pope's body in the choir.

The gates of the Sacrament Chapel were thrown back. Noble
Guards raised the bier shoulder high. The papal choir chanted
the ancient prayers of the Church while the body was carried
first to the Confession of the Apostles, then to the Chapel of
the Choir. Many Cardinals and bishops, robed in copes of black
and silver, followed the bier.

John Mary's body was lifted reverently and placed in the
inner of the three coffins. The officiating prelates could hardly
see through their tears while they arranged everything in perfect order and put into the inner coffin at the Pope's feet a bag
of medals of gold, silver, and bronze, signalizing the outstand-
ing event in each year of his reign. With the medals was a history
of John Mary's reign written on fine parchment.

The lead coffin was slowly soldered. The Cardinals then placed five seals on it and the archivist added one more.

A last Absolution was sung. It echoed in the dome like an irrevocable farewell spoken by a lover. The coffin was gently placed in slings. Slowly it moved out and high up into the niche prepared for it in the temporary tomb above the east door.

The waiting masons began to brick up the opening. Cardinals and guards waited in sadness while the work went on. Long before the bells of Saint Peter's struck the hour of midnight a marble slab was set before the rough wall of brick.

It carried a simple inscription:

PIUS IX, P.M.

EPILOGUE

THE will of Pius IX permitted an unusual innovation—the Cardinals were allowed to discuss the merits of the various candidates before the election of a new Pope. Permission was also granted to hold the conclave outside of Rome if the new authorities should attempt to impede the access of the Cardinals or try to control the election.

The conclave was short. Cardinal Pecci, who had been Bishop of Perugia for thirty-two years, became the new Pope and assumed the title of Leo XIII. The new Pope proved to be mentally brilliant; he was equally social-minded.

During the three years in which the new reign was developing with astonishing dynamism, the body of Pius IX rested in its high niche over the east door of Saint Peter's.

Many people prayed to the dead Pope for special favors. Among these was John Bosco. He had long revered the profound spirituality, sanctity, and heroic charity of Pius IX. In his school paper he published a number of articles and bulletins describing the inner beauty of the Pope's last years and the many favors obtained through his intercession. From all over the world, particularly from France and Italy, came innumerable testimonies that spoke in trumpet tones the celestial power of Pius IX. Some examples from this moving record are of exceptional interest.

At the time of the Pope's death in Rome, a Belgian child, dying from an undiagnosed illness, told his mother he had a vision of Pius IX being crowned by the Virgin in heaven. The child was instantly cured. Since news of the Pope's death had not yet reached Belgium, the mother sent a telegram to Rome. The answer indicated the child had been cured at the very moment of the Pope's death.

In September, 1878, Sister Agnes Serafina of Jesus, aged twenty-five, was ill of typhus. Doctor Monti, her physician, said there was no possible chance of recovery. The nuns started a novena to Pius IX. On the last day of the novena Sister Agnes felt a tingling sensation all over her body. She was cured immediately, and Doctor Monti issued a statement that the cure could only have been supernatural.

During the same month, Salvatore de Angelis, a layman, was suffering terrible agony from a tumor on the liver. Doctors Topai and Scalzi said an immediate operation was the only possible way of saving the young man's life. A friend of the family, Carlo Insegna, urged the family to pray to Pius IX. Insegna brought a relic of the dead Pope, which was applied to the affected spot. De Angelis fell into a deep sleep. Within two hours the tumor had disappeared, the young man's temperature was normal. The doctors were amazed and quite willingly gave their testimony to a cure beyond nature.

The succeeding circumstances are interesting. De Angelis became a priest and spent most of his clerical life as pastor of Sassia. Father de Angelis was noted for his lifelong devotion to Pius IX.

Achille Beccalori, a poor farmer, aged sixty-four, of Borgo San Donnino, was skinning a calf that had died of a malignant disease. In the hasty process of skinning the animal, Beccalori cut his arm with the knife. Within twenty-four hours the man became desperately ill; his arm was swollen to enormous size. At the hospital to which he was moved, Doctor Cenci, the resident physician, and Professor Ingami of Parma, said there was no hope of Beccalori's recovery. Sister Anna Maria Valentina, a nurse, urged Beccalori to pray to Pius IX. She applied a relic to the swollen arm. Beccalori at once went to sleep, and by morning was cured.

In the same town, in March of 1878, a young man, Giuseppe Flori, was dying of cancer of the liver. The doctor said the boy could not possibly live. A neighbor, Mrs. Elena Papini, begged the family to pray to the Pope, so recently dead. Mrs. Papini applied a picture of Pius IX to the diseased spot. Flori was cured within a few hours.

These wonders, carefully documented, and many others too numerous to mention, impelled thousands to pay private honor to Pius IX. Many groups made novenas at his temporary tomb in the high arch, and everyone longed for the time when the Pope could be moved to his final resting place in a more accessible spot.

Pius IX always loved Santa Maria Maggiore. The most ancient shrine of Our Lady, the mother church of the Mother, was woven into the very fabric of his heart. In his last days John Mary asked the Roman authorities for permission to be buried in Santa Maria Maggiore.

The request was refused with a rudeness that spoke volumes. It was alleged that any further burials in the center of the city would endanger the health of the citizens, though it was less than a month since Victor Emmanuel had been entombed in the Pantheon with John Mary's forgiving permission.

"Very well, then," Pius IX said. "If I cannot be buried inside the walls of Rome I will choose the poorest church outside the walls." After some consideration, the Pope selected the Church of Saint Laurence. It was noted for its antiquity and unpretentious charm. Once again John Mary asked for a plain tomb in keeping with the simplicity of his private life, that had so enchanted Saint John Bosco.

For a long time, the Vatican tried to obtain permission for the work of construction. It was finally given, and the tomb was built. Gifts poured in from the entire world. Princes and paupers sent money or rich gifts, indicating their love for the dead Pope.

His enemies among the revolutionary groups in Rome were equally active. In books and pamphlets, in private meetings and public speeches they vilified the memory of Pius IX. They went to insane lengths to fabricate stories that might serve to soil his reputation and minimize his tremendous achievements.

Because of this active and vitriolic hatred, the Cardinal-Executors of the Pope's will were forced to wait three years for an opportunity to transfer the body to the church he had chosen. The Cardinals, in arranging the funeral, were in close touch with the civil authorities. They in turn consulted the proper ministries of the government.

July 13, 1881 was the appointed day. The Vatican had agreed that the funeral should be kept very quiet. To insure this result the hour was set for midnight.

The night of July 13th was heavy and still. The jets of the tinkling fountains before Saint Peter's were woven with star-light. From the bell-cote of the basilica the ancient bells chimed out the hour of twelve. On the echo of the last note a simple cortege formed in the wide piazza. There were two closed carriages following the hearse. After these walked a small number of Saint Peter's clergy, the diplomats accredited to the Holy See, and a considerable group of Roman citizens who loved Pius IX and had somehow got wind of his funeral. The mourners all carried massive, lighted candles.

The slow procession went down the Borgo di Santo Spirito (now the Via della Conciliazione). A crowd suddenly materialized along the narrow sidewalks. They shouted ugly words and made obscene gestures of derision.

In the wider space before the Castle of Sant' Angelo a larger crowd waited, ugly in temper and armed with knives, stones and clubs. There was a rush toward the hearse and carriages, there were organized blasphemies, and torrents of horrible invective swept from the sewers of the mind. Above all this foul background rose a concerted scream.

"Throw the old pig in the Tiber! Throw the old pig in the Tiber!" Knives flashed, clubs rose and fell. The screams of the injured knifed through the shouting.

The attending prelates, ambassadors, and groups of the faithful formed a thick cordon about the hearse. They used their massive wax candles to good advantage in defense of their lives and the Pope's body.

At last they were across the bridge. The most serious rioting was over. No more than a token police effort had been made in attempting to control the passions of the organized mob.

The remaining distance across the city was dogged with shouted insults and blasphemies. An occasional stick or stone fell with a thud on the simple hearse.

By the time the filth-spattered procession had reached the Piazza Verano, wiser heads in the government had decided to stage a face-saving incident. Files of soldiers were in waiting. The mob leaders faded away in the crowd.

The mortal remains of Pius IX were entombed in eloquent silence while time began the slow process of sifting the massive lies against his memory. The next day, July 14th, Mancini, the Foreign Minister, imposed a rigid censorship on all telegrams describing the disgraceful episode. Meanwhile, Mancini, by note, instructed his ambassadors abroad, indicating the false light in which they were to represent the sordid affair.

On July 15th the story made front-page news in the great newspapers of the world. *The London Times,* which had no particular love of things Catholic, spoke of the riot as a "grave scandal" and fixed the blame squarely on the civil authorities. The *Berliner Tageblatt,* Lutheran in inspiration, pointed out that "Leo XIII may well declare henceforth with complete justice that he cannot leave the Vatican for reasons of personal safety."

In Italy itself all decent people were thoroughly enraged. Their feelings were summed up in a blunt editorial in the *Gazzetta d'Italia,* on August 1st, which pointed the finger at those in the highest reaches of the government: "the cabinet, silly and weak, is afraid to antagonize a handful of agitators who have representatives and accomplices in the government itself."

Some seventy-five years have passed since Pius IX was buried in an orgy of hate. Today a battered and chastened world has been forced to weigh the deeds and slogans that sparked the "age of progress."

The House of Savoy reigns no more; Italian politics have become the prey of sinister forces. History is beginning to declare its truth that falls like a nimbus about the head of Pius IX. It is all too clear, too tragically clear, that the evil forces he fought, almost single-handed, are like a breath from the regions of eternal evil. And the cross on which his enemies crucified Pius IX is shown to be the great rood on which humanity today is being crucified.

In recognition of this fact, our Holy Father, Pope Pius XII, on December 8, 1954, a feast on which many significant acts of Pius IX had taken place, signed the Decree for the opening of the Apostolic Process for the beatification of the great Pope, who was called by those who knew him best, *Papa Angelico.*

BIBLIOGRAPHY

Summarium (Super Dubio) S.C. Rites, Rome: 1954.

Aubert, R. *Le Pontificat de Pie IX* (1846–1878) Paris: Bloud & Gay, 1952.

Berkeley, G. F.-H., *The Irish Battalion in the Papal Army of 1860*, Dublin: 1929.

Berkeley, G. F.-H., *Italy in the Making* (1815–1846) Cambridge, 1936.

Besson, Mgr., *Frederick Francis Xavier de Mérode* (English Translation by Lady Herbert) London: W. H. Allen, 1887.

Bourgeois, E., et Clermont, E., *Rome et Napoléon III*, Paris: 1907.

Butler, Cuthbert, *The Vatican Council*, London: Longmans, 2 Vols. 1930.

Campana, *Il Concilio Vaticano*, Lugano: 1926.

Cani, Mgr., *Procès Romain pour la Cause du Pape Pie IX*, Memoire de Mgr. Cani, Paris: 1910.

Crispolti, *Pio IX-Leone XIII-Pio X-Benedetto XV-Pio XI. (Ricordi Personali)* Milan: 1939.

Crispolti, *Pio IX*, Milan: 1928.

Dalla Torre, Paolo. *L' Opera Riformatrice ed Amminstrativa di Pio IX Fra il 1850 e il 1870*, Rome: 1945.

De Cesare, R., *The Last Days of Papal Rome*, Translated by Helen Zimmern, Boston: Houghton Mifflin & Company, 1909.

Faraoni, Vincenzo, Msgr. *Brevi Cenni della Vita del Servo di Dio, Pio IX*, Naples: 1910.

Granderath, T., S.J., *Geschichte des Vatikanischen Konzils*, Fribourg: 1903–1906 (French Translation—*Histoire du Vatican*) 5 Vols. Brussels: 1908.

257

Halperin, S. W. *Italy and the Vatican at War: A Study of their Relations from the Outbreak of the Franco-Prussian War to the Death of Pius IX.* Chicago: Chicago University Press, 1939.

Hayward, Fernand, *Pie IX et Son Temps,* Paris: Librarie Plon, 1948.

Hayward, Fernand, *Le Dernier Siècle de la Rome Pontificale,* Paris: Payot, 2 Vols. 1927–1928.

Hergenröther, *Storia Universale della Chiesa,* Vol. VII, Parte II. Pagges 585–617.

Huguet, R. P., S.M. *L'Esprit de Pie IX,* Lyon et Paris: Felix Girard, 1866.

Keller, Joseph E., S.J. *The Life and Acts of Pope Leo XIII* (Preceded by a sketch of *The Last Days of Pius IX*) New York: Benziger Brothers, Inc., 1882.

La Gorce, P. de la, *Histoire de la Seconde République Française,* Vol I. Paris: 1887.

Maguire, J. F. *The Pontificate of Pius IX,* London: Longmans, Green & Co., 1870.

Maguire, J. F., *Rome: its Ruler, and its Institutions* (2nd Edition) London: Longmans, Green & Company, 1859.

Maioli, G., *Pio IX da Vescovo a Pontefice* (*Lettere al Card. Luigi Amat*) Modena: 1949.

Marocco, *Pio IX* 4 Vols. Torino: 1861–1864.

Monti, Antonio, *Pio IX nel Risorgimento Italiano,* Bari: Gius. Laterza & Figli, 1928.

Morosi, Dario (Rev.), *Vita di Sua Santità Pio Papa Nono,* Florence: Tipogratfia Della Concezione 3 Vols. 1883, 1884, 1885.

Mourret, F., *Le Concile du Vatican D'après des Documents Inédits,* Paris: 1919.

Pastor, Ludwig von, *The History of the Popes,* London: Kegan Paul, Trench Trübner & Company 20 Vols.

Pelczar, G. S., *Pio IX e il Suo Pontificato* 3 Vols. Turin: 1909, 1910, 1911.

Petroncelli, *Pio IX—Il Sillabo.* ecc. Florence: 1927.

Purcell, E. S. *Life of Cardinal Manning,* Vol. II. London: Macmillan Company, 1896.

Rappini, Raphael (Éditeur), *Enseignments et Conseils du Souverain Pontife Pie IX aux Catholiques,* Bologna: 1878.

Stepischnegg, Jakob Maximilian, *Papa Pius IX Eine Feine Beit,* Wien: Wilhelm Braumüller, 1879.

Trollope, T. Adolphus, *The Story of the Life of Pius IX,* London: Richard Bentley & Son 2 Vols. 1877.

Veuillot, L., *Vita Di Sua Santità Pio IX,* Bologna: 1863.

Wallace, Lillian Parker, *The Papacy in European Diplomacy* (1869–1878) Chapel Hill: University of North Carolina Press, 1948.

Ward, W. *William George Ward and the Catholic Revival,* London: Longmans, Green & Company, 1912.

The Syllabus for the People, By a Monk of St. Augustine's (Ramsgate), London: Burns & Oates, 1874.

Senigallia e Pio IX nel Cinquantenario della Morte, Scuola Tipografia, Marchigiana, 1928.

Il Palazzo Mastai, Tipografia Marchigiana, Senigallia: 1953.

Grâces Obtenues par l'Intercession de Pie IX depuis l'Epoque de sa Mort, Traduit de l'Italien, Bologna: Imprimerie Felsinienne, 1879.

SET UP, PRINTED AND BOUND BY BENZIGER BROTHERS, INC., NEW YORK

INDEX

SET UP, PRINTED, AND BOUND BY BENZIGER BROTHERS, INC.